Holiday Calendar 2021

Published for BIMCO in 2021 by:

Witherby Publishing Group Ltd
Navigation House,
3 Almondvale Business Park,
Almondvale Way,
Livingston EH54 6GA,
Scotland, UK

info@witherbys.com
witherbys.com
+44(0)1506 463 227

BIMCO Head Office
Bagsværdvej 161
2880 Bagsværd
Denmark
+45 4436 6800

holidays@bimco.org
www.bimco.org

Book ISBN: 978-1-85609-961-5
eBook ISBN: 978-1-85609-962-2

Printed and bound by Trade Colour Printing, Penrith, UK

Printed in compliance with
Enviromental Certificate DS/ES ISO 14001

Contents

Introduction

One of the cornerstones of BIMCO is to support members' businesses by delivering practical tools, advice and guidance. An example is the indispensable voyage planning tool: the BIMCO Holiday Calendar. Access to the Holiday Calendar data is offered to members on the BIMCO website. The printed version is available for purchase for everyone in the industry and offered with a discount to BIMCO members. Support and advice relating to holiday information – a benefit exclusive to BIMCO members – is not included when purchasing the printed holiday calendar. Should our members prefer a direct connection between their systems and the BIMCO Holiday database, we suggest utilising our public released API. To get access please forward your request to holidays@bimco.org, and we will guide you through the application process.

It is not unusual that charterers and owners agree to be guided by the BIMCO Holiday Calendar in order to avoid any doubt over what is considered a holiday under the charter party. Where differences occur between what is stated in the Holiday Calendar and actual experience, either about holidays or working hours, we recommend members to seek information on the BIMCO website which is continually updated. This may initially explain a discrepancy.

Should there still be disagreements about the actual dates, we recommend that members contact BIMCO for advice using holidays@bimco.org. We will utilise our network and reliable sources and provide assistance and guidance to the extent applicable information is available to us.

The Holiday Calendar provides details on holidays on the following levels:
- National / Federal
- Regional / State / Provincial
- Local

In general, holidays can be categorized as follows:
- Fixed
- Movable
- Relative

Fixed holidays in context of the Holiday Calendar are fixed in accordance with the Gregorian/western calendar. As such, they will fall on the same date each year in the calendar. Movable holidays might as well be fixed, but in accordance with other calendars such as the Islamic lunar calendar which itself is subject to observations – not calculations. Relative holidays are fixed in accordance with other events – e.g. Ascension Day – or calculated – e.g. (western) Easter.

Additional information on the port working hours are provided for various ports. The details for working hours may include:

- Ordinary/overtime hours
- Shift work possibilities
- Restrictions or limitations on certain days

Please find below a summary of notes and definitions for terms frequently encountered:

Holidays:

A British Arbitration Award defined holidays in the context of laytime as follows:
"A holiday, by law and accepted practice, is a day which the competent authority has declared or decreed to be a holiday. It is irrelevant whether work is or is not performed on such holiday, or whether work is charged at normal or overtime rates [...]What matters and the only point which matters is whether the competent authority has declared the day in question to be a holiday."

Holidays are days that have been elevated to having the legal status of holidays by the competent local, regional or national authority with the authority to elevate certain days to the status of legalised holidays.

Labour agreement holidays: (for instance, longshore holidays in the USA)
Holidays that extent from agreements between employers and employees may or may not coincide with public holidays. If they do not coincide with public holidays, they constitute days free of work according to a labour agreement and cannot be regarded as holidays in terms of laytime computing.

Conditional holidays:

Conditional holidays have a limited public appliance but are irrespective of legislative support derived for matters concerning the individual. For this reason, conditional holidays are excluded from BIMCO holidays, and BIMCO continuously advises not to regard conditional holidays as holidays in terms of laytime computing.

Conditional holidays are usually only applicable to followers of a certain religion, e.g.: Eid al-Fitr in Argentina and the Armenian Christmas in Lebanon. Some public holidays can easily be confused with conditional holidays – e.g. Christmas Day in Iraq. In case of doubt, BIMCO recommends members to seek our guidance for clarification.

BIMCO holidays:

Parties agreeing to use the term "BIMCO Holidays" should kindly notice that BIMCO reserves every right to amend the information contained in the BIMCO holiday database. Not only will the Islamic holidays subject to lunar observations be adjusted, but holidays may be decreed or declared with short notice.

Super holidays:

BIMCO is not aware of a universally recognised definition for this term and strongly recommends it is avoided all together. As far as BIMCO is concerned, a day is either a holiday or not. There is no need to make contractual separation of holidays into different categories. Should the parties nevertheless find it necessary to use the term, we invariably recommend they define exactly what days this term covers.

Charter party holidays:

India operates extensive two-tier holiday schedules. Laytime allowed would be artificially inflated if all these holidays were to be excepted from laytime. Shipowners would then have to hold out for correspondingly higher freight rates. For this reason, a system of declaring "charter party holidays" has existed for many years. This is mostly done by the local chamber of commerce. It is generally acknowledged that only holidays that are declared "charter party holidays" have a bearing on counting of laytime. As outlined by the Bombay Chamber of Commerce and Industry:

"The Chamber as empowered by the resolution passed at its General Committee Meeting held on July 22, 1881 declares the Charter Party Holidays for the Mumbai Port."

In general, this procedure has been accepted by charterers, and disputes on these matters have been very few. Unfortunately, it has on an earlier occasion been reported to BIMCO that in a laytime dispute concerning a ship discharging at Indian ports, the charterers had totally disregarded this time-honoured position and, based on a British arbitration award, claimed that any holiday in India, regardless of its status, has the effect of interrupting counting of laytime.

To avoid similar disputes, we recommend that only "charter party holidays" will be excepted from the running of laytime, and that this point should be discussed and covered adequately in the charter party.

Weekends and weekend clauses:

There are generally two weekend schedules based on either:
*   Friday, or
*   Sunday

While many Western countries observe a Saturday-Sunday weekend, with Sunday sometimes being gazetted as a public holiday, it is common in Islamic and Judaic countries to observe a Friday-Saturday weekend, with Friday sometimes being gazetted as a public holiday.

The duration of weekends is another topic, as well as the legal definitions of working weeks, weekly days of rest and weekends. Where such information is available to BIMCO, please find this as a general note for the applicable national, regional or local entity.

Considering the above, we strongly advise shipowners to be careful not to agree on "Saturday-clauses" or extensive weekend clauses. Due investigations of the possibility to work all days of the week should be made prior to agreeing on such terms. The only way to avoid disputes is to cover the question of e.g. weekly days of rest, etc. adequately, clearly and expressly in chartering negotiations and in the charter party. A suitable clause to cover this subject clearly could read as follows:

"In ports of loading or discharging where a day other than Sunday is the recognised weekly day of rest, such a day takes the place of Sunday in this context and is excepted (unless used), and Sunday is counted as a normal layday."

Several countries will observe a substitution of holidays falling on non-working day, be it either:

- Other holidays
- Weekly days of rest
- Weekends

Any case of holiday observation offset – if any – is subject to legislation. In cases where such information is available to BIMCO, please find it mentioned in the notes for the applicable governing level.

Ramadan:
Ramadan is the ninth month of the Islamic year and is observed as a thirty-day fast during the hours of daylight by Muslims. As a result, labour conditions may be difficult and, in any event, the labourers' working capacity will decrease. The month of Ramadan is not in itself a holiday, but the first day(s) of the following month, Shawwal, is usually a holiday – often called "Eid-el-Fitr", "Ramadan Bairam" or just "Ramadan" – in celebration of the end of fasting.

In the Islamic year 1442 – correlating partly with the year 2021 in the Gregorian calendar – Ramadan is expected to last from approximately 12 April to 11 May 2021. It must be noted that Islamic holidays are usually listed as "approximate" dates deliberately as they depend upon the actual appearance of the moon.

Check your contract before fixing:
Holidays can cause disputes and unnecessary cost. This book will help parties avoid many pitfalls even though knowledge about holidays around the world cannot rescue a badly worded contract. BIMCO therefore strongly advices parties to prepare contracts well. Professional advice on what to do and what to avoid can be found in the BIMCO publication "Check Before Fixing". The next version will be published in spring 2021.

Disclaimer:
The printed Holiday Calendar is intended as and can only ever serve as a guide. It must be understood that any details given in no way override charter parties or the established interpretation of charter parties.

Albania

General holidays

January	1-2	New Year's Days
March	14	Summer Day
-	22	Nevruz
April	4	Easter (Catholic)
May	1	Labour Day
-	2	Easter (Orthodox)
-	13[1]	Eid al-Fitr
July	20[1]	Eid al-Adha
September	5	Saint Teresa Canonisation Day
November	28	Independence Day
-	29	Liberation Day
December	8	Youth Day
-	25	Christmas Day

[1] Exact date(s) subject to sighting of the moon.

Durazzo (Durres)
Working hours:
Monday - Saturday: 24 hours per day, non-stop.
Sunday and holidays: Workable upon request at extra payment.

Algeria

General holidays

January	1	New Year's Day
-	12	Yennayer
May	1	Labour Day
-	13[1]	Eid-ul-Fitr
July	5	Independence Day
-	20[1]	Eid Al Adha
August	10[1]	Awal Muharram
-	19[1]	Ashura
October	19[1]	Birthday of the Prophet
November	1	Anniversary of the Revolution

[1] Exact date(s) subject to sighting of the moon.

Algiers
Working hours:
Saturday - Thursday: 07:00-19:00.
Shift work times: First shift 07:00-13:00 and second shift 13:00-19:00 at normal rates.
Third shift 19:00-01:00, fourth shift 01:00-07:00, possible on overtime at double rates.
Friday and holidays: Shift work is possible at overtime rates.
All port operations are at double rates 21.00-05.00.

Annaba
Working hours:
Saturday - Thursday: First shift 06:00-12:45 and second shift 12:45-19:00.
Night shift: First shift 19:00-01:00, second shift 01:00-06:00.
Friday and holidays: First and second shift on overtime. No night shift.
Port authority, pilot station, mooring labour and tug boats available on a 24-hour basis.

Arzew
Working hours:
First shift 07:00-13:00 and second shift 13:00-19:00 at normal rates. Third shift
19:00-01:00 and fourth shift 01:00-07:00 possible on overtime at double rates.
Friday and holidays: Shift work is possible at overtime rates.

Bejaia
Working hours:
Saturday - Thursday: 07:00-19:00.
Shift work times: First shift 07:00-13:00 and second shift 13:00-19:00 at normal rates.
Third shift 19:00-01:00 and fourth shift 01:00-07:00 possible on overtime at 150% rates.
Friday and holidays: Shift work is possible at overtime rates.

Djen - Djen
Working hours:
Saturday - Thursday: 07:00-19:00.
Shift work times: First shift 07:00-13:00 and second shift 13:00-19:00 at normal rates.
Third shift 19:00-01:00 and fourth shift 01:00-07:00 possible on overtime at double rates.
Friday and holidays: Shift work is possible at overtime rates.

Ghazaouet
Working hours:
Saturday - Thursday: 06:30-18:30.
First shift 06:30-12:30 and second shift 12:30-18:30 at normal rates. Third shift
18:30-00:30 and fourth shift 00:30-06:30 can be worked on requested double rates.
Friday and holidays: Shift work is possible at overtime rates.
All port operations are at double rates.

Mostaganem
Working hours:
Saturday - Thursday: 07:00-19:00.
First shift 07:00-13:00 and second shift 13:00-19:00 at normal rates. Third shift
19:00-01:00 and fourth shift 01:00-07:00 possible on overtime at double rates.
Friday and holidays: Shift work is possible at overtime rates.
All port operations are at double rates 21.00-05.00.

Oran
Working hours:
Saturday - Thursday: 07:00-19:00.
First shift 07:00-13:00 and second shift 13:00-19:00 at normal rates. Third shift
19:00-01:00 and fourth shift 01:00-07:00 possible on overtime at 100% extra.
Friday and holidays: Shift work is possible at overtime rates.
All port operations are at normal rates.

Skikda
Working hours:
Saturday - Thursday: 06:00-18:30.
Saturday - Thursday: First shift 06:00-12:00 and second shift 13:00-18:30. Third shift 19:00-01:00 and fourth shift 01:00-05:00 possible on overtime at double rates.
Friday and holidays: Shift work is possible at 175% rates.
All port operations are at 175% rates.

Tenes
Working hours:
Saturday - Thursday: 07:00-19:00.
Shift work times: First shift 07:00-13:00 and second shift 13:00-19:00 at normal rates.
Third shift 19:00-01:00 and fourth shift 01:00-07:00 possible on overtime at double rates.
Friday and holidays: Shift work is possible at double rates.

Angola
General holidays

January	1	New Year's Day
February	4	Liberation Day
-	16	Carnival
March	8	International Women's Day
-	23	Liberation of Southern Africa
April	2	Good Friday
-	4	Peace Day
May	1	Labour Day
September	17	National Heroes' Day
November	2	All Souls' Day
-	11	Independence Day
December	25	Christmas Day

Local holidays

Cabinda

May	28	Cabinda City Anniversary

Working hours:
Monday - Sunday: Normal working hours 00:00-00:00.
Meal breaks: 12:30-13:30 and 20:00-21:00.
Work available on holidays on request of overtime.

Lobito

September	2	Lobito City Anniversary

Working hours:
Monday - Sunday: Normal working hours 07:30-17:00. Work available 17:00-07:30 on request. Meal breaks: 12:30-13:30 and 19:00-20:30.
Work available on weekends and holidays.

Luanda
Working hours:
Commercial port
Monday - Friday: Normal working hours 07:00-16:00, 15:30-00:00, and 23:00-08:00.
Saturday - Sunday 07:00-16:00, 15:30-00:00, and 23:00-08:00 at overtime
Meal breaks 12:30-13:30 and 20:00-21:00.
Sonils oil base.
Monday - Sunday: Normal working hours 00:00-00:00.
Meal breaks 12:30-13:30 and 20:00-21:00.
Work available holidays at additional cost.

Namibe

August	4	Namibe City Anniversary

Working hours:
Monday - Sunday: Normal working hours 07:30-21:00.
Work available 21:00-00:00 on request.
Meal breaks: 12:30-13:30 and 20:00-21:00.
Work available weekends and holidays at additional cost.

Palanca Oil Terminal
Working hours:
Mooring: 06:00-15:00. Unmooring: 24 hours a day.

Soyo

April	5	Soyo City Anniversary

Working hours:
Monday - Sunday: Normal working hours 08:00-17:00.
Work available 17:00-08:00 on request.
Meal breaks: 12:30-13:30 and 19:00-20:30.
Work available on weekends and holidays.

Antigua and Barbuda

General holidays

January	1	New Year's Day
April	2	Good Friday
-	5	Easter Monday
May	3	Labour Day
-	24	Whit Monday
August	2-3	Carnival
November	1	Independence Day
December	9	V.C. Bird Day
-	25	Christmas Day
-	26	Boxing Day

The following holiday will be observed with an offset in certain cases:

If January 1 is a Sunday, New Year's Day will be observed the following Monday.

If November 1 is a Saturday or a Sunday, Independence Day will be observed the following Monday.

If Christmas Day is a Saturday or Sunday, a holiday will be substituted December 27.

All Sundays are Common Law holidays.

Argentina

General holidays

January	1	New Year's Day
February	15-16	Carnival
March	24	Day of Remembrance for Truth and Justice
April	2	Malvinas Islands Day
-	2	Good Friday
May	1	Labour Day
-	25	Anniversary of the 1810 Revolution
June	21[1]	Commemoration of the death of General Martín Miguel de Güemes
-	20	Commemoration of the death of General Manuel Belgrano
July	9	Independence Day
August	16[1]	Commemoration of the death of General José de San Martin
October	11[1]	Respect for Cultural Diversity Day
November	20[1]	Argentinean Sovereignty Memorial Day
December	8	Immaculate Conception
-	25	Christmas Day

[1] Movable holiday
If a movable holiday falls on a Tuesday or Wednesday, it will be observed the preceding Monday. If a movable holiday falls on a Thursday or Friday, it will be observed the following Monday.

Local holidays

Buenos Aires

Buenos Aires

November	10	City Founding Day

Working hours:
Southdock and Newport:
Monday - Friday: 07:00-13:00 and 13:00-19:00. No meal breaks. Overtime can be worked at extra cost 19:00-01:00 and 01:00-07:00.
Saturday: 07:00-13:00. Overtime can be worked at extra cost 13:00-19:00 and 19:00-01:00.
Sunday and holidays: 07:00-13:00, 13:00-19:00, 19:00-01:00 and 01:00-07:00 all at overtime on request. No work 24 to 26 December and 31 to 2.

Bahia Blanca

April	11	City Founding Day
September	24	City's Saints Day

Working hours:

Monday - Friday: 07:00-19:00 at normal. 19:00-01:00 can be worked on request.
Saturday: 07:00-13:00 at normal. 13:00-01:00 on request.
Sunday: 01:00-07:00 at 135% extra. 07:00-01:00 can be worked at 85% extra.
National holidays: Work is possible at 200% extra.
There is no work after 13:00 on 24 December (Christmas Eve) and 31 December (New Year's Eve).

Campana

July	6	Foundational memorial day of Campana city

Working hours:

Monday - Friday: 07:00-19:00 at normal rates. 19:00-01:00 workable at 100% extra.
Saturday: 07:00-13:00 at normal rates. 13:00-01:00 workable at 100% extra.
Sunday: Workable at 100% extra.
National holidays: Work is possible at 200% extra.
There is no work after 19:00 on 24 December (Christmas Eve) and 31 December (New Year's Eve).

La Plata

November	19	City Anniversary

Working hours:

Monday - Friday: 07:00-13:00 and 13:00-19:00 at normal rates. Overtime 19:00-01:00 and 01:00-07:00 at 100% extra.
Saturday: 01:00-07:00, 07:00-13:00 and 13:00-19:00 at 100% extra. 19:00-01:00 at 150% extra.
Sunday and holidays: 07:00-13:00 and 13:00-19:00 at 100% extra. 19:00-01:00 and 01:00-07:00 at 150% extra.

Mar del Plata

February	14	City Founding Day
November	22	St. Cecilia - Patron of the City

Working hours:
Monday - Friday: 07:00-19:00 at normal rates. Overtime can be arranged on request.
Saturday: 07:00-13:00 at normal rates. 13:00-19:00 at 100% extra. 19:00-01:00 and 01:00-07:00 at 150% extra.
Sunday: 07:00-13:00 and 13:00-19:00 at 100% extra. 19:00-01:00 and 01:00-07:00 at 200% extra.

Necochea - Quequen

July	16	Patron of the City (Necochea)
September	24	Patron of the City (Quequen)
October	12	City Anniversary (Necochea)

Working hours:
Monday - Friday: 07:00-19:00 at normal rates. Overtime can be arranged on request.
Saturday: 07:00-13:00 at normal rates. 13:00-19:00 at 100% extra. 19:00-01:00 and 01:00-07:00 at 150% extra.
Sunday: 07:00-13:00 and 13:00-19:00 at 100% extra. 19:00-01:00 and 01:00-07:00 at 200% extra.

Puerto Rosales
Working hours:
24 hours per day, 7 days per week (Saturday, Sunday and holidays included).

Ramallo
Working hours:
Monday - Friday: 06:00-18:00 at normal rates. 18.00-06.00 overtime on request.
Saturday: 06:00-12:00 at normal. 12.00-06.00 overtime on request.
Sunday: All times are on request overtime.

San Nicolas

Working hours:
Monday - Friday: 06:00-18:00 at normal rates. 18:00-06:00 workable at extra rates.
Saturday: 06:00-12:00 at normal rates. 12:00-00:00 at 100% extra.
Sunday: Can be worked at 100% extra.
National holidays: Work is possible at 200% extra.
There is no work after 13:00 on 24 December (Christmas Eve) and 31 December (New Year's Eve).

San Pedro

June	25	City Foundation Day
September	8	Patron of the City

Working hours:
Monday - Friday: 06:00-18:00 at normal rates. 18.00-06.00 work is available at overtime rates.
Shift working times: First shift 06:00-12:00. Second shift 12:00-18:00.
No meal breaks.
Saturday: 06:00-12:00 at normal rates. 12.00-06.00 work is available at overtime rates.
Sunday and holidays: Work is available at overtime rates.

Chubut

April	30	Demarcation day
July	28	Anniversary of the first Welsh settlement
December	13	Día del Petróleo Nacional

Comodoro Rivadavia

February	23	City Anniversary
December	13	Dia del Petroleo

Working hours:
Monday - Friday: 07:00-13:00 and 13:00-19:00 at normal rates. 19:00-01:00 and 01:00-07:00 at overtime rates. No meal breaks.
Saturday: 07:00-13:00 at normal rates. 13:00-00:00 overtime can be arranged on request.

Puerto Madryn

July	28	City Anniversary

Working hours:
Monday - Friday: 07:00-13:00, 13:00-19:00 at normal rates. 19:00-01:00 at 100% extra.
Saturday: 07:00-13:00 at normal rates. 13:00-01:00 overtime on request.
Sunday and holidays: Work is available at 100% extra.

Entre Rios

February	3	Batalla de Caseros
June	27	Día del Trabajador Estatal
September	29	San Miguel Arcángel

Diamante

February	27	City Founding Day
September	16	Patron of Diamante

Working hours:
Monday - Friday: 07:00-13:00 and 13:00-19:00 at normal rates. 19:00-01:00 and 01:00-07:00 workable at 100% extra.
Saturday: 07:00-13:00 at normal rates. 13:00-19:00 and 19:00-01:00 workable at 100% extra.
Sunday: 01:00-07:00, 07:00-13:00, 13:00-19:00 and 19:00-01:00 workable at 100% extra.
National holidays: Work possible 07:00-13:00 and 13:00-19:00 at 100% extra.
There is no work after 13.00 on 24 December (Christmas Eve) and 31 December (New Year's Eve).

Rio Negro

San Antonio Este

July	10	City Anniversary

Working hours:

Monday - Friday: 07:00-23:00 at normal rates. 23:00-07:00 at extra rates.

Saturday: 07:00-15:00 at normal rates. 15:00-01:00 at 50% extra.

Sunday and holidays: Work is available at overtime rates except for 1 May (Labour Day), when there is no work.

There is no work after 13:00 on 24 December (Christmas Eve) and 31 December (New Year's Eve).

Santa Cruz

Deseado

June	15	City Foundation Day
August	16	Patron of State of Santa Cruz

Working hours:

Monday - Friday: 07:00-19:00 at normal rates. 19:00-07:00 at 50% extra.

Saturday: 07:00-13:00 at normal rates. 13:00-19:00 at 100% extra and 19:00-01:00 at 150% extra.

Sunday and holidays: Work is available 24 hours a day at overtime rates.

There is no work after 13:00 on 24 December (Christmas Eve) and 31 December (New Year's Eve).

Puerto Punta Quilla

Working hours:

Monday - Friday: 07:00-13:00 and 13:00-19:00.

Saturday: 07:00-13:00.

All other periods are at overtime rates of 100%.

National holidays: Work possible 07:00-13:00 and 13:00-19:00 at 200% extra.

No work after 13:00 on following days: 24 December (Christmas Eve) and 31 December (New Year's Eve).

Rio Gallegos

August	16	Patron of State of Santa Cruz
December	19	City Founding Day

Working hours:
Monday - Friday: 07:00-13:00 and 13.00-19.00 at normal rates. 19.00-01.00 and 01.00-07.00 overtime on request.
Shift working times: First shift 01:00-07:00. Second shift 07:00-13:00. Third shift 13:00-19:00. Fourth shift 19:00-01:00.
Saturday, Sunday and holidays: Work is available at an overtime rate of 100%.

San Julian
Working hours:
Monday to Friday: 07:00-13:00 and 13:00-19:00 at normal rates.
Shift working times: First shift 01:00-07:00. Second shift 07:00-13:00. Third shift 13:00-19:00. Fourth shift 19:00-01:00.
Saturday, Sunday and holidays: Work is available at an overtime rate of 100%.

Santa Fe

November	15	Administrative holiday

Rosario

October	7	Day of the Virgin

Working hours:
Monday - Friday: 06:00-12:00 and 12:00-18:00 at normal rates. 18:00-00:00 and 00:00-06:00 at 50% extra.
Saturday: 06:00-12:00 at normal rates. 00:00-06:00 at 50% extra. 12:00-00:00 at 100% extra.
Sunday and holidays: 00:00-00:00 at 100% extra.

San Lorenzo
Working hours:
Monday - Friday: 06:00-12:00 and 12:00-18:00 at normal rates. 18:00-00:00 and 00:00-06:00 at 50% extra.
Saturday: 06:00-12:00 at normal rates. 12:00-18:00, 18:00-00:00 and 00:00-06:00 at overtime rates.
Shift working times: First shift 00:00-06:00. Second shift 06:00-12:00. Third shift 12:00-18:00. Fourth shift 18:00-00:00.
Sunday and holidays: Work is available at an overtime rates.

Santa Fe

Working hours:

Monday - Friday: 06:00-18:00 at normal rates. 19:00-01:00 and 01:00-07:00 workable at 100% extra.

Saturday: 06:00-13:00 at normal rates. 13:00-19:00 and 19:00-01:00 at 100% extra.

Sunday: Can be worked at 100% extra.

National holidays: Work is possible at 100% extra.

There is no work after 13:00 on 24 December (Christmas Eve) and 31 December (New Year's Eve).

Villa Constitucion

February	14	City Anniversary
June	29	St. Paul – Patron of the City

Working hours:

Acindar (ING Acevedo Berth): 24 hours per day. Shift work: Starting at 06:00 and 18:00. No meal breaks.

Servicio Portuarios Berths: Normal hours 06:00-18:00. Shift work: Personnel change every three hours. No meal breaks.

Holidays: 24 hours per day. Shift work: Starting at 06:00 and 18:00. No meal breaks.

Tierra del Fuego

April	2	Provincial holiday

Aruba

General holidays

January	1	New Year's Day
-	25	G.F. Croes (Betico) Day
February	15	Carnival Monday
March	18	Aruba Day
April	2	Good Friday
-	5	Easter Monday
-	27	King's Day
May	1	Labour Day
-	13	Ascension Day
December	25	Christmas Day
-	26	Boxing Day

Barcadera
Working hours:
Monday - Friday: 07:30-00:00 at regular rates. 00:00-07:30 at overtime rates.
Saturday, Sunday and holidays: Work available 24 hours per day at overtime rates.
Holidays: Availability of work can be reduced to half a day.

Oranjestad
Working hours:
Monday - Friday: 07:30-00:00 at regular rates. 00:00-07:30 at overtime rates.
Saturday, Sunday and holidays: Work available 24 hours per day at overtime rates.
Holidays: Availability of work can be reduced to half a day.

San Nicholas
Working hours:
24 hours per day, 7 days per week, 365 days per year.
Holidays: Availability of work can be reduced to half a day.

Australia

General holidays

All holidays are applied at state level.

Territorial holidays

New South Wales

January	1	New Year's Day
-	26	Australia Day
April	2	Good Friday
-	3	Easter Saturday
-	4	Easter Sunday
-	5	Easter Monday
-	25	ANZAC Day
June	14	Queen's Birthday
October	4	Labour Day
December	25	Christmas Day
-	26	Boxing Day

If January 1 coincides with a Saturday or Sunday, the following Monday shall be a holiday.

If Australia Day coincides with a Saturday or Sunday, the following Monday shall be a holiday instead.

If Christmas Day coincides with a Friday, the following Monday shall be a holiday. If it coincides with a Saturday, the following Monday and Tuesday shall be public holidays.

Northern Territory

January	1	New Year's Day
-	26	Australia Day
April	2	Good Friday
-	3	Easter Saturday
-	5	Easter Monday
-	25	ANZAC Day
May	3	May Day
June	14	Queen's Birthday
August	2	Picnic Day
December	24[1]	Christmas Eve
-	25	Christmas Day
-	26	Boxing Day
-	31[1]	New Years Eve

[1] From 7PM.

If January 1 coincides with a Saturday or Sunday, the following Monday shall be a holiday.

If Australia Day coincides with a Saturday or Sunday, the following Monday shall be a holiday instead.

If ANZAC Day coincides with a Sunday, the following Monday shall be a holiday instead.

If Christmas Day coincides with a Friday, the following Monday shall be a holiday. If it coincides with a Saturday, the following Monday and Tuesday shall be public holidays.

Darwin

Working hours:

24 hours' operations, 7 days a week.

East ARM Wharf is 24 hours operational.

Fort Hill Wharf is 24 hours operational.

Stokes Hill Wharf operates from 08:00-21:00.

Queensland

January	1	New Year's Day
-	26	Australia Day
April	2	Good Friday
-	3	The day after Good Friday
-	4	Easter Sunday
-	5	Easter Monday
-	25	ANZAC Day
May	3	Labour Day
October	4	Queen's Birthday
December	24[1]	Christmas Eve
-	25	Christmas Day
-	26	Boxing Day

[1] Christmas Eve from 6 pm.

If January 1 coincides with a Saturday or Sunday, the following Monday shall be a holiday.

If Australia Day coincides with a Saturday or Sunday, the following Monday shall be a holiday instead.

If ANZAC Day coincides with a Sunday, the following Monday shall be a holiday instead.

If Christmas Day coincides with a Friday, the following Monday shall be a holiday. If it coincides with a Saturday, the following Monday and Tuesday shall be public holidays.

Abbot Point
Working hours:
24 hours a day, 7 days a week, 365 days a year.

June	22	Show holiday

Brisbane

August	11	Brisbane show holiday

Working hours:
24 hours per day, 7 days per week if required by the party ordering services, with flexible start and finish times.

DP World Brisbane:
First shift 07:00-15:00, second shift 15:00-23:00 and third shift 23:00-07:00.

Patrick:
First shift 03:30-07:00 break 10:45-11:30, second shift 07:00-10:45 break 10:45-11:30, third shift 11:30-15:00, fourth shift 15:00-18:45, break 18:45-19:30 fifth shift 19:30-23:00, sixth shift 23:00-02:45, break 02:45-03:30.

Brisbane Container Terminals: Works on all the shifts as above.

Berths number: Brisbane Container Terminals occupies Berth 11 and 12.

Bundaberg
Working hours:
24 hours per day, 7 days per week, 365 days per year.

May	27	Annual Show

Cairns
Working hours:
The port operates 24 hours a day seven days a week.

July	16	Annual Show

Dalrymple Bay
Working hours:
24 hours per day, 7 days a week, 365 days per year.

June	17	Show holiday

Gladstone

August	9	Annual Show

Working hours:
24 hours per day, 7 days a week, 365 days a year.
All bulk cargoes – 24 hours.
Boyne Smelter Berth – Normal working hours 07:00-19:00; 19:00-07:00.
Bulk Coal Terminals – 24/7, 363 days per year. There is no work on 2 April (Good Friday) and 25 December (Christmas Day) and also no work 00:00-07:00 on 3 April (The day after Good Friday), 23:00-00:00 on 24 December (Christmas Eve).
Conventional and container ships can start at any time and work 3 x 8-hour shifts.

Hay Point
Working hours:
24 hours per day, 7 days a week, 365 days a year.

June	17	Show holiday

Mackay
Working hours:
Shift work times: First shift 07:00-15:00 and second shift 15:00-23:00 at normal rates.
Third shift 23:00-07:00 possible on overtime by request.

June	17	Show holiday

Rockhampton
Working hours:
Normal working hours 08:00-16:30, meal break 12:00-12:30.
Overtime by request on any day 16:30-19:30.

June	10	Annual Show

Townsville
Working hours:
First shift 08:00-16:00, meal 12:35-13:00. Second shift 16:00-01:00, meal 20:35-21:00.
Third shift 00:00-08:00.
Townsville is a 24-hour port on holidays.
Overtime by request on Good Friday and Christmas days.

July	5	Annual Show

South Australia

January	1	New Year's Day
-	26	Australia Day
April	2	Good Friday
-	3	Easter Saturday
-	5	Easter Monday
-	25	ANZAC Day
May	17	State Holiday
June	14	Queen's Birthday
October	4	Labour Day
December	24	Christmas Eve
-	25[1]	Christmas Day
-	26	Boxing Day
-	31[1]	New Year's Eve

[1] Christmas Eve and New Year's Eve from 7pm.

If ANZAC Day coincides with a Sunday, the following Monday shall be a holiday.

If any of the following holiday coincides with a Saturday or Sunday, the following Monday will be a holiday instead:
New Year's Day
Australia Day
Christmas Day.

If Boxing Day coincides with a Saturday, the following Monday shall be a holiday instead. If Boxing Day coincides with a Sunday or Monday the following Tuesday shall be a holiday.

All Sundays are holidays.

Adelaide
Working hours:
Patrick: First shift 07:30-15:30, second shift 15:30-23:30 and third shift 23:30-07:30.
DP World Adelaide: First shift 07:00-15:00, second shift 15:00-23:00 and third shift 23:00-07:00.
Meal breaks: First shift: 09:30-09:50 and 12:00-12:25. Second shift: 17:00-17:20 and 19:30-19:55. Third shift: 00:30-00:50 and 03:00-03:25.
Applied shifts are nominal. All shifts is with variable duration 7-12 hours, starting any time.

Port Giles
Working hours:
08:00-15:00 and 15:00-22:00, including Saturday, Sunday and holidays.

Port Lincoln
Working hours:
08:00-15:00 and 15:00-22:00, including Saturday, Sunday and holidays.

AUSTRALIA

Port of Ardrossan
Working hours:
08:00-15:00 and 15:00-22:00, including Saturday, Sunday and holidays.

Port Pirie
Working hours:
Day shift 08:00-15:00, with up to three hours (15:00-18:00) overtime. Evening shift 15:00-22:00 and night shift 00:00-07:00.
Holidays: All shifts workable on request of overtime.
Shifts may start with an offset up to -2/+4 hours with no penalty.

Thevenard
Working hours:
Monday - Friday: Day shift 08:00-15:00, evening shift 15:00-22:00 and night shift 22:30-08:00.
Saturday, Sunday and holidays: All shifts workable.

Wallaroo
Working hours:
Monday - Sunday: 08:00-15:00 and 15:00-22:00.
Holidays: All shifts workable on request of overtime.

Tasmania

January	1	New Year's Day
-	26	Australia Day
March	8	Eight Hours Day
April	2	Good Friday
-	5	Easter Monday
-	6	Easter Tuesday
-	25	ANZAC Day
June	14	Queen's Birthday
December	25	Christmas Day
-	26	Boxing Day

If any of the following holidays coincides with a Saturday or Sunday, the following Monday shall be a holiday instead:
New Year's Day
Australia Day.
If Christmas Day coincides with a Saturday, the following Monday shall be a holiday. If it coincides with a Sunday, the following Tuesday shall be a public holiday.
If Boxing Day coincides with a Saturday, the following Monday shall be a holiday instead. If it coincides with a Sunday, the following Tuesday shall be a holiday instead.

Victoria

January	1	New Year's Day
-	26	Australia Day
March	8	Labour Day
April	2	Good Friday
-	3	Easter Saturday
-	4	Easter Sunday
-	5	Easter Monday
--	25	ANZAC Day
June	14	The Queen's Birthday
September	24[1]	Friday before the AFL Grand Final
November	2[2]	Melbourne Cup
December	25	Christmas Day
	26	Boxing Day

[1] To be confirmed.
[2] May be substituted locally
If New Year's Day falls on a weekend, it is observed the following Monday.
If Christmas Day or Boxing Day falls during the weekend, additional holidays will be observed with a two-day delay.

Geelong
Working hours:
First shift 08:00-15:00, breaks 10:00-10:20 and 12:30-12:55. Second shift 15:00-22:00, breaks 17:00-17:25 and 19:30-19:50. Third shift 23:00-06:00.

Melbourne
Working hours:
24 hours per day, 7 days a week.

Portland
Working hours:
First shift 08:00-15:00, breaks 10:00-10:15 and 12:30-13:00. Second shift 15:00-22:00, breaks 17:00-17:15 and 19:30-20:00. Third shift 23:00-06:00, breaks 01:00-01:15 and 03:30-04:00.
Woodchip ships: First shift 07:00-15:00. Second shift 15:00-23:00. Third shift 23:00-07:00.
Ingot ships: First shift 08:00-15:00. Second shift 15:30-22:30. Third shift 23:00-06:00.

Western Australia

January	1	New Year's Day
-	26	Australia Day
March	1	Labour Day
April	2	Good Friday
-	5	Easter Monday
-	25	ANZAC Day
June	7	Western Australia Day
September	27	Queen's Birthday
December	25	Christmas Day
-	26	Boxing Day

If any of the following holidays coincides with a Saturday or Sunday, the following Monday shall be a holiday instead: Australia Day.

If Christmas Day Coincides with a Friday, the following Monday shall be a holiday. If it coincides with a Saturday or Sunday, the following Monday and Tues shall be holidays.

Azerbaijan

General holidays

January	1-2	New Year Holiday
March	8	Women's Day
-	20-24[1]	Novruz
May	9	Victory Day
-	13-14[1]	Ramazan Bayrami Holiday
-	28	Republic Day
June	15	National Salvation Day
-	26	Armed Forces Day
July	20-21[1]	Gurban Bayrami Holiday
October	18	National Independence Day
November	9	Flag Day
-	12	Constitution Day
-	17	National Revival Day
December	31	World Azerbaijanis Solidarity Day

[1] To be confirmed.

Baku

Working hours:

Monday - Friday: 08:00-17:00. Shift work times: First shift 08:00-20:00 and second shift 20:00-08:00. Meal break 12:30-13:30.

Saturday, Sunday and holidays: Work is available at double overtime rate.

Azores

General holidays

January	1	New Year's Day
April	2	Good Friday
-	4	Easter Sunday
-	25	Anniversary of the Revolution
May	1	Labour Day
-	24[1]	Whit Monday
June	10	Portugal Day
-	3	Corpus Christi
August	15	Ascension Day
October	5	Implementation of the Republic
November	1	All Saints Day
December	1	Independence Restoration
-	8	Immaculate Conception
-	25	Christmas Day

[1] Regional holiday..

Local holidays

Angra do Heroismo

June	24	Dia de Sao João

Working hours:
Monday - Friday: 00:00-00:00. Meal hours 12:00-13:00 and 17:00-18:00.
Saturday, Sunday and holidays: Overtime 00:00-00:00 at 151% extra. No work on
1 January and 25 December. On 24 and 31 December, work stops at 17:00.

Horta

June	24	Dia de Sao João

Working hours:
Harbour personnel and stevedores:
Monday - Friday: 08:00-17:00. Overtime 17:00-00:00 and 00:00-08:00 at extra cost.
Meal hours 12:00-13:00, 17:00-18:00 and 02:00-03:00.
Saturday, Sunday and holidays: Overtime 24 hours per day at overtime cost.

Ponta Delgada

May	10	Local Holiday

Working hours:
Monday - Friday: 08:00-17:00. Overtime 17:00-20:00, 20:00-00:00 and 00:00-08:00.
Meal hours 12:00-13:00, 20:00-21:00 and 02:00-03:00.

Praia da Vitoria

August	11	Municipal Holiday

Working hours:
Monday - Friday: 08:00-00:00. First shift 08:00-17:00, second shift 18:00-00:00.
Meal hours 12:00-13:00 and 17:00-18:00.

Harbour personnel work 24/7

Bahamas

General holidays

January	1	New Year's Day
-	10	Majority Rule Day
April	2	Good Friday
-	5	Easter Monday
May	24	Whit Monday
June	4	Labour Day
July	10	Independence Day
August	2	Emancipation Day
October	12	National Heroes Day
December	25	Christmas Day
-	26	Boxing Day

If a public holiday falls on a Sunday, the following day shall be a public holiday.

Freeport

Working hours:

Monday - Friday: 08:00-12:00 and 13:00-17:00. 17:00-00:00 can be worked at 50% extra. 00:00-08:00 can be worked at 100% extra.

Saturday, Sunday and holidays: Workable at 100% extra.

CEMEX Bahamas Ltd.

Work at this dock can be done throughout the year on a 24 hour basis or as terminal operators decide.

Bahamas Oil Refining Company

These facilities are not affected by holidays and operations are carried on throughout the year 24/7.

Grand Bahama Shipyard

These facilities are not affected by holidays and operations are carried on throughout the year 24/7.

Bahrain

General holidays

January	1	New Year's Day
May	1	Labour Day
-	14[1]	Eid Al Fitr
July	20[1]	Eid Al Adha
August	9[1]	Hijri New Year
-	18[1]	Ashoora
October	18[1]	Prophet's Birthday
December	16	National Day

[1] Exact date(s) subject to sighting of the moon.

Bangladesh

General holidays

February	21	Language Martyrs' Day
March	17	Sheikh Mujibur Rahman's Birthday
-	26	Independence Day
-	29[1]	Shabe Barat
April	14	Bengali New Year
May	1	Labour Day
-	7	Jumatul Bidah
-	10[1]	Shabekdar
-	13-15[1]	Eid-al-Fitr
-	26[1]	Buddha Purnima
July	20-22[1]	Eid-ul-Azha
August	15	National Mourning Day
-	19[1]	Ashura
-	30	Janmastami
October	15	Durga Puja
-	19[1]	Maulud Nabi
December	16	Victory Day
-	25	Christmas Day

[1] Exact date(s) subject to sighting of the moon.

Chittagong

Working hours:

Saturday - Thursday: Day shift 08:00-12:00 and 14:00-16:30. Night shift 20:00-04:00.
Overtime 16:30-19:30 and 04:00-07:30.

Friday: Weekly holiday, but no overtime charged. Day shift 08:00-11:30 and 13:30-17:00.
Night 20:00-04:00.

Food Grain Vessels discharge:

In three shifts without overtime:

Saturday - Thursday: 07:30-16:00, 16:00-00:00 and 00:00-07:30.
Meal break 13:00-14:00.

Friday: as Saturday - Thursday but midday meal 12:30-14:00.

Holidays: Work possible at double the normal overtime rates.

Mongla

Working hours:

Saturday - Thursday: 07:00-16:00 and 19:00-03:00. Meal break 11:00-12:00.
Night shift 19:00-03:00. Overtime possible 16:00-19:00 and 03:00-07:00.

Friday: Weekly day of rest, but no overtime charged, 07:00-16:00.
Meal break 11:00-14:00. Overtime possible 16:00-19:00 and 03:00-07:00.

Holidays: Work possible at triple the normal overtime rates.

Barbados

General holidays

January	1	New Year's Day
-	21	Errol Barrow Day
April	2	Good Friday
-	5	Easter Monday
-	28	National Heroes' Day
May	1	May Day
-	24	Whit Monday
August	1[1]	Emancipation Day
-	2	Kadooment Day
November	30	Independence Day
December	25	Christmas Day
-	26[2]	Boxing Day

The following holidays will offset on certain conditions:

If January 1 or 21, April 28, May 1, November 30 or December 26 falls on a Sunday the following Monday will be observed as a holiday.

If December 25 falls on a Sunday, the following Tuesday will be observed as a holiday.

If August 1 falls on a Sunday or Monday, the following Tuesday will be observed as a holiday.

[1] Observed 3 August

[2] Observed 27 December

Belgium

General holidays

January	1	New Year's Day
April	5	Easter Monday
May	1	Labour Day
-	13	Ascension Day
-	25	Pentecost Monday
July	21	Independence Day
August	15	Assumption Day
November	1	All Saints' Day
-	11	Armistice Day
December	25	Christmas Day

Antwerp
Working hours:
Monday - Friday: First shift 06:00-13:45 with a break 10:00-10:30. Second shift 14:00-21:45 with break 18:00-18:30. Third shift 22:00-5:45 with break 02:00-02:30.
Saturday: Ordinary working day but overtime rates apply.
Sunday and holidays: Work possible at double rates.
No work on Christmas (25/12) and one on New Year's Day (01/01).

Ghent
Working hours:
Monday - Friday: 07:45-11:30 and 13:30-17:00 regular working hours.
Morning shift at 5% extra 06:15-10:00 and/or 10:30-14:00. Afternoon shift at 15% extra 14:00-17:45. Night shift at 50% extra 22:00-05:45 with meal break from 01:45-02:15.
Saturday and Sunday: Work possible at overtime by request.
Holidays: Work possible at 100% extra.
Saturday: Work possible with a minimum of 3 3/4 hours.
Sunday and holidays: Work possible with a minimum of 3 3/4 hours.

Oostende

Working hours:

Monday - Friday: First shift 08:00-15:45, day shift 06:00-13:45, second shift 14:00-21:45 and third shift 22:00-05:45.

Meal breaks 10:00-10:30, 12:00-12:30, 18:00-18:30 and 02:00-02:30.

Saturday: Same working hours but 50% overtime rates apply.

Sunday and holidays: Same working hours but 100% overtime rates apply.

Zeebrugge and Brugge

Working hours:

Monday - Friday (Day shift): 08:00-15:45, with meal break 12:00-12:30.

Morning shift at 5% extra 06:00-13:45 with meal break 10:00-10:30.

Afternoon shift at 15% extra 14:00-21:45 with meal break 18:00-18:30.

Night shift at 50% extra 22:00-05:45 with meal break 02:00-02:30.

Saturday: Work possible at 50% extra on day shift, 55% extra on morning shift, 65% extra on afternoon shift and 100% extra on night shift.

Sunday: Work possible at 100% extra on day shift, 105% extra on morning shift, 115% extra on afternoon shift and 150% extra on night shift.

Holidays: Work possible at 100% extra.

Belize

General holidays

January	1	New Year's Day
March	9	Baron Bliss Day
April	2	Good Friday
-	3	Holy Saturday
-	5	Easter Monday
May	1	Labour Day
-	24	Sovereign's Day / Commonwealth Day
September	10	St. George's Caye Day
-	21	Independence Day
October	12	Day of the Americas
November	19	Garifuna Settlement Day
December	25	Christmas Day
-	26	Boxing Day

If a holiday coincides with a Sunday, the following Monday will be observed as a holiday.

If any of the following holidays coincides with a Tuesday, Wednesday or Thursday they will be observed the preceding Monday. If they coincide with a Friday, they will be observed the following Monday:

Baron Bliss Day
Sovereign's Day
Day of the Americas
Boxing Day

Benin

General holidays

January	1	New Year's Day
-	10	Traditional Religion's Day
April	5	Easter Monday
May	1	Labour Day
-	13	Ascension Day
-	13[1]	Korite
	24	Whit Monday
July	20[2]	Tabaski
August	1	Independence Day
-	15	Assumption Day
October	19[3]	Prophet's Birthday
November	1	All Saints' Day
December	25	Christmas Day

[1] Refered to as Ramadan Day or Eid al-Adha.
[2] Refered to as Eid el-Fitr
[3] Referred to as Maouloud Day.

Cotonou

Working hours:

Monday - Friday: First shift 07:00-15:00 and second shift 15:00-23:00. Third shift at overtime and by written request from 23:00-07:00.

Saturday and Sunday: Overtime rates apply.

Holidays: Day time 50% extra and night time 100% extra.

Bermuda

General holidays

January	1	New Year's Day
April	2	Good Friday
May	28	Bermuda Day
June	21	National Heroes' Day
July	29	Emancipation Day
-	30	Mary Prince Day
September	6	Labour Day
November	11	Remembrance Day
December	25	Christmas Day
-	26	Boxing Day

Holidays falling on a Saturday or Sunday will be observed the following Monday.
If two holidays coincide the following non-holiday will be kept a public holiday.
Sundays are public holidays.

Hamilton Harbour
Working hours:
Monday - Friday: 08:00-16:30. Overtime 17:30-22:00 at double time.
Meal breaks 12:00-13:00 and 16:30-17:30.
Saturday: Overtime 08:00-16:00 at double time. Meal break 12:00-13:00.
Sunday: Overtime 08:00-16:30 and 17:30-22:00 at double time.
Meal breaks 12:00-13:00 and 16:30-17:30. Meal hours: Can be worked at overtime rates, double time.
Holidays: Workable at overtime rates, double time, with the following exceptions: There is no work except for line handling on Good Friday, Labour Day and Christmas Day.

Bonaire

General holidays

January	1	New Year's Day
April	2	Good Friday
-	4	Easter Sunday
-	5	Easter Monday
-	27	King's Birthday
-	30	Dia di Rincon
May	1	Labour Day
-	13	Ascension Day
-	23	Whit Sunday
September	6	Bonaire Day
December	15	Kingdom Day
-	25	Christmas Day
-	26	2nd Christmas Day

Brazil

General holidays

January	1	New Year's Day
April	21	Martyrdom of Tiradentes
May	1	Labour Day
September	7	Independence Day
October	12	Our Lady Aparecida - Patroness of Brazil
November	2	All Souls' Day
-	15	Proclamation of the Republic
December	25	Christmas Day

Local holidays

Alagoas

June	24	São João
-	29	São Pedro
September	16	Emancipation Day
November	20	Zumbi dos Palmares
-	30	State Evangelical Day

Maceio

April	2	Good Friday
June	29	Marshal Floriano Peixoto Memorial Day
-	3	Corpus Christi
August	27	Patroness of the City
December	8	Our Lady of Conceição

Amapa

March	19	São José
May	15	Dia de Cabralzinho
July	25	Dia de São Tiago
November	20	Dia da Consciência Negra

Santana

July	26	St. Ana Day
November	30	Day of the Evangelical
December	17	City Anniversary

Amazonas

September	5	Data Magna

Itacoatiara

April	25	Aniversário de Itacoatiara
June	29	Dia de São Pedro
September	5	Amazon elevation to the category of Province

Manaus

February	16[1]	Carnival Tuesday
-	17[1]	Ash Wednesday
September	5	Elevation of Amazon to Province
October	24	Elevation of Manaus to City
November	20	Black Conscience Day
December	8	Our Lady of Conception

[1] Until 12 PM.

Bahia

July	2	Data Magna

Aratu

February	2	Municipal holiday
April	2	Good Friday
June	3	Corpus Christi
-	24	Dia de Festa Junina
August	14	City anniversary

Ilheus

April	23	São Jorge
June	24	São João
-	28	Dia da Cidade
August	15	Nossa Senhora da Vitória

Working hours:
Monday - Saturday: Day shift 07:00-13:00 and 13:00-19:00 at ordinary rates. Night shift 19:00-01:00, 01:00-07:00 at 50% extra.
Sunday: Work from 07:00 Sunday to 07:00 Monday at 100% extra.

Salvador-Bahia Port

April	2	Good Friday
June	24	São João
-	3	Corpus Christi
December	8	Nossa Senhora da Conceição

Working hours:
Monday - Friday: Day shift 07:00-13:00 and 13:00-19:00 at ordinary rates. Night shift 19:00-01:00 and 01:00-07:00 at 50% extra.
Saturday: Day shift 07:00-13:00 at ordinary rates. From 13:00-19:00 at 50% extra. From 19:00-01:00 and 01:00-07:00 at 100% extra.
Sunday: Workable from 07:00 Sunday to 07:00 Monday at 200% extra.

Ceara

March	25	Data Magna

Mucuripe (Fortaleza)

March	19	São José
April	2	Good Friday
June	3	Corpus Christi
August	15	Nossa Senhora de Assunção

Espirito Santo

April	2	Data Magna

Barra do Riacho

April	2	Good Friday
-	3	Emancipação Política
June	3	Corpus Christi
-	24	Dia de São João Batista

Ponta do Ubu

April	2	Good Friday
June	29	São Pedro
-	9	Santo José de Anchieta
August	15	Nossa Senhora da Assunção

Vitoria

April	2	Good Friday
-	12	Nossa Senhora da Penha
June	3	Corpus Christi
September	8	Nossa Senhora da Vitória

Maranhao

July	28	Data Magna

Ponta da Madeira

April	2	Good Friday
June	29	São Pedro
September	8	Natividade de Nossa Senhora
December	8	Nossa Senhora da Conceição

Para

August	15	Data Magna

Belem

April	2	Good Friday
June	3	Corpus Christi
November	2	All Saints' Day
December	8	Nossa Senhora da Conceição

Munguba

April	2	Good Friday
June	3	Corpus Christi
-	28	São Benedito
December	8	Nossa Senhora da Conceição

Santarem

April	2	Good Friday
June	22	City Anniversary
December	8	Nossa Senhora da Conceição

Paraiba

August	5	Data Magna

Parana

Data Magna in Parana is explicitly not a civil holiday.

Paranagua

April	2	Good Friday
June	3	Corpus Christi
July	29	Dia de Nossa Senhora do Santíssimo Rosário
-	29	Dia do Evangelho

Pernambuco

March	6	Data Magna

Recife

April	2	Good Friday
June	24	Dia de São João
July	16	Nossa Senhora do Carmo
December	8	Nossa Senhora da Conceição

Working hours:

Monday - Friday: Day shift 08:00-14:00 and 14:00-20:00 at normal rates. Night shift 20:00-02:00 and 02:00-08:00 at 50% extra.

Saturday: 08:00-14:00 at normal rates. 14:00-20:00 at 50% extra. 20:00-02:00 and 02:00-04:00 at 100% extra.

Sunday and holidays: 08:00-14:00 and 14:00-20:00 at 100% extra. 20:00-02:00 and 02:00-08:00 at 250% extra.

Piaui

October	19	Data Magna

Rio de Janeiro

February	16	Carnival Tuesday
April	23	Dia de São Jorge

Angra Dos Reis

January	6	City Anniversary
April	2	Good Friday
-	5	Dia de São Benedito
December	8	Nossa Senhora da Conceição

Itaguai

April	2	Good Friday
-	2	Dia de adoração a Jesus Cristo
-	23	Dia de São Jorge
June	3	Corpus Christi
July	5	County's Emancipation
November	30	Dia do Evangélico
December	3	Dia do São Francisco Xavier

Rio de Janeiro

January	20	Dia de São Sebastião
April	23	Dia de São Jorge
November	20	Zumbi dos Palmares

Working hours:

Monday - Friday: First shift 07:00-13:00, second shift 13:00-19:00. Third shift 19:00-01:00. Fourth shift 01:00-07:00.

Saturday: First shift 07:00-13:00, second shift 13:00-19:00 at ordinary rates. Third shift 19:00-01:00, fourth shift 01:00-07:00 at overtime rates.

Sunday: First shift 07:00-13:00, second shift 13:00-19:00, third shift 19:00-01:00, fourth shift 01:00-07:00, all at overtime rates.

Rio Grande do Norte

October	3	Martyrs of Cunhaú and Uruaçu

Natal

January	6	Dia de Santos Reis
April	2	Good Friday
June	3	Corpus Christi
November	21	Nossa Senhora da Apresentação
-	20	Dia da Consciência Negra

Rio Grande do Sul

September	20	Data Magna

Itaqui

March	17	São Patrício
April	2	Good Friday
June	3	Corpus Christi
September	20	Farroupilha Revolution

Working hours:
First shift 07:30-11:30, second shift 13:30-23:30 and third shift 01:30-07:30. Meal breaks from 11:30-13:30, 23:30-01:30.

Porto Alegre

February	2	Nossa Senhora dos Navegantes
April	2	Good Friday
June	3	Corpus Christi
November	20	Dia da Consciência Negra

Working hours:
Monday - Saturday: 07:30-11:30 and 13:00-17:00. Meal break 11:30-13:00, workable at 100% extra.
Overtime 01:00-07:30 and 17:00-19:00 at 50% extra, and 19:00-01:00 at 20% extra.
Sunday and holidays: Overtime at 100% extra 07:30-11:30, 13:00-17:00, 17:00-19:00, 19:00-01:00 and 01:00-07:30.
Meal break 11:30-13:00 can be worked at 100% extra.

Rio Grande

February	2	Nossa Senhora dos Navegantes
April	2	Good Friday
June	29	São Pedro
-	3	Corpus Christi

Working hours:

New Port:

Monday - Saturday: 08:00-13:45 and 13:45-19:30. Overtime 19:30-01:15 at 25% extra, 01:15-07:00 at 50% extra and 07:00-08:00 at 200% extra.

Sunday and holidays: Overtime 08:00-13:45 and 13:45-19:30 at 100% extra, 19:30-01:15 at 125% extra, 01:15-07:00 at 150% extra and 07:00-08:00 at 200% extra.

Private Terminals:

Work available 24 hours per day, Sunday and holidays included.

Carnival days: Normal working conditions.

Santa Catarina

August	11	Data Magna

Observed the following Sunday.

Imbituba

April	2	Good Friday
June	3	Corpus Christi
November	2	All Souls' Day
December	8	Nossa Senhora da Conceição

Itajai

April	2	Good Friday
June	3	Corpus Christi
-	15	City's Foundation
November	2	All Souls' Day

Sao Francisco do Sul

April	2	Good Friday
-	15	City's Foundation
June	3	Corpus Christi
September	8	Dia da Padroeira

Working hours:
Port/terminals/stevedores working round the clock.
Day shift: 07:00-13:00 and 13:00-19:00.
Night shift: 19:00-01:00 and 01:00-07:00.

Sao Paulo

July	9	Data Magna

Santos

January	26	Dia da Cidade
April	2	Good Friday
June	3	Corpus Christi
September	8	Nossa Senhora do Monte Serrat
November	20	Dia da Consciência Negra

Sao Sebastiao

January	20	Padroeiro de São Sebastião
March	16	Emancipation day
June	3	Corpus Christi
November	20	Dia da Consciência Negra

Sergipe

July	8	Data Magna

Aracaju

March	17	City foundation
June	24	Dia de São João
-	3	Corpus Christi
December	8	Nossa Senhora da Conceição

British Virgin Islands

General holidays

January	1	New Year's Day
March	1	The Anniversary of the Birth of Hamilton Lavity Stoutt
-	8	Commonwealth Day
April	2	Good Friday
-	5	Easter Monday
May	24	Whit Monday
June	12	Sovereign's Birthday
July	1	Territory Day
August	2	Festival
October	21	St. Ursula's Day
December	25	Christmas Day
-	26	Boxing Day

Brunei

General holidays

January	1	New Year's Day
February	12	Chinese New Year
-	23	National Day Holiday
March	11	Isra' Dan Mi'raj
April	13[1]	First Day of Ramadan
-	29[1]	Nuzul Al-Quran
May	13-15[1]	Hari Raya Aidil Fitri
-	17[2]	Hari Raya Aidil Fitri
-	31	Royal Brunei Armed Forces Day
July	15	H.M. The Sultan's Birthday
-	20[1]	Hari Raya Aidil Adha
August	10	Al-Hijra
October	19	Prophet Muhammad's Birthday
December	25	Christmas Day

[1] Exact date(s) subject to sighting of the moon.
[2] Exact date(s) subject to sighting of the moon. Substitutes 14 May.
Holidays falling on a Sunday will be observed on Monday.

Bulgaria

General holidays

January	1	New Year's Day
March	3	Liberation Day
April	30	Orthodox Easter
May	1	Labour Day
-	6	St. George's Day
-	24	Culture and Literacy Day
September	6	Unification Day
-	22	Independence Day
December	24	Christmas Days

If a holiday coincides with a Saturday or Sunday, the following working day will be a holiday.

Bourgas
Working hours:
Bourgas: Shift work Monday - Sunday 08:00-20:00 and 20:00-08:00. Meal breaks 12:00-12:45 and 00:00-00:45.
Holidays: Overtime possible at 100% extra.
Terminal Bourgas East - 2: Shift work Monday - Sunday 08:00-20:00 and 20:00-08:00. Meal breaks 12:00-12:45 and 00:00-00:45.
Holidays: Overtime possible at 100% extra.

Varna
Working hours:
Varna East: Shift work 07:00-19:00 and 19:00-07:00. Meal breaks 12:00-12:30 and 00:00-00:30.
Varna West: Shift work 07:00-19:00 and 19:00-07:00. Meal breaks 12:00-12:30 and 00:00-00:30.
The ports will not operate from 19:00 on 24 December till 19:00 on 25 December and from 19:00 on 31 December till 19:00 on 1 January.

Cambodia

General holidays

January	1	New Year's Day
-	7	Victory over Genocide Day
March	8	International Women's Day
April	13-16	Khmer New Year Holiday
May	1	International Labour Day
-	6	Visak Bochea Day
-	10	Royal Plowing Day
-	14	King's Birthday
June	18	King's Mother's Birthday
September	16-18	Pchum Ben Festival
-	24	Constitutional Day
October	15	Commemoration Day of King's Father's
-	29	King's Coronation Day
November	9	National Independence Day
-	18-20	Bon Om Touk

Phnom Penh
Working hours:
Monday - Friday: First shift 07:00-11:30, second shift 14:00-17:30. Overtime available on request at 00:00-07:00.
Saturday and Sunday: Overtime work available. Night shift 19:00-23:00.
Holidays: Overtime work available at 50% extra.
Boxships usually not affected by overtime charges

Sihanoukville Port
Working hours:
Monday - Sunday: First shift 08:00-16:00, second shift 16:00-00:00, third shift 00:00-08:00. Meal breaks 12:00-13:00, 18:00-19:00, 07:00-08:00.
Holidays: Work available at 30% extra.
Saturday, Sunday and holidays: Charges for Pilot service increase 50%.
Night services: Charges for tug assistance, mooring and unmooring increase 25%.

Cameroon

General holidays

January	1	New Year's Day
February	11	Youth Day
April	2	Good Friday
May	1	Labour Day
-	13	Ascension Day
-	13[1]	Djouldé Soumaé
	20	National Day
July	20[1]	Djouldé Laihadji
August	15	Assumption Day
December	25	Christmas Day

[1] Exact date(s) subject to sighting of the moon.

If any of the following secular holidays coincide with another holiday or a Sunday, the following day will be observed as a holiday:

New Year's Day - January 1.

Youth Day - February 11.

Labour Day - May 1.

National Day - May 20.

Douala

Working hours:

Monday to Sunday: 07:00-17:30 as normal and 17:30 to 06:00 overtime on request.

Holidays: Work available on request of overtime.

No work on Labour Day and National Day 06:00-00:00.

No work from 18:00 on 24 December to 06:00 on 26 December.

No work from 18:00 on 31 December to 06:00 on 2 January.

Canada

General holidays

May	24	Victoria Day
July	1	Canada Day
November	11	Remembrance Day

If 1 July coincides with a Sunday, 2 July will be a legal holiday throughout Canada

Provincial holidays

British Columbia

January	1	New Year's Day
February	15	Family Day
April	2	Good Friday
August	2	British Columbia Day
September	6	Labour Day
October	11	Thanksgiving Day
December	25	Christmas Day

The following are not statutory holidays in British Columbia:
Easter Sunday
Easter Monday
Boxing Day

Manitoba

January	1	New Year's Day
February	15	Louis Riel Day
April	2	Good Friday
September	6	Labour Day
October	11	Thanksgiving Day
December	25	Christmas Day

If a holiday falls on a weekend, the following working day will be a day off.
The following days are not general holidays:
Easter Sunday
Terry Fox Day
Remembrance Day
Boxing Day

Churchill MAN
Working hours:
Monday - Friday: 08:00-16:00.
Overtime: 16:00-20:00 at 50% extra and 20:00-08:00 at 100% extra.
Saturday and Sunday: 08:00-12:00 at 50% extra and 12:00-08:00 at 100% extra.
Holidays: Double overtime rate is applied on Canada Day, Civic Holiday, Thanksgiving Day and Remembrance Day.

New Brunswick

January	1	New Year's Day
February	15	Family Day
April	2	Good Friday
August	2	New Brunswick Day
September	6	Labour Day
December	25	Christmas Day

Saint John NB
Working hours:
Monday - Friday: 08:00-17:00 straight time. Meal break 12:00-13:00. Overtime 19:00-23:00 at 50% extra.
Saturday: Same hours as Monday - Friday at 50% extra and 19:00-23:00 at 100% extra.
Sunday: Same hours as Monday - Friday, all at 100%.
Holidays: Work is available 08:00-17:00 at 100%, except for 26 December (Boxing Day).

Newfoundland

January	1	New Year's Day
April	2	Good Friday
June	21	June Holiday
September	6	Labour Day
December	25	Christmas Day

Botwood NL
Working hours:
24 hours per day. Two 12-hour shifts. First shift 08:00-20:00. Second shift 20:00-08:00. Meal breaks 12:00-12:30, 17:30-18:00, 00:00-00:30, 05:30-06:00.
Holidays at overtime: There is no work on 26 December (Boxing Day).

Corner Brook NL

Corner Brook Pulp and Paper
Working hours:
Monday - Saturday: First shift 08:00-16:30 and second shift 16:30-01:00.
Meal breaks from 12:00-12:30 and 20:30-21:00.
Sunday: Workable at 50% overtime.

St Johns NL

Working hours:
Monday - Friday: 08:00-12:00 and 13:00-17:00. Overtime 18:00-22:00 and 23:00-07:00.
Meal breaks from 07:00-08:00, 12:00-13:00, 17:00-18:00 and 22:00-23:00.
Saturday and Sunday: Double overtime rates apply.
Holidays: 150% overtime rates apply.
If New Year's Day, Canada Day, Remembrance Day, Christmas Day or Boxing Day fall on a Saturday or Sunday, the following Monday will be observed as a holiday. These Mondays are workable at double rates.

Nova Scotia

January	1	New Year's Day
February	15	Heritage Day
April	2	Good Friday
September	6	Labour Day
December	25	Christmas Day

Halifax NS

Working hours:
Monday to Friday Shift working times: First shift 08:00-12:00. Second shift 13:00-17:00. Third shift 18:00-23:00. Fourth shift 00:00-05:00.
Overtime/Finishing hours: 12:00:00-13:00:00, 17:00:00-18:00:00, 23:00:00-0:00:00 and 5:00:00-8:00:00.
Saturday: Work available at 50% overtime rate.
Sunday and holidays: Work available at 100% overtime rate.
No work to be performed on 26 December (Boxing Day).

Ontario

January	1	New Year's Day
February	15	Family Day
April	2	Good Friday
September	6	Labour Day
October	11	Thanksgiving Day
December	25	Christmas Day
-	26	Boxing Day

Hamilton ONT

Working hours:

Monday - Friday: 08:00-12:00 and 13:00-17:00 at straight time. 18:00-22:00 at 50% overtime rates.

Saturday and Sunday: Same hours as above. Work between 08:00-22:00 at 50% overtime rate and thereafter 200% overtime rates applies.

Holidays: Work available on request of overtime.

Thunder Bay ONT

Working hours:

General cargo: Monday - Friday: 08:00-12:00 and 13:00-17:00.
Overtime 18:00-22:00, Saturday, Sunday, holidays.
Grain: Monday - Friday: 08:00-16:00.
Overtime 16:00-21:00 and Saturday, Sunday.
Thunder Bay Terminal: Monday - Sunday: 00:00-00:00 – no overtime.

Toronto ONT

Working hours:

Monday - Friday: 08:00-12:00 and 13:00-17:00 at straight time. 18:00-22:00 overtime at 50% extra.

Saturday and Sunday: Work possible on overtime at 50% rate and work between 22:00-08:00 at 200% overtime rates applies.

Holidays: Work is possible on all holidays at overtime by request.

Prince Edward Island

January	1	New Year's Day
February	15	Islander Day
April	2	Good Friday
September	6	Labour Day
December	25	Christmas Day

Quebec

January	1	New Year's Day
May	24	National Patriots' Day
June	24	National Holiday
September	6	Labour Day
October	11	Thanksgiving
December	25	Christmas Day

If 1 July coincides with a Sunday, 2 July is a statutory holiday instead.

Becancour QUE

Working hours:

Dry bulk cargoes: Monday - Friday: 08:00-16:00 straight time. 16:00-00:00 and 00:00-08:00 at overtime rates.

Saturday, Sunday and holidays: Work available 24 hours per day at overtime rates.

General cargo: Monday - Friday: 08:00-17:00 straight time. Break 12:00-13:00. 18:00-22:00 at overtime rates.

Saturday, Sunday and holidays: Work available 08:00-22:00 at overtime rates.

Montreal QUE

Working hours:

Bulk: Monday - Friday: 07:00-15:00 straight time. 15:00-23:00 at overtime rates.
Two-hour extensions: 15:00-17:00 and 23:00-01:00, both available basis two hours at
overtime rates. Four-hour extensions: 15:00-19:00 and 23:00-03:00, both available basis
four hours at overtime rates.

Saturday and Sunday: Work available 24 hour at overtime rates.

Grain: Monday - Friday: 07:00-15:00 straight time. Extension: 15:00-23:00 at overtime
rates.

Saturday, Sunday: Same options, but all at overtime rates.

Steel, General Cargo & Breakbulk: Monday - Friday: 07:00-15:00 straight time.
15:00-23:00 at overtime rates. Breaks 10:30-11:30 and 18:30-19:30.

Saturday and Sunday: Work available at overtime rates.

Variations in working hours might occur depending on the season.

Sorel QUE

Working hours:

Section 15, Richardson International (grain)

Monday - Friday: 08:00-17:00 normal working hour, 18:00-22:00 at overtime rates and
22:00-00:00 at overtime to finish a ship.

Saturday, Sunday and holidays: 08:00-17:00 and 18:00-22:00 at overtime rates.
22:00-00:00 at overtime to finish a ship.

Section 19, Sorel-Tracy Maritime terminals

Monday - Friday: 08:00-17:00 normal woking hours and 18:00-22:00 at overtime rates.
22:00-00:00 at overtime to finish a ship.

Saturday, Sunday and holidays: 08:00-17:00 and 18:00-22:00 at overtime. 22:00-00:00
at overtime to finish a ship.

Sections 20 & 21, Rio Tinto Fer et Titane inc

Rio Tinto's own stevedores work 24 hours per day, 7 days per week with no holidays.

Trois-Rivieres QUE

Working hours:

Bulk cargoes

Monday - Friday: 08:00-16:00 normal working hours. 16:00-00:00 and 00:00-08:00 at overtime rates.

Saturday, Sunday and holidays: Work available 24 hours per day at overtime rates.

Grain

Monday - Friday: 08:00-16:00 normal working hours. 16:00-00:00 at overtime rates.

Saturday, Sunday and holidays: 08:00-00:00 at overtime rates.

General cargoes

Monday - Friday: 08:00-17:00 straight time. Meal break 12:00-13:00. 18:00-22:00 at overtime rates.

Saturday, Sunday and holidays: 08:00-22:00 at overtime rates.

Cape Verde

General holidays

January	1	New Year's Day
-	13	Democracy Day
-	20	Heroes' Day
April	2	Good Friday
May	1	Labour Day
June	1	Youth Day
July	5	Independence Day
August	15	Assumption Day
November	1	All Saints' Day
December	25	Christmas Day

Porto da Praia

April	29	Day of the City

Working hours:
Monday - Sunday: 08:00-13:00 and 14:00-22:00. Breaks 13:00-14:00 and 19:00-20:00.

Porto Grande

January	22	St. Vincent's Day

Working hours:
Monday - Friday: 08:00-12:00, 13:00-19:00 and 20:00-00:00. Breaks 12:00-13:00 and 19:00-20:00.
Saturday, Sunday and holidays: Work available at overtime rates.

Cayman Islands

General holidays

January	1	New Year's Day
-	25	National Heroes Day
February	17	Ash Wednesday
April	2	Good Friday
-	5	Easter Monday
May	17	Discovery Day
-	26	Election Day
June	14[1]	Queen's Birthday
July	5	Constitution Day
November	15	Remembrance Day
December	25	Christmas Day
-	26	Boxing Day

[1] TBC

If Christmas Day coincides with a Saturday or Sunday, it will be observed the following Monday.
If Boxing Day coincides with a Saturday it will be observed the following Monday.
If Boxing Day coincides with a Sunday or Monday it will be observed the following Tuesday.

Chile

General holidays

January	1	New Year's Day
April	2	Good Friday
-	3	Holy Saturday
May	1	Labour Day
-	21	Day of the glorious Navy
June	28	Saint Peter and Saint Paul Day
July	16	Our Lady of Mount Carmel
August	15	Assumption Day
September	18	Independence Day
-	19	Day of the glorious Army
October	11	Discovery of the New World
-	30	Evangelical and Protestant Churches Day
November	1	All Saints' Day
December	8	Immaculate Conception Day
-	25	Christmas Day

The following holidays will be observed with an offset:
   If New Year's Day falls on a Sunday it will be observed the following Monday
   If Independence Day falls on a Saturday the preceding Friday will be observed as a holiday.
Sundays are public holidays.
Elections and referendums are public holidays.

China

General holidays

January	1	New Year
February	11-17	Spring Festival
April	3-5	Ching Ming Festival
May	1-5	Labour Day
June	12-14	Dragon Boat Festival
September	19	Mid-Autumn Festival
October	1-7	National Day

The following will be extraordinary working days:
7 and 20 February
25 April
8 May
18 and 26 September
9 October

Dalian

Working hours:

Monday - Sunday: 06:00-14:00, 14:00-22:00 and 22:00-06:00. Breaks 07:00-08:00, 12:00-13:00, 19:00-20:00.

Holidays: 00:00-00:00 overtime by request.

Hong Kong

February	12	Lunar New Year
-	13	The second day of Lunar New Year
-	14	The third day of Lunar New Year
April	2	Good Friday
-	3	The day following Good Friday
-	4	Ching Ming Festival
-	6	The day following Easter Monday
May	1	Labour Day
-	19	The Birthday of the Buddha
June	14	Tuen Ng Festival
July	1	Hong Kong Special Administrative Region Establishment Day
September	22	The day following the Chinese Mid-Autumn Festival
October	1	Chinese National Day
-	14	Chung Yeung Festival
December	25	Christmas Day
-	27	First weekday after Christmas Day

If a holiday coincides with a Sunday it shall be transferred to the following Monday with the following exceptions:
  If either the first, second or third day of the Lunar New Year coincides with a Sunday, that day shall be transferred to the fourth day of the Lunar New Year
  If Christmas Day coincides with a Sunday, it shall be transferred to the second weekday after Christmas Day.
All Sunday are holidays

Working hours:

Monday - Sunday: 06:00-14:00, 14:00-22:00 and 22:00-06:00. Breaks 07:00-08:00, 12:00-13:00, 19:00-20:00.
Holidays: 00:00-00:00 overtime by request.

The islands of Kinmen, Matsu, Penghu and Taiwan

January	1	Founding Day of the Republic of China
February	10-16	Chinese Lunar New Year
-	28	Peace Memorial Day
April	4	Children's Day
-	5	Tomb Sweeping Day
June	14	Dragonboat Festival
October	20	Mid-Autumn Festival
-	10	National Day

Working hours:

Monday - Friday: 08:00-13:00, 13:00-20:00 and 20:00-08:00. Breaks 07:00-08:00, 12:00-13:00, 19:00-20:00.

Saturday, Sunday and Holidays: 00:00-00:00 overtime by request.

Colombia

General holidays

January	1	New Year's Day
-	6	Epiphany
March	19	St. Joseph
April	1	Maundy Thursday
-	2	Good Friday
May	1	Labour Day
-	13	Ascension Day
June	3	Corpus Christi
-	11	Sacred Heart of Jesus
-	29	St. Peter and St. Paul
July	20	Independence Day
August	7	Battle of Boyacá
-	15	Assumption of B.V. Mary
October	12	Columbus Day
November	1	All Saints' Day
-	11	Independence of Cartagena
December	8	Immaculate Conception
-	25	Christmas Day

If any of the following days do not fall on a Monday, they will be observed the following Monday:
6 January, 19 March, 29 June, 15 August, 12 October, 1 November, 11 November, Ascension Day, Corpus Christi and Sagrado Corazón de Jesús.

Local holidays

Barranquilla
Working hours:
Monday - Sunday: 24 hours including holidays.

Buenaventura
Working hours:
Monday - Sunday: 24 hours including holidays.

Cartagena
Working hours:
Monday - Sunday: 24 hours including holidays.

Puerto Bolivar
Stevedore's working hours are normal during local holidays.
Only port administration staff usually work half day during local holidays.

Santa Marta
Working hours:
Monday - Sunday: 24 hours including holidays.

Congo, Dem. Rep. of

General holidays

January	1	New Year's Day
-	4	Martyrs of Independence
-	16	Laurent Désiré's Day
-	17	Patrice Emery's Day
May	1	Labour Day
-	17	Revolution Day
June	30	Independence Day
August	1	Parents' Day
December	25	Christmas Day

Congo, Republic of

General holidays

January	1	New Year's Day
April	5	Easter Monday
May	1	Labour Day
-	13	Ascension Day
-	24	Pentecost Monday
June	10	Reconciliation Day
August	15	National Day
November	1	All Saints' Day
-	28	Republic Day
December	25	Christmas Day

Cook Island

General holidays

January	1	New Year's Day
-	2	Day after New Year's Day
April	2	Good Friday
-	5	Easter Monday
-	25	ANZAC Day
June	1	Queen's Birthday
July	6	Ra o te Ui Ariki Day
August	4	Constitution Day
October	26	Gospel Day
December	25	Christmas Day
-	26	Boxing Day

All Sundays are holidays. If another holiday coincides with a Saturday or Sunday, it will be observed the following Monday.
If Christmas Day and New Years Day coincide with a Saturday, the following Tuesdays will be observed as holidays.
Each island observes a local holiday known as Gospel Day for that island.

Costa Rica

General holidays

January	1	New Year's Day
April	1	Maundy Thursday
-	2	Easter Friday
-	11	Juan Santamaria Day
May	1	Labor Day
July	25	Nicoya Annexation Day
August	2	Virgin of Los Angeles Day
-	15	Mothers' Day
September	15	Independence Day
December	1	Abolition of the Armed Forces
-	25	Christmas Day

Golfito
Working hours:
24 hours per day, 7 days per week.

Puerto Caldera
Working hours:
24 hours per day, 7 days per week.

Puntarenas
Working hours:
24 hours per day, 7 days per week.
Meal breaks are taken sometime between 11:00 and 13:00, between 17:00 and 19:00 and between 22:00 and 06:00.

Croatia

General holidays

January	1	New Year's Day
-	6	Epiphany
April	4	Easter
-	5	Easter Monday
May	1	Labour Day
-	30	Statehood Day
June	3	Corpus Christi
-	22	Anti-Fascist Struggle Day
August	5	Victory and Homeland Thanksgiving Day
-	15	Assumption of Mary
November	1	All Saints' Day
-	18	Remembrance day
December	25	Christmas Day
-	26	St. Stephen's Day

Dubrovnik
Working hours:
Monday - Sunday: 00:00-00:00.
Overtime for mooring/unmooring from Monday - Sunday: 22:00-06:00 at 25 % extra, on holidays at 50% extra.

Ploce
Working hours:
Monday - Friday: First shift 06:00-14:00 and second shift 14:00-22:00 at normal rates. Third shift 22:00-06:00 at 50% extra. Breaks: 09:00-09:30 and 18:00-18:30.
Saturday: First shift 6:00-14:00 at normal rates. Second shift 14:00-22:00 at 50% extra. Third shift 22:00-06:00 at 75% extra.
Sunday and holidays: First shift 06:00-14:00 and second shift 14:00-22:00 at 100% extra. Third shift 22:00-06:00 at 150% extra.

Pula
Working hours:
Monday - Friday: 07:00-15:00. Break 10:00-10:30. Overtime by request at 15:00-07:00.
Saturday, Sunday and holidays: Work available 00:00-00:00 overtime by request.

Rasa (Trget-Brsica)
Working hours:
Monday - Friday: Shifts 06:30-14:30 and 14:30-22:30. Breaks 09:00-10:00 and 18:00-19:00. Overtime by request at 22.30-06:30.
Saturday and Sunday: Work available 00:00-00:00 overtime by request.

Rijeka
Working hours:
Monday - Friday: 06:30-14:30 and 14:30-22:30. Breaks 09:30-10:00 and 18:00-18:30.
Overtime: Monday - Friday 22:30-06:30 at 50% extra.
Saturday: 06:30-14:30 at 50% extra. 14:30-22:30 at 75% extra. 22:30-06:30 at 100% extra.
Sunday: 06:30-14:30 at 100% extra. 14:30-22:30 and 22:30-06:30 at 150% extra.
Holidays: 06:30-14:30 at 150% extra. 14:30-22:30 at 200% extra.

Sibenik
Working hours:
First shift 07:00-15:00, second shift 15:00-23:00, third shift 23:00-07:00.
Breaks: 10:30-11:00, 18:00-18:30, 03:00-03:30.
Saturdays, Sundays and holidays: 00:00-00:00 working overtime by request.
General cargo is handled during daylight only. Usually first and second shift.

Split
Working hours:
Monday - Friday: First shift 06:00-13:00 and second shift 13:00-20:00.
Breaks: 09:00-09:30 and 16:00-16:30.
Saturday: 06:00-16:00 break 09:00-09:30.
Overtime: Monday - Friday: 20:00-03:00 at 50% extra. Saturday: 16:00-20:00 at 50% extra. Sunday: 06:00-20:00 at 100% extra.
Holidays: 06:00-13 and 13:00-20:00 overtime at 150% extra.

Zadar

Working hours:

Monday - Friday: 07:00-15:00 and 15:00-22:00. Breaks: 10:30-11:00 and 18:30-19:00.
Saturday: 07:00-15:00 at 50% extra. 15:00-22:00 at 75% extra.
Sunday at 100% extra and holidays at 150% extra.

Cuba

General holidays

January	1	Triumph of the Revolution
-	2	Victory Day
May	1	Labour Day
July	25-27	Anniversary of National Rebellion
October	10	Independence Day
December	25	Christmas Day
-	31	New Year's Eve

When 1 May or 10 October coincides with a Sunday, the rest associated with the Sunday is transfered to the following Monday.

Curacao

General holidays

January	1	New Year's Day
February	15	Carnival Monday
April	2	Good Friday
-	4	Easter Sunday
-	5	Easter Monday
-	27	King's Birthday
May	1	Labour Day
-	13	Ascension Day
July	2	Flag Day
October	10	Curacao Day
December	25	Christmas Day
-	26	Boxing Day
-	31	New Year's Eve

There is no work on New Year's Day, Carnival Sunday, Good Friday, Labour Day, Christmas Day. On all other national holidays work is possible at overtime wages and conditions.
On 24 December (Christmas Eve) and 31 December (New Year's Eve) work is possible at overtime rates and conditions until 11.00.
Labour Day is observed the following day, should it coincide with the King's Birthday or a Sunday.

Curacao
Working hours:
Monday - Friday: 07:00-15:00 and 15:00-23:00. 23:00-07:00 at overtime by request.
Containers:
Monday - Friday: 07:00-15:00. 15:00-23:00 at overtime by request.
Saturday, Sunday and holidays: 07:00-15:00 and 15:00-21:00 at overtime by request.
General cargo:
Monday - Friday: 07:00-23:00.

Willemstad
Working hours:
Monday - Friday: 07:00-15:00 and 15:00-23:00.
Saturday and Sunday: 00:00-00:00 at overtime by request.
Containers:
Monday - Friday: 07:00-15:00. 15:00-23:00 at overtime by request.
Saturday, Sunday and holidays: 07:00-15:00 and 15:00-21:00 at overtime by request.
General/breakbulk cargoes:
Monday - Friday: 07:00-23:00.

Cyprus

General holidays

January	1	New Year's Day
-	6	Epiphany Day
March	15	Green Monday
-	25	Greek Independence Day
April	1	Cyprus National Day
-	4	Catholic Easter
-	30	Orthodox Good Friday
May	1	Labour Day
-	2	Orthodox Easter Day
-	3	Orthodox Easter Monday
June	21	Orthodox Whit Monday
August	15	Assumption Day
October	1	Cyprus Independence Day
-	28	Greek National Day
December	24	Christmas Eve
-	25	Christmas Day
-	26	Boxing Day

Larnaca
Working hours:

Monday - Friday: First shift 08:00-12:00 and 13:00-17:00. Second shift 17:00-23:00. Work is possible after 23:00 on an overtime basis.

Saturday, Sunday and holidays: Workers may abstain from work or work on an overtime basis with the following exceptions: No work is possible on New Year's Day, Easter Sunday, Labour Day and Christmas Day.

Limassol
Working hours:

Monday - Friday: First shift 08:00-12:00, second shift 13:00-17:00, third shift 17:00-23:00. And fourth shift 23:00-08:00 at overtime by request.

Saturday, Sunday and holidays: 00:00-00:00 overtime by request.

No work on New Year's Day, Easter Sunday, Labour Day and Christmas Day.

Denmark

General holidays

January	1	New Year's Day
April	1	Maundy Thursday
-	2	Good Friday
-	4	Easter Day
-	5	Easter Monday
-	30	Prayer Day
May	13	Ascension Day
-	23	Whit Sunday
-	24	Whit Monday
December	25	Christmas Day
-	26	Boxing Day

Aalborg
Working hours:
Monday - Thursday: 07:00-15:00. Friday: 07:00-14:30.
Breaks 09:00-09:30, 12:00-12:30 and 17:30-18:30.
Overtime: Monday 15:00-00:00 and 00:00-07:00. Tuesday - Thursday 15:00-00:00.
Friday 14:00-00:00.
Saturday, Sunday and holidays: overtime by request at 100% extra.
1 May (Labour Day) 07:00-12:00 normal working.

Aarhus
Working hours:
Monday - Thursday: 07:00-16:00. Overtime 06:00-07:00 and 16:00-19:00 at 50% extra.
00:00-06:00 and 19:00-06:00 at 100% extra.
Friday: 07:00-15:30. Overtime 06:00-07:00 and 15:30-18:30 at 50% extra. 18:30-06:00 at
100% extra.
Saturday: 06:00-10:00 at 50% extra. 10:00-00:00 at 100% extra.
Sundays and holidays: 00:00-00:00 at 100% extra.
Work 12:00-00:00 at 100% extra on 1 May (Labour Day) and 5 June (Constitution Day).

Assens
Working hours:
Monday - Sunday: 07:00-15:00.

Bandholm
Working hours:
Monday - Thursday: 07:00-15:30.
Friday: 07:00-15:00.

Copenhagen
Working hours:
Monday - Thursday: 07:00-15:00. Overtime 15:00-05:30 and 06:00-07:00.
Friday: 07:00-14:30. Overtime 15:00-05:30 and 06:00-07:00.
Saturday, Sunday and holidays: 06:00-06:00 at overtime by request.
No work on New Year's Day, Good Friday, Easter Day and Monday, Whit Monday and Christmas Day.

Esbjerg
Working hours:
Monday - Thursday: 07:00-16:00. Friday: 07:00-15:30. Breaks 08:30-09:00 and 12:00-13:00.
Overtime: 16:00-19:00 and 19:00-07:00. Breaks 18:00-19:00 and 00:00-01:00.
Saturday: Overtime by request at 07:00-10:30 and 10:30-07:00. Breaks 08:30-9:00, 18:00-19:00, 00:00-01:00 and 12:00-13:00.
Saturday: 00:00-00:00 at overtime by request.
Overtime rates:
Monday - Thursday: 16:00-19:00 at 50% extra, 19:00-07:00 at 100% extra.
Friday: 15:30-18:30 at 50% extra and 18:30-07:00 at 100% extra.
Saturday: 07:00-10:30 at 50% extra and 10:30-07:00 at 100% extra.
Sunday and holidays: 00:00-00:00 at 100% extra.

Fredericia
Working hours:
Monday - Thursday: 07:00-15:30, breaks 08:30-09:00 and 12:00-12:30.
Friday: 07:00-15:00, breaks 08:30-09:00 and 12:00-12:30.
Overtime: Monday 15:30-07:00 and 00:00-07:00. Tuesday - Thursday 15:30-07:00. Friday 15:00-00:00.
Saturday and Sunday: 00:00-00:00 at overtime by request.

Grenaa
Working hours:
Monday, Tuesday and Wednesday 07:00-16:00, Thursday and Friday 07:00-15:00.
Breaks: 9:00-9:30 and 12:00-12:30.

Kalundborg
Working hours:
Monday - Thursday: 08:00-15:30. Friday: 08:00-15:00.
Breaks 08:30-09:00 and 12:00-12:30.

Middelfart
Working hours:
Monday - Thursday: 07:00-15:30. Friday: 07:00-15:00.
Breaks 08:30-09:00 and 12:00-12:30.
Overtime: Monday 00:00-7:00 and 15:30-07:00. Tuesday - Thursday 15:30-07:00. Friday 15:00-00:00.
Saturday, Sunday: 00:00-00:00 at overtime by request.

Odense
Working hours:
Monday - Thursday: 07:00-15:30, break 08:30-09:00 and 12:00-12:30.
Friday: 07:00-15:00, break 08:30-09:00 and 12:00-12:30.
Overtime: Monday - Friday: 06:00-07:00 and 16:30-19:30 at 50% extra. 20:00-06:00 at 100% extra.
Breaks 15:30-16:30, 19:30-20:00, 23:30-00:00, 03:30-04:00 and 06:00-06:30.
Saturday: 07:00-10:00 at 50% extra, and 10:00-07:00 at 100% extra with same breaks.
Sunday and holidays: overtime by request 00:00-00:00 at 100% extra.

Roedbyhavn
Working hours:
Monday - Thursday: 07:00-15:30.
Friday: 07:00-15:00.

Djibouti

General holidays

January	1	New Year's Day
March	11[1]	Prophet's Ascension
May	1	Labour Day
-	13-14[1]	Aid-al-Fitr
June	27	Independence Day
July	20-21[1]	Aid-al-Adha
August	9[1]	Islamic New Year
October	18[1]	Birthday of Prophet Mohammed
December	25	Christmas Day

[1] Exact date(s) subject to sighting of the moon.

Djibouti
Working hours:
Monday - Sunday: Three shifts 07:00-14:00, 15:00-22:00 and 23:00-06:00.
During Ramadan: Shifts 06.00-11.00, 13.00-17.00, 19.00-23.00 and 01.00-06.00.

Dominica

General holidays

January	1	New Year's Day
February	15-16	Carnival
April	2	Good Friday
-	5	Easter Monday
May	4	Labour Day
-	24	Whit Monday
August	3	Emancipation Day
November	3	National Day
-	4	Community Service Day
December	25	Christmas Day
-	26	Boxing Day

Holidays coinciding with a Sunday will be observed the following Monday. If two holidays would thereby coincide, the latter will be observed the following day

Dominican Republic

General holidays

January	1	New Year's Day
-	6	Epiphany
-	21	Dia de la Altagracia
-	26	Duarte's Day
February	27	Independence Day
April	2	Good Friday
May	1	Labour Day
June	3	Corpus Christi
August	16	Restoration Day
September	24	Our Lady of Las Mercedes Day
November	6	Constitution Day
December	25	Christmas Day

The leave associated with holidays will shift as per the following:
   For holidays coinciding with Tuesday or Wednesday, the leave will shift to the preceding Monday.
   For holidays coinciding with Thursday or Friday, the leave will shift to the following Monday.
This provision do not apply to:
   1 January,
   21 January
   27 February
   16 August
   24 September
   25 December
   Corpus Christ
   Good Friday

Boca Chica
Working hours:
Monday - Friday: 8:00-12:00 and 14:00-18:00. Saturday: 08:00-12:00.
Overtime: Monday 12:00-14:00, 18:00-08:00 and 24:00-08:00. Tuesday - Friday 12:00-14:00 and 18:00-08:00. Saturday 12:00-24:00.
Sunday and holidays: 00:00-00:00 overtime at request, except on New Year's Day and Christmas Day.

Cabo Rojo
Working hours:
Monday - Sunday and holidays: 00:00-00:00.

Caucedo
Monday - Sunday and holidays: 00:00-00:00.

La Romana
Working hours:
General cargo
Monday - Friday: 08:00-12:00 and 14:00-18:00
Saturday: 08:00-12:00.
Overtime: Monday 00:00-08:00, 12:00-14:00 and 18:00-08:00. Tuesday - Friday 12:00-14:00 and 18:00-08:00. Saturday 12:00-00:00.
Sunday and holidays: 00:00-00:00 at overtime by request except on New Year's Day and Christmas Day.

Puerto Manzanillo
Working hours:
Monday - Friday: 08:00-12:00 and 14:00-18:00.
Saturday: 08:00-12:00.
Overtime: Monday 00:00-08:00, 12:00-14:00 and 18:00-08:00. Tuesday - Friday 12:00-14:00 and 18:00-08:00. Saturday 12:00-00:00 except on New Year's Day and Christmas Day.
Sunday and holidays: 00:00-00:00 at overtime by request.

San Pedro de Macoris
Working hours:
Monday - Friday: 08.00-12.00 and 14.00-18.00
Saturday: 08.00-12.00.
Overtime: Monday 00:00-08:00, 12:00-14:00 and 18:00-08:00. Tuesday - Friday 12:00-14:00 and 18:00-08:00. Saturday 12:00-00:00.
Sunday and holidays: 00:00-00:00 at overtime by request except on Good Friday, Labour Day, Christmas Day and New Year's Day.

Viejo de Azua
Working hours:
Monday - Friday: 08.00-12.00 and 14.00-18.00
Saturday: 08.00-12.00.
Overtime: Monday 00:00-08:00, 12:00-14:00 and 18:00-08:00. Tuesday - Friday 12:00-14:00 and 18:00-08:00. Saturday 12:00-00:00.
Sunday and holidays: 00:00-00:00 at overtime by request except on New Year's Day, Good Friday and Christmas Day.
Except on major holidays (New Year, Easter and Christmas) overtime work may be ordered all days and work can be carried out round the clock and on weekends.

Ecuador

General holidays

January	1	New Year's Day
February	15	Carnival Monday
-	16	Carnival Tuesday
April	2	Good Friday
May	1	Labour Day
-	24	Anniversary of the Battle of Pichincha
August	10	Independence Day
October	9	Independence of Guayaquil
November	2	All Soul's Day
-	3	Independence of Cuenca
December	25	Christmas Day

Holidays will shift according to the below rules:
  If Tuesday and the following Wednesday are holidays, the Wednesday holiday will shift to the preceding Monday.
  If Wednesdays and the following Thursday are holidays, the Wednesday holiday will shift to the following Friday.
  If Friday and the following Saturday are holidays, the Saturday holiday will shift to the preceding Thursday.
  If Sunday and the following Monday are holidays, the Sunday holiday will shift to the following Tuesday.
The exceptions to these rules are:
  January 1
  December 25
  Carnival Tuesday

Local holidays

Balao Oil Terminal

August	5	Esmeraldas' Independence Day
November	21	Province anniversary

Esmeraldas

August	5	Esmeraldas' Independence Day
November	21	Province anniversary

Working hours:
24 hours, 365 days. Breaks 6:00-7:00, 11:30-12:30, 18:00-19:00 and 23:00-00:00.
Holidays: 00:00-00:00 overtime by request.
Likely observed 6 August.
Likely observed 22 November.

Guayaquil

July	25	Guayaquil Foundation Day

Working hours:
24 hours, 365 days. Breaks 6:00-7:00, 11:30-12:30, 18:00-19:00 and 23:00-00:00.
Holidays: 00:00-00:00 overtime by request.
Likely observed 26 July.

La Libertad

April	14	City anniversary
November	7	Province anniversary

Likely observed 8 November.

Manta

November	4	Manta Canton Anniversary

Working hours:
24 hours, 365 days. Breaks 6:00-7:00, 11:30-12:30, 18:00-19:00 and 23:00-00:00.
Holidays: 00:00-00:00 overtime by request.
Likely observed 5 November.

Egypt

General holidays

January	7	Coptic Christmas
-	25	Police Day
April	25	Sinai Liberation Day
May	2	Coptic Easter Sunday
-	13-17[1]	Eid el-Fitr
June	30	30 June Revolution
July	20-24[1]	Eid al-Adha
-	23	23 July Revolution
August	10[1]	Islamic New Year
October	6	Victory Day
-	19[1]	Prophet's Birthday (Moulid El Nabi)

[1] Exact date(s) subject to sighting of the moon.

El Salvador

General holidays

January	1	New Year's Day
April	1	Maundy Thursday
-	2	Good Friday
-	3	Holy Saturday
May	1	Labour Day
June	17	Father's Day
August	6	St. Saviour's Day
September	15	Independence Day
November	2	All Souls' Day
December	25	Christmas Day

Local holidays

Acajutla
Working hours:
Monday - Friday: 07:00-15:00 and 15:00-23:00. Overtime by request 23:00-07:00.
Saturday and Sunday: Same shifts as Monday - Friday but on overtime by request.
Holidays: Overtime by request 07:00-07:00. No work on Good Friday.

Eritrea

General holidays

January	1	New Year's Day
-	19	Orthodox Epiphany
March	8	International Women's Day
May	1	Labour Day
-	24	Independence Day
June	20	Martyrs' Day
September	1	Revolution Day

Estonia

General holidays

January	1	New Year's Day
February	24	Independence Day
April	2	Good Friday
-	4	Easter Sunday
May	1	May Day
-	23	Whit Sunday
June	23	Victory Day
-	24	Midsummer Day
August	20	Independence Restoration Day
December	24	Christmas Eve
-	25	Christmas Day
-	26	Boxing Day

Falkland Islands

General holidays

January	1	New Year's Day
April	2	Good Friday
-	21	Queen's Birthday
June	14	Liberation Day
October	4	Peat Cutting Day
December	8	Battle Day
-	25	Christmas Day
-	26	Boxing Day
-	27	Christmas Holiday

If a holiday falls on a Saturday or Sunday the following working day shall be a public holiday.

Faroe Islands

General holidays

January	1	New Year's Day
April	1	Maundy Thursday
-	2	Good Friday
-	4	Easter Sunday
-	5	Easter Monday
-	25	National Flag Day
-	30	Prayer Day
May	13	Ascension Day
-	23	Whit Sunday
-	24	Whit Monday
July	28	St. Olav's Eve
-	29	St. Olav's Day
December	24	Christmas Eve
-	25	Christmas Day
-	26	Boxing Day
-	31	New Year's Eve

Local holidays

Torshavn

Working hours:

Monday - Friday: 08:00-17:00. Overtime by request 17:00-21:00 at 35%, and 21:00-8:00 at 60%.

Saturday: Overtime by request 08:00-00:00 at 65% extra.

Sunday and holidays: Overtime by request 00:00 - 00:00 at 100% extra.

Fiji

General holidays

January	1	New Year's Day
April	2	Good Friday
-	3	Easter Saturday
-	5	Easter Monday
June	26[1]	National Sports Day
September	7	Constitution Day
October	10	Fiji Day
-	19[2]	Birthday of Prophet Muhammad
November	4	Diwali
December	25	Christmas Day
-	26	Boxing Day

[1] To be confirmed.

[2] Exact date(s) subject to sighting of the moon.

If any of the following holidays fall on a Saturday or Sunday, the following Monday will be a public holiday:

  Christmas Day
  New Year's Day
  Diwali
  Prophet Mohammed"s Birth Day

If Boxing Day falls on a Saturday, the following Monday will be a public holiday.

If Boxing Day falls on a Sunday or Monday, the following Tuesday will be a public holiday.

Finland

General holidays

January	1	New Year's Day
-	6	Epiphany
April	2	Good Friday
-	4	Easter
-	5	Easter Monday
May	23	Whit Sunday
December	6	Independence Day
-	25	Christmas Day
-	26	Boxing Day

Hamina
Working hours:
Monday - Friday: Day shift 06:00-14:00 and evening shift 14:00-22:00.
Saturday: 06:00-14:00.

Hanko
Working hours:
Monday - Friday: Day shift 07:00-15:30 and evening shift 15:30-22:30.
Saturday: 07:00-15:30.

Helsinki
Working hours:
West Harbour: Monday - Sunday: 05:30-01:00.
Eckerö Line Ab Oy: Monday - Friday: 07:30-21:00. Saturday: 07:30-14:00.
Sunday: 07:30-21:00.
Tallink Silja Oy: Monday - Sunday: 06:15-00:30.
HTG Stevedoring: Monday - Friday: 06:15-22:30. Saturday: 06:15-15:00. Sunday:
No work.
South Harbour: Monday - Sunday: 06:00-21:00.
Tallink Silja Oy: Monday - Friday: 09:15-17:15, Saturday and Sunday: 09:15-11:00,
15:00-17:15.
HTG Stevedoring: Monday - Friday: 09:30-17:30. Saturday: 09:30-12:30.
Katajanokka: Monday - Sunday: 06:00-22:00.
Vuosaari harbour: Monday - Sunday: 00:00-00:00.

Inkoo
Working hours:
Monday - Friday: 06:00-14:00 and 14:00-22:00.

Jakobstad
Working hours:
Monday - Friday: 06:00-14:00 and 14:00-22:00 normal shift and 23:00-06:00 overtime by request.
Saturday, Sunday and holidays: 00:00-00:00 overtime by request.

Kalajoki
Working hours:
Monday - Friday: 07:00-15:30 and 15:30-00:00. Breaks: 11:00-11:30 and 19:30-20:00.
Saturday: 07:00-15:30.
Sunday: No work.

Kantvik
Working hours:
Monday - Friday: 07:00-15:00 and 15:00-23:00.
Saturday: 07:00-15:00.

Kaskinen
Working hours:
Monday - Friday: 07:30-16:30.

Kemi
Working hours:
Monday - Friday: 06:00-14:30 and 14:30-22:30. 22:30-06:00 overtime by request.
Saturday: 07:00-15:30 and 22:30-06:00 overtime by request.
Sunday: 22:30-06:00 overtime by request.

Kokkola
Working hours:
Monday - Friday: Day shift 07:00-16:00 and evening shift 16:00-00:00. Breaks 11:00-12:00 and 19:30-20:00. 00:00-07:00 nights work available at extra cost.
Saturday: 07:00-15:00. 00:00-07:00 nights work available at extra cost.
Sundays: 00:00-00:00 work available at extra cost.

Kotka
Working hours:
Monday - Friday: Day shift 06:00-14:00 and evening shift 14:00-22:00.
Saturday: 06:00-14:00.

Koverhar
Working hours:
Monday - Friday: 07:00-23:00.
Saturdays, Sundays and holidays: No work.

Kristiinankaupunki
Working hours:
Monday - Friday: 07:00-22:00.
Saturday: No work.

Loviisa and Valkom
Working hours:
Monday - Friday: Day shift 07:00-15:10 and evening shift 15:10-23:20.
Saturday: 07:00-15:10.

Oulu
Working hours:
Monday - Friday: Day shift 07:00-16:00 and evening shift 16:00-00:00.
Saturday: 07:00-15:00.
Labour usually works only one shift on New Year's Eve, 30 April and on 5 of December.

Pori
Working hours:
Monday - Friday: Day shift 07:00-15:30 and evening shift 15:30-00:00.
Saturday: 07:00-15:30.

Porvoo
Working hours:
Monday - Friday: Day shift 07:00-16:00 and evening shift 16:00-00:00.
Saturday: No work.

Raahe
Working hours:
Monday - Friday: 07:00-15:00 and 15:00-23:00.

Rauma
Working hours:
Monday - Friday: Day shift 07:00-15:30 and evening shift 15:30-00:00.
Saturday: 07:00-15:30.

Tornio - Roytta
Working hours:
Monday - Friday: 07:00-16:00 and 16:00-00:00.
Saturday: 07:00-15:30 overtime by request.

Turku
Working hours:
Monday - Friday: 06:30-15:00 and 15:00-23:00. Break 10:30-11:00.
Sunday and holidays: 00:00-00:00 overtime by request.
No work on New Year's Day.

Uusikaupunki
Working hours:
Monday - Friday: Day shift 07:00-15:00 and evening shift 15:00-23:30.
Saturday: 07:00-15:30.

Vaasa
Working hours:
Monday - Friday: 07:00-15:30 and 15:30-23:30
Saturday: No work.

France

General holidays

January	1	New Year's Day
April	5	Easter Monday
May	1	Labour Day
-	8	Victory Day 1945
-	13	Ascension
-	24	Pentecôte Monday
July	14	National Day
August	15	Assumption
November	1	All Saints' Day
-	11	1918 Armistice Day
December	25	Christmas Day

Regional holidays may apply.

Local holidays

Bayonne
Working hours:
Monday - Friday: 06:00-14:00 and 14:00-22:00. Breaks 09:00-09:30 and 18:00-18:30.
Saturday: 06:00-14:00 overtime by request.
Sunday and holidays: No work.
Chemical Berth
Monday - Sunday: 00:00-00:00.
Sulphur Berth
Monday - Friday: 08:05-16:20.
Saturday, Sunday and holidays: Work possible 05:00-21:00 at overtime rates.
Silo Berth
Monday - Friday: Shift work 06:00-14:00 and 14:00-22:00.
Saturday: 00:00-00:00 overtime by request.
Sunday and holidays: No work.

Boulogne-sur-Mer
Working hours:
Monday - Friday: 07:00-12:00 and 14:00-19:00 and Saturday: 07:00-12:00 as regular working hours.
Overtime: 06:00-14:00, 14:00-22:00 and 22:00-06:00 at overtime by request on any days and holidays.

Brest
Working hours:
Monday - Friday: 08:00-12:00 and 14:00-18:00 regular working hours.
Shift work: Monday - Friday: 06:00-14:00, and 14:00-22:00, breaks 10:00-10:30 and 18:00-18:30.
Saturday: 06:00-14:00 overtime by request. Break 10:00-10:30.
Sunday and holidays: 00:00-00:00 overtime by request.
No work on 1 May (Labour Day). On 24 December (Christmas Eve) and 31 December (New Year's Eve) there is only shift work 06:00-14:00, with a meal break 10:00-10:30.

Calais
Working hours:
Monday - Friday: 06:15-12:15 and 14:00-20:00. 21:00-03:00 overtime by request.
Saturday: 06:15-12:15. 14:00-20:00 overtime by request.
Sunday: 06:15-12:15 overtime by request.
No work after 12:15 on Christmas Eve and New Year's Eve.

Cannes
Working hours:
Monday - Saturday: 08:00-12:00 and 14:00-18:00. 50% extra 06:00-08:00, 12:00-14:00 and 18:00-22:00. 100% extra 22:00-06:00.
Sunday and holidays: 100% extra applies 00:00-00:00.

Dieppe
Working hours:
Monday - Saturday: 06:00-11:45, 14:00-17:45 and 18:30-22:00.
Sunday and holidays: No work.
There is no work available on 24 December (Christmas Eve) and 31 December (New Year's Eve).

Dunkerque
Working hours:

Monday - Saturday: 06:00-14:00, 14:00-22:00 and 22:00-06:00. Breaks 10:00-10:30, 18:00-18:30 and 02:00-02:30.

0:00:00-6:00:00 is normal working hours for Monday and Sunday.

Sunday and holidays: 06:00-12:00, 12:00-18:00, 18:00-00:00 and 00:00-06:00. There is no work on 1 May (Labour Day).

QPO:

Monday - Saturday: 06:00-00:00.

Sunday: 00:00-06:00 normal and 06:00:00 overtime by request.

No work on: 1 January (New Year's Day), 1 May (Labour Day) and 25 December (Christmas Day).

Arcelor:

Monday - Sunday: 00:00-00:00.

Tanker:

Monday - Sunday: 00:00-00:00.

Fecamp
Working hours:

Monday - Friday: 08:00-12:00, 13:30-17:30. 17:30-20:00 overtime by request.

Saturday: 08:00-20:00 overtime by request.

Sunday and holidays: No work.

Fos
Working hours:

FOS public ore berth and Caronte terminal:

Monday - Friday: 06:00-13:00, 13:00-20:00 and 20:00-03:00.

Saturday: 13:00-00:00 overtime by request. Sunday: 00:00-06:00 overtime by request.

Sollac:

05:00-13:00, 13:00-21:00 and 21:00-05:00.

No work on: New Year's Day, Easter Monday, Labour Day, National Day, Assumption Day and Christmas Day.

Granville
Working hours:

Monday - Friday: 08:00-12:00 and 14:00-18:00. 06:00-08:00 and 18:00-22:00 overtime by request.

Saturday: 06:00-12:00 overtime by request.

Sunday and holidays: No work.

Honfleur
Working hours:
Shift work: 06:00-13:00 and 13:00-20:00.
Saturday: 07:00-19:00 overtime by request.

La Nouvelle
Working hours:
General Cargo:
Monday - Saturday: 08:00-12:00 and 14:00-18:00. Sunday: 08:00-12:00 overtime by request.
Grain Silo:
Monday - Friday: 08:00-12:00 and 14:00-18:00. 05:30-07:30 and 18:00-20:00 overtime by request.
Saturday: 08:00-12:00 overtime by request.
Sunday: 05:30-12:00 overtime by request.
Holidays: Overtime by request 08:00-12:00, except 1 January, 1 May, 14 July and 25 December.

Le Havre
Working hours:
Crude oil - Terminal: Monday - Sunday: 00:00-00:00.
No holidays affect the loading and discharging of petroleum products, which are carried out 24 hours per day.
Dry cargo and container: Monday - Sunday: Morning shifts 06:00-14:00, 07:00-15:00 and 08:00-16:00. Afternoon shifts 14:00-22:00 and 15:00-23:00. Night shifts 22:00-06:00 and 23:00-06:00.
Perishable goods: Sunday and holidays 07:00-13:00 overtime by request.
Product tankers - Terminal: Monday - Friday: 07:00-20:00 normal and 20:00-07:00 overtime by request. Saturday: 00:00-00:00 overtime by request.
Sunday and holidays: No work.
Operations can only commence between 06:00 and 15:00.
Terminaux de Normandie - Operator: Monday - Friday: 07:30-20:00. Saturday: No work.
GMP - Operator: Monday - Friday: 07:00-21:00. Saturday: No work.
CNMP - Operator: Monday - Friday: 07:00-20:30. Saturday: No work.

Lorient
Working hours:
Monday - Friday: 06:00-13:00 and 13:00-20:00. 20:00-03:00 overtime by request.
Saturday: 06:00-13:00. 13:00-20:00 overtime by request.
Sunday and holidays: No work.

Marseilles

Working hours:
East harbours: 06:30-11:30, 13:30-19:30, 20:00-02:00 and 08:30-11:30.
West harbours: 06:00-12:00, 13:00-20:00, 20:00-03:00 and 08:00-12:00.
No work on: New Year's Day, Labour Day, National Day, Assumption Day and Christmas Day.
On Christmas Eve and New Years Eve work only 06:30-12:30 at East harbours, and 06:00-13:00 at West harbours.

Port Saint-Louis

Working hours:
Monday - Friday normal: 06:00-13:00, 13:00-20:00 and 20:00-03:00. Special shifts 03:00-06:00, 08:30-12:00, 13:30-17:00 and 20:00-23:30.
Saturday: 06:00-13:00. 13:00-20:00 overtime by request.
No work on: New Year's Day, Labour Day, National Day and Christmas Day.
Work 06:00-13:00 on Christmas Eve and New Year's Eve.

Rochefort

Working hours:
Monday - Friday: 05:00-13:00 and 14:00-22:00. Break 13:00-14:00.
Saturday: 05:00-13:00 overtime by request.
Sunday: 05:00-13:00 and 13:00-21:00 overtime by request.

Rouen

Working hours:
Monday - Friday: Long shift 07:30-13:30; 13:30-19:30.
Saturday: 07:30-12:00.
Holidays: Work stop at 13:30 on 31 December (New Year's Eve) and 12:00 on 24 December (Christmas Eve).
Working hours depend on the terminal.

Saint Malo

Working hours:
Monday - Friday: 08:00-12:00 and 14:00-18:00.
Saturday and Sunday: No work.

Saint Nazaire
Working hours:
Monday - Friday: 06:00-14:00 and 14:00-22:00. Break: 10:00-10:30 and 18:00-18:30.
Saturday, Sunday and holidays: 06:00-14:00 and 14:00-22:00. 22:00-06:00 overtime by request.
No work on Labour Day.

Sete
Working hours:
Monday - Friday: 06:00-13:00, 13:00-20:00 and 20:00-23:00.
Saturday: 06:00-13:00. 13:00-20:00 and 20:00-23:00 overtime by request.
Sunday: 00:00-00:00 overtime by request.

Tonnay-Charente
Working hours:
Monday - Friday: 05:00-13:00 and 13:00-21:00. 05:00-08:00 and 18:00-20:00 overtime by request. Saturday: 05:00-13:00 overtime by request. 13:00-00:00 no work.
Sunday and holidays: No work.

French Guiana

General holidays

January	1	New Year's Day
April	5	Easter Monday
May	1	Labour Day
-	8	Victory Day
-	13	Ascension Day
June	10	Abolition Day
-	24	Whit Monday
July	14	French National Day
August	15	Assumption Day
November	1	All Saints' Day
-	11	Armistice Day
December	25	Christmas Day

Gabon

General holidays

January	1	New Year's Day
April	5	Easter Monday
-	17	Women's Day
May	1	Labour Day
-	13[1]	Aid El Fitr
-	24	Whit Monday
July	20[1]	Aid El Adha
August	15	Assumption Day
-	16-17	Independence Days
November	1	All Souls' Day
December	25	Christmas Day

[1] Exact date(s) subject to sighting of the moon.

Libreville
Working hours:
Monday - Friday ordinary: 06:00-18:00. Meal hours 12:00-13:00.
Saturdays ordinary: 08:00-12:00.
Shift work: 06:00-18:00 and 18:00-06:00. Meal hours 12:00-13:00 and 00:00-01:00.
Holidays: Workable at overtime by request.

Port Gentil
Working hours:
Monday - Wednesday: 06:00-18:00. Meal hours 12:00-13:00.
Saturdays: 08:00-12:00.
Shift work: 06:00-18:00 and 18:00-06:00. Meal hours 12:00-13:00 and 00:00-01:00.
Holidays: Workable at overtime double rate.

Gambia

General holidays

January	1	New Year's Day
February	18	Independence Day
April	2	Good Friday
-	5	Easter Monday
May	1	Labour Day
-	13-14[1]	Koriteh
-	25	African Liberation Day
July	20[1]	Tobaski
August	15	Assumption Day
-	18[1]	Yawmul Ashura
October	18[1]	Maulud Nabi
December	25	Christmas Day

[1] Exact date(s) subject to sighting of the moon.

Georgia

General holidays

January	1-2	New Year's Days
-	7	Christmas (Orthodox)
-	19	Epiphany (Orthodox)
March	3	Mother's Day
-	8	International Women's Day
April	9	Memorial Day
-	30	Easter Friday (Orthodox)
May	1	Easter Saturday (Orthodox)
-	2	Easter Sunday (Orthodox)
-	3	Easter Monday (Orthodox)
-	9	Victory Day
-	12	St. Andrew's Day
-	26	Independence Day
August	28	St. Mary's Day
October	14	Day of Svetistskhovloba
November	23	St. George's Day (Giorgoba)

Batumi
Working hours:
08:00-20:00 and 20:00-08:00 seven days per week, including holidays. No overtime charges are applied.
Break times: 12:00-13:00 and 16:30-17:00.

Poti
Working hours:
08:00-20:00 and 20:00-08:00 seven days per week, including holidays. No overtime charges are applied.
Break time: 13:00-14:00.

Germany

General holidays

January	1	New Year's Day
April	2	Good Friday
-	5	Easter Monday
May	1	Labour Day
-	13	Ascension Day
-	24	Whit Monday
October	3	Day of German Unity
-	31	Reformation Day
December	25	Christmas Day
-	26	Second Christmas Day

Local holidays

Brake

Working hours:

Monday - Friday: First shift 06:00-14:00 and second shift 14:00-22:00. Third shift 22:00-06:00 at overtime rates. Breaks 09:30-10:00, 17:30-18:00 and 01:30-02:00.

Saturdays: First shift 06:00-14:00, second shift 14:00-22:00 and third shift 22:00-06:00 all at overtime rates. Breaks 08:30-09:00, 17:30-18:00 and 01:30-02:00.

Sundays: First shift 06:00-12:00, second shift 12:00-18:00, third shift 18:00-00:00 and fourth shift 00:00-06:00 all at overtime rates. Breaks 09:30-10:00, 15:00-15:30, 21:00-21:30 and 03:00-03:30.

No work on the following holidays: New Year's Day, Labour Day and Christmas Day.

On the following days only one shift workable 06:00-12:00 with break 08:30-09:00: Day before Labour Day, Christmas Eve and New Year's Eve.

On the following holidays, overtime can be arranged against extra payment: Good Friday, Easter Monday, Ascension Day, Whit Monday, Day of German Unity, Second Christmas and Reformation Day.

Bremen

Working hours:

Monday - Friday: First shift 06:00-14:00, second shift 08:30-16:30, third shift 14:30-22:30 and fourth shift 22:30-06:00. Breaks 09:45-10:15, 12:15-12:45, 18:15-18:45 and 02:00-02:30.

Saturday: First shift 14:30-20:30 and second shift 20:30-02:30. Breaks 09:45-10:15, 17:15-17:45 and 23:15-23:45.

Sunday: First shift 06:00-12:00, second shift 12:00-18:00, third shift 18:00-00:00 and fourth shift 00:00-06:00. Breaks 08:45-09:15, 14:45-15:15, 20:45-21:15 and 02:45-03:15.

No work on the following holidays: New Year's Day, Labour Day and Christmas Day.

Bremerhaven

Working hours:

Monday - Friday: First shift 06:00-14:00, second shift 08:30-16:30, third shift 14:30-22:30 and four shift 22:30-06:00. Breaks 09:45-10:15, 12:15-12:45, 18:15-18:45 and 18:45-02:30.

Saturday: First shift 06:00-14:00, second shift 14:30-20:30 and third shift 20:30-02:30. Breaks 09:45-10:15, 17:15-17:45 and 23:15-23:45.

Sunday: First shift 06:00-12:00, second shift 12:00-18:00, third shift 18:00-00:00 and fourth shift 00:00-06:00. Breaks 08:45-09:15, 14:45-15:15, and 02:45-03:15.

No work on the following holidays: New Year's Day, Labour Day and Christmas Day.

Brunsbuttel

Working hours:

Monday - Friday: 07:00-16:00.

The following shifts may be ordered: Monday - Sunday: 06:00-14:00 and 14:00-22:00.

Night shift 22:00-06:00 overtime by request.

Saturday and Sunday: All shifts overtime by request.

On the following holidays no work is available: New Year's Day, Labour Day and Christmas Day.

There is no work after 12:00 on 24 December (Christmas Eve) and 31 December (New Year's Eve).

Cuxhaven

Working hours:

Cuxport Terminal

Monday - Friday: 07:00-21:00 and 21:00-0700. Overtime can be arranged.

Saturday: 07:00-13:00. Overtime can be arranged.

Sunday: 00:00 overtime by request.

Holidays: Work can be arranged on a voluntary basis at overtime rates.

Overtime can be arranged from 13:00-00:00 on the following days: New Year's Day, day before Labour Day, 24 December (Christmas Eve), 31 December (New Year's Eve).

Duisburg

Working hours:

Working hours Christmas Eve 24 December and New Years Eve 31 December workable 06:00-14:00.

Monday - Saturday: First shift 06:00-14:00, second shift 14:00-22:00. Third shift 22:00-06:00 overtime by request at 25% extra.

Sunday: Work can be arranged overtime by request at 50% extra.

Dusseldorf

Working hours:

Reisholz Wharf

Monday - Friday: 07:30-16:30 normal working. 16:30-07:30 overtime by request.

Saturday - Sunday: 24 hours overtime by request.

Main port and Heerdt Wharf

Monday - Friday: 08:00-16:00 normal working. 16:00-08:00 overtime by request.

Saturday: 07:30-12:30 Normal working. 12:30-07:30 overtime by request.

Sunday: 12:30-08:00 overtime by request.

Emden

Working hours:

Monday - Friday: First shift 06:00-14:00 and second shift 14:00-22:00. Third shift 22:00-06:00 can be arranged on overtime by request against extra payment. Breaks 10:00-10:30, 18:00-18:30, 02:00-02:30.

Saturday and Sunday: Same hours as Monday - Friday but third shift Saturday and all work on Sunday against extra payment, on a voluntary basis and by special request only.

Holidays: Work can be arranged at overtime rates, except for those holidays listed.

No work on the following holidays: New Year's Day, Labour Day and Christmas Day.

Flensburg

Working hours:

Monday - Thursday: 07:00-16:00.

Friday: 07:00-13:15.

Shift work: Monday - Friday: First shift 07:00-14:30 and second shift 14:30-22:00 overtime by request.

Saturday: First shift 07:00-14:30. Overtime work beyond ordinary working hours/shift times at extra cost: 06:00-07:00 and 16:00-20:00 at 33% extra. 20:00-06:00 at 50% extra.

Sunday: Workable at 100% extra.

Gluckstadt

Working hours:

The following shifts may be ordered: Monday - Friday: 06:00-14:00 and 14:00-22:00. Night shift 22:00-06:00 overtime by request.

Saturday-Sunday: 06:00-14:00, 14:00-22:00 and 22:00-06:00 overtime by request.

On the following holidays no work is available: New Year's Day, Labour Day and Christmas Day.

There is no work after 12:00 on 24 December (Christmas Eve) and 31 December (New Year's Eve).

Hamburg

Working hours:

Monday - Friday: First shift 06:50-15:00, second shift 09:00-17:10, third shift 15:00-23:10 and fourth shift 23:10-06:50. Breaks 11:00-11:30, 13:00-13:30, 19:00-19:30 and 03:00-03:30.

Saturday - Sunday: First shift 07:00-13:00, second shift 13:00-19:00, third shift 19:00-01:00 and fourth shift 01:00-07:00.

No work on the following holidays, except in urgent cases such as bunkering, passenger ships and ships damaged at sea: New Year's Day, Labour Day and Christmas Day.

Days preceding the above holidays worked on 01:00-07:00, 07:00-13:00, 13:00-19:00 and 19:00-01:00.

Shifts are extendable to complete ship.

Kiel

Working hours:

Monday - Friday: 07:00-16:00. 16:00- 07:00 and 00:00-07:00 can be arranged on overtime by request.

Saturday: 07:00-13:00 normal and 13:00-00:00 can be arranged on overtime by request.

Sunday 24 hour overtime by request.

Leer

Working hours:

Monday - Friday: First shift 06:00-18:00, second shift 18:00-00:00 and third shift 00:00-06:00 overtime by request.

Saturday - Sunday: 00:00-00:00 overtime by request.

Oil Mill Terminal W. Connemann

Monday - Sunday and Holidays: 00:00-00:00 normal.

Lubeck - Travemunde

Working hours:

Seelandkai and Nordlandkai

Monday - Saturday: First shift 07:00-16:00, second shift 16:00-23:00 and third shift 23:00-06:00. Breaks 11:30-12:00, 19:00-19:30 and 02:00-02:30.

Sunday and holidays: First shift 07:00-13:00, second shift 13:00-19:00, third shift 19:00-01:00 and fourth shift 01:00-07:00. Breaks 10:00-10:30, 16:00-16:30, 22:00-22:30 and 04:00-04:30.

Schlutup

Monday - Friday: First shift 07:00-16:00, second shift 16:00-23:00.

Saturday: First shift 07:00-16:00.

Breaks 11:30-12:00, 19:00-19:30.

Sundays and holidays: 00:00-00:00 can be arranged on overtime by request.

Travemunde

Monday - Sunday and Holidays: First shift 06:00-23:00, second shift 23:00-06:00 overtime by request at 40% extra.

Neustadt

Working hours:

Monday - Thursday: 07:00-16:00. Breaks from 12:00-12:45. 06:00-07:00 and 16:00-20:00 overtime by request at an additional cost of 30%.

Friday: 07:00-12:00. 06:00-07:00 and 12:00-20:00 overtime by request at an additional cost of 30%.

Saturdays: Work can be arranged at an additional cost of 50%.

Sundays and holidays: No work.

Nordenham
Working hours:
General cargo
Monday - Friday: First shift 06:00-14:00 and second shift 14:00-22:00 at normal rates. Third shift 22:00-06:00 at overtime by request. Breaks 09:30-10:00, 02:00-02:30 and 18:00-18:30.
Saturday: First shift 06:00-14:00. Breaks 09:30-10:00.
Holidays: 00:00-00:00 at overtime by request. No work on the following holidays: New Year's Day, Labour Day and Christmas Day from 12:00-00:00.
Sunday: Overtime by request.
Bulk cargo
Monday - Friday: First shift 06:00-14:00, second shift 14:00-22:00 and third shift 22:00-06:00. Breaks 09:30-10:00, 18:00-18:30 and 02:00-02:30.
Saturday: First shift 06:00-14:00. Breaks 09:30-10:00.
Holidays: 00:00-00:00 at overtime by request. No work on the following holidays: New Year's Day, Labour Day and Christmas Day from 12:00-00:00.
Sunday: 06:00-14:00, 14:00-22:00 and 22:00-06:00 at overtime by request.
General cargo and bulk cargo
On the following holidays, overtime can be arranged against extra payment: Good Friday, Easter Monday, Ascension Day, White Monday, Day of German Unity and Christmas Day. On the following days no work after 12:00, unless in exceptional cases for completion of vessels by special agreement: Day before Labour Day, Christmas Eve and New Year´s Eve.

Papenburg
Working hours:
Monday - Friday: 07:00- 16:00. Meal break 12:00-12:45.
Saturday: 07:00- 16:00 at overtime by request.
On these days work available 07:00-12:00: Christmas Day and New Year's Day.
Wintertime: October - March from 07:00-18:00.
Summertime: April - September from 06:00-20:00. Openings outside normal hours can be facilitated.

Rendsburg
Working hours:
Monday - Thursday: Day shift 07:00-21:00. Meal break 12:00-13:00.
Friday: Day shift 07:00-19:30.
Saturday: 06:00-12:00 at overtime by request. Breaks 09:00-09:30.
Holidays: No work.

Rostock

Working hours:

Monday - Friday: 05:00-21:00. 21:00-00:00 at overtime by request.

Saturday and days before holidays: 06:00-14:00 at normal rates. Work beyond 14:00 is possible but only on request and at overtime rates.

No work available on the following holidays: New Year's Day, Easter Monday, Labour Day, Whit Monday and Christmas Day.

Holidays: : 00:00-00:00 at overtime by request.

Oil terminals:

Monday - Sunday: 00:00-00:00 at normal rate.

Holidays: No work.

Working times of other terminals may differ from the above.

Ferry services and oil port: Work available every day around the clock.

Stralsund

Working hours:

Monday - Friday: First shift 06:00-14:30 and second shift 14:30-23:00. 23:00-06:00 at overtime by request.

Saturday: 06:00-14:30. 14:30-23:00 and 23:00-06:00 at overtime by request.

Sunday: 06:00-14:30, 14:30-23:00 and 23:00-06:00 at overtime by request.

Holidays: 00:00-00:00 at overtime by request.

No work on the following holidays: New Year's Day, Labour Day and Christmas Day Stop work at 14:30 - 00:00 on the Reformation Day.

Wilhelmshaven

Working hours:

Rhenus Midgard Terminals

Monday - Friday: First shift 06:00-14:00, second shift 14:00-22:00 and third shift 22:00-06:00.

Saturday: First shift 06:00-14:00 and second shift 14:00-22:00. Overtime can be arranged for third shift 22:00-06:00.

Sunday: Overtime can be arranged for all three shifts.

No work on the following holidays: New Year's Day, Labour Day and Christmas Day.

Holiday: Overtime can be arranged for all three shifts.

Oil and chemical Terminals

Monday - Sunday and Holiday: First shift 06:00-14:00, second shift 14:00-22:00 and third shift 22:00-06:00.

Wismar

Working hours:

Monday - Friday: First shift 06:00-14:00 and second shift 14:00-22:00. Third shift 22:00-06:00 at overtime rates. Breaks 10:00-10:30, 18:00-18:30 and 02:00-02:30.

Saturday: First shift 06:00-14:00. Second shift 14:00-20:00 and third shift 20:00-02:00 at overtime rates and on request only.

Sunday: First shift 06:00-12:00, second shift 12:00-18:00, third shift 18:00-00:00 and fourth shift 00:00-06:00, all at overtime rates and on request only.

No work on the following holidays: New Year's Day, Labour Day and Christmas Day.

Ordinary work stops at 12:00 on the day before the holidays above.

On all other holidays, work is possible on request and by special arrangement at overtime rates.

Ghana

General holidays

January	1	New Year's Day
-	7	Constitution Day
March	6	Independence Day
April	2	Good Friday
-	5	Easter Monday
May	1	Labour Day
-	13[1]	Eid ul-Fitr
July	21[1]	Eid al-Adha
August	4	National Founder's Day
September	21	Kwame Nkrumah Memorial Day
December	3	National Farmers Day
-	25	Christmas Day
-	26	Boxing Day

[1] Exact date(s) subject to sighting of the moon.

Takoradi
Working hours:
Monday - Saturday: 07:30-12:30, 14:00-17:00 and 19:30-03:30.
Overtime: First shift 12:30-14:00 and 17:00-19:30. Second shift 03:30-07:30.
Sunday and holidays: Shift work at overtime rates 07:30-19:30 and 19:30-07:30.

Tema
Working hours:
Monday - Saturday: 07:30-12:30, 14:00-17:00 and 19:30-03:30.
Overtime: First shift 12:30-14:00 and 17:00-19:30. Second shift 03:30-07:30.
Sunday and holidays: Shift work at overtime rates 07:30-19:30 and 19:30-07:30.

Gibraltar

General holidays

January	1	New Year's Day
March	8	Commonwealth Day
April	2	Good Friday
-	5	Easter Monday
-	28	Workers' Memorial Day
May	1	May Day
-	31	Spring Bank Holiday
June	14	Queen's Birthday
August	30	Late Summer Bank Holiday
September	10	Gibraltar National Day
December	25[1]	Christmas Day
-	26[2]	Boxing Day

[1] Observed 27 December (2021 only).

[2] Observed 28 December (2021 only).

Gibraltar

Working hours:

Monday - Thursday: 08:00-13:00 and 14:00-17:00. Monday 00:00-08:00 at 100% extra.
Friday: 08:00-13:00 and 14:00-16:00. Overtime 17:00-08:00.
Saturday: 08:00-00:00 at 50% extra.
Sunday: 00:00-00:00 at 100% extra.
When the usual date of a bank or public holiday falls on a Saturday or Sunday, a substitute day is given, normally the following Monday.

Greece

General holidays

January	1	New Year's Day
-	6	Epiphany
February	15	Ash Monday
March	25	Independence Day/Annunciation of Virgin Mary
April	30	Good Friday (Orthodox)
May	1	Labour Day and Holy Saturday (Orthodox)
-	3	Easter Monday (Orthodox)
June	21	Whit Monday (Orthodox)
August	15	Assumption B.V. Mary
October	28	Anniversary of War Outbreak
December	24[1]	Christmas Eve
-	25	Christmas Day
-	26	Second Christmas Day
-	31[1]	New Year's Eve

[1] From noon.

Chalkis

July	26	St. Paraskevi

Working hours:
Winter (Monday - Friday): 08:00-16:00. Overtime 16:00-19:00 at 50% extra.
Summer (Monday - Friday): 07:00-15:00. Overtime 15:00-18:30 at 50% extra.
Saturday: Overtime 07:00-15:00 and 15:00-18:30 at 50% extra.

Corfu

May	21	Union of Ionian Islands with Greece
August	11	St. Spyridon Procession
December	12	St. Spyridon

Working hours:
Summer (Monday - Saturday): 07:00-14:00. Overtime 14:00-00:00 at 25% extra.
Winter (Monday - Saturday): 08:00-15:00. Overtime 15:00-00:00 at 25% extra.
Sunday and holidays: Work available at 75% extra.

Eleusis

April	23	St. George's Day

Working hours:
Monday - Friday: 07:30-15:00. 15:00-18:00 at 20% extra. 18:00-22:00 at 30% extra.
22:00-06:00 at 50% extra.
Saturday: 07:30-12:00 at 40% extra, 12:00-22:00 and 22:00-06:00 at 75% extra.
Sunday: Work available at 75% extra.

Heraklion

November	11	St. Minas

Working hours:
Monday - Friday: 07:30-15:00. Work available 15:00-00:00 at overtime by request.
Saturday, Sunday and holidays: Work available at overtime by request.

Itea

December	6	St. Nicholas

Kalamata

February	2	B. V. Mary (Ypapanti)
June	10	Ascension Day
December	17	St. Denis

Working hours:
Winter (Monday - Friday): 08:00-12:00 and 13:00-17:30.
Summer (Monday - Friday): 08:00-12:00 and 14:00-18:00.
Saturday and holidays: Work available at overtime by request.

Mytilene

November	8	Michael and Gabriel

Working hours:
Monday - Saturday: 07:00-15:00 at normal rates. 15:00-20:00 at 25% extra. 20:00-07:00
at 50% extra.
Sunday and holidays: Work available 22:00-07:00 at 100% extra.

Patras

November	30	St. Andrew

Working hours:
Monday - Friday: 08:00-17:00 at normal rates. 17:00-08:00 at 100% extra.
Sunday and holidays: Work available 00:00-00:00 overtime by request at 100% extra.

Piraeus

December	12	St. Spyridon

Working hours:
Monday - Sunday: First shift 07:30-14:30, second shift 15:00-22:00, third shift 22:00-05:00.
No work 22:00-07:00 following days New Year's Day, Good Friday (Orthodox), Holy Saturday (Orthodox) and Christmas Day.
No work in Labour Day.
The Passenger Terminal
Monday - Sunday: 00:00-00:00.

Souda

November	21	Eisodia of Virgin Mary
December	6	St. Nicholas

Working hours:
Summer (Monday - Friday): 08:00-12:00 and 14:00-18:00. Overtime 18:00-08:00 at 25% extra.
Winter (Monday - Friday): 08:00-12:00 and 13:30-17:30. Overtime 17:30-08:00 at 25% extra.
Saturday: Work available at 25% extra cost.
Sunday and holidays: Work available at 75% extra cost.
Winter: October - April
Summer: May - September

Thessaloniki

October	26	St. Demetrius

Working hours:

Conventional cargo terminal

Monday - Friday: First shift 08:00-15:00, second shift 15:00-22:00 at normal rate and third shift 22:00-08:00 overtime by request.

Saturday: 08:00-15:00 at normal working hours and second shift 15:00-22:00 and third shift 22:00-08:00 overtime by request.

Sunday and Holidays workable on request of overtime.

Container terminal

Monday - Sunday: First shift 08:00-15:00 second shift 15:00-22:00, third shift 22:00-05:30. Overtime 05:30:08:00 by request.

All Holidays 00:00-00:00 overtime by request.

Volos

Working hours:

Monday - Friday: 07:00-14:00 at normal rates. 14:00-21:00 at 25% extra. 21:00-06:00 at 50% extra.

Saturday and Sunday: 07:00-21:00 at 25% extra. 21:00-06:00 at 50% extra.

Holidays: 08:00-13:30, 14:00-22:00 and 22:00-04:00 overtime by request at 75% extra.

Greenland

General holidays

January	1	New Year's Day
-	6	Epiphany
April	1	Maundy Thursday
-	2	Good Friday
-	5	Easter Monday
-	30	Prayer Day
May	13	Ascension Day
-	24	Whit Monday
June	21	Ullortuneq
December	24	Christmas Eve
-	25	Christmas Day
-	26	Boxing Day
-	31	New Year's Eve

Grenada

General holidays

January	1	New Year's Day
February	7	Independence Day
April	2	Good Friday
-	5	Easter Monday
May	1	Labour Day
-	24	Whit Monday
June	3	Corpus Christi
August	2	Emancipation Day
-	9	Carnival
-	10[1]	Carnival Tuesday
October	25	Thanksgiving Day
December	25	Christmas Day
-	26	Boxing Day

[1] Half day - until noon.
The mentioned holidays are Bank Holidays.
If a Bank Holiday falls on a Sunday, the following Monday shall be a Bank Holiday

St Georges Harbour
Working hours:
Monday - Friday: 07:00-16:00. Breaks 12:00-13:00 and 18:00-19:00. Overtime 16:00-23:00.

Saturday - Sunday and holidays: Work available at 100%.

There is no work on Independence Day, Good Friday, Labour Day and 25 December (Christmas Day).

Guadeloupe

General holidays

January	1	New Year's Day
April	5	Easter Monday
May	1	Labour Day
-	8	Memorial Day 1945
-	13	Ascension Day
-	24	Whit Monday
-	27	Emancipation Day
July	14	National Day
August	15	Assumption B.V. Mary
November	1	All Saints' Day
-	11	Armistice Day
December	25	Christmas Day

Guatemala

General holidays

January	1	New Year's Day
April	1	Maundy Thursday
-	2	Good Friday
-	3	Holy Saturday
May	1	Labour Day
June	30	Army Day
September	15	Independence Day
October	20	Revolution Day
November	1	All Saints' Day
December	24[1]	Christmas Eve
-	25	Christmas Day
-	31[1]	New Year's Eve

[1] Half-day holiday.
When a holiday falls on a Tuesday, it will be observed on the preceding Monday.
When a holiday falls on a Wednesday or Thursday, it will be observed the following Friday.
These provision do not apply to the following:
1 January, Maundy Thursday, Good Friday and Easter Saturday, 15 September, 1 November, December 24, December 25, December 31 and the day of the local festival.

Local holidays

Puerto Barrios

May	28	Patron's Feast Day

Working hours:
Monday - Friday: 07:00-15:00 and 15:00-19:00 at normal. 19:00-23:00 and 23:00-07:00 at overtime rates.
The holiday above is workable at overtime rates.

Puerto Quetzal

March	19	St. Joseph's Day

Working hours:
Monday - Friday: First shift 07:00-14:30, second shift 14:30-21:30, third shift 21:30-07:00.
The local holidays above are workable at overtime rates.

San Jose

March	19	St. Joseph's Day

Working hours:
Monday to Friday: 07:00-14:30, 14:30-21:30 and 21:30-07:00.

Santo Tomas de Castilla

May	28	Santa Cruz

Working hours:
Monday - Friday: 06:00-13:00, 13:00-19:00, 19:00-00:00 and 00:00-06:00.
The local holidays above are workable at overtime rates.

Guinea Equatorial

General holidays

January	1	New Year's Day
April	2	Good Friday
May	1	Labour Day
June	3	Corpus Christi
-	5	President's Birthday
August	3	Freedom Day
-	15	Constitution Day
October	12	Independence Day
December	8	Immaculate Conception
-	25	Christmas Day

Guinea, Republic of

General holidays

January	1	New Year's Day
April	5	Easter Monday
May	1	Labour Day
-	13[1]	Korite
-	25	Africa Day
July	20[1]	Tabaski
August	15	Assumption Day
October	2	Independence Day
-	19[1]	Mouloud
December	25	Christmas Day

[1] Exact date(s) subject to sighting of the moon.

Information provided to BIMCO by the Ministry in charge of Investments and Public-Private Partnerships

Working hours for all ports in Republic of Guinea:

Monday - Thursday: 08:00-16:30. Meal break 12:00-13:00. Overtime 16:30-08:00.

Friday: 08:00-13:00. Overtime 13:00-08:00.

Saturday: Workable at overtime rates.

Sunday: Workable at overtime rates.

Holidays: All Saints' Day workable at overtime rates.

General cargo handling is slower during rainy season.

Guinea-Bissau

General holidays

January	1	New Year's Day
-	20	National Hero's Day
March	8	Women's Day
May	1	Labour Day
-	13[1]	Korité
July	20[1]	Tabaski
August	3	Pidjiguiti Day
September	24	Independence Day
November	14	Readjustment Movement Day
December	25	Christmas Day

[1] Exact date(s) subject to sighting of the moon.

Guyana

General holidays

Month	Day	Holiday
January	1	New Year's Day
February	23[1]	Republic Day
March	29[2]	Phagwah
April	2	Good Friday
-	5	Easter Monday
May	1	Labour Day
-	26[1]	Independence Day
July	5[1]	Caricom Day
-	20[2]	Eid-ul-Adha
August	1[1]	Emancipation Day
-	2	Commonwealth Day
October	19[2]	Youman Nabi
November	4[2]	Deepavali
December	25	Christmas Day
-	26	Boxing Day

[1] Subject to public announcement.
[2] Exact date(s) subject to sighting of the moon.
All Sundays are public holidays.
If a holiday falls on a Sunday, the following day is observed a holiday.
If Christmas Day falls on a Sunday, the following Tuesday is a holiday.

Georgetown

Working hours:
Monday - Friday: 07:00-15:00. Overtime 15:00-23:00, 23:00-03:00 and 03:00- 07:00.
Saturday, Sunday and holidays: 07:00-15:00, 15:00-23:00, 23:00-03:00 and
03:00- 07:00, all at overtime rates.

Haiti

General holidays

January	1	New Year's Day
-	2	National Heroes' Day
February	15[1]	Lundi Gras
-	16	Mardi Gras
April	2	Good Friday
-	14	Day of the Americas
May	1	Labour Day
-	13	Ascension Day
-	18	Flag Day
-	22	Sovereignty Day
June	3	Corpus Christi
August	15	Assumption of Mary
October	17	Dessalines death anniversary
-	24	United Nations Day
November	1	All Saints' Day
-	2[1]	All Souls' Day
-	18	Vertiere Battle
December	5	Discovery Day
-	25	Christmas Day

[1] Half day.

Honduras

General holidays

January	1	New Year's Day
April	1	Holy Thursday
-	2	Good Friday
-	3	Holy Saturday
-	14	Panamerican Day
May	1	Labour Day
September	15	Independence Day
October	7	Francisco Moranzan's Birthday
-	12	Columbus Day
-	21	Army Day
December	25	Christmas Day

Local holidays

Puerto Castilla
Working hours:
Monday - Friday: 07:00-12:00 and 13:00-17:00. Overtime 18:00-23:00 and 23:30-06:00.
Breaks 06:00-07:00, 12:00-13:00, 17:00-18:00 and 23:00-23:30.
Saturday: 07:00-12:00 and 13:00-17:00 at ordinary on-board stevedoring rates.
Sunday: Work negotiable and up to double rates, subject to labour availability.
There is no work from 06:00-18:00 on Labour Day and Good Friday.
There is no work from 18:00-18:00 on New Year's Day and Christmas Day. All holidays overtime by request.

Puerto Cortez

August	15	Assumption Day

Working hours:
Monday - Friday: 07:00-12:00 and 13:00-17:00. Overtime 18:00-23:00 and 23:30-06:00.
Breaks 06:00-07:00, 12:00-13:00, 17:00-18:00 and 23:00-23:30.
Saturday: 07:00-12:00 at normal.
Saturday 12:00-00:00. Sunday and holidays, overtime 50% extra.
There is no work from 06:00-18:00 on Labour Day and Good Friday.
There is no work from 18:00-18:00 on New Year's Day and Christmas Day. All holidays overtime by request.

San Lorenzo

August	10	San Lorenzo Day

Working hours:
Monday - Friday: 07:00-12:00 and 13:00-17:00. Overtime 18:00-06:00.
Breaks 06:00-07:00, 12:00-13:00, 17:00-18:00 and 23:00-23:30.
Saturday: 07:00-12:00 at normal.
Sunday: Overtime rate of 100% extra.
There is no work from 06:00-18:00 on Labour Day and Good Friday.
There is no work from 18:00-18:00 on New Year's Day and Christmas Day.

Hungary

General holidays

January	1	New Year's Day
March	15	Memorial Day of the Revolution of 1848
April	2	Good Friday
-	5	Easter Monday
May	1	Labour Day
-	24	Whit Monday
August	20	Memorial Day of Saint Stephen, the first King of Hungary
October	23	Memorial Day of the Revolution of 1956
November	1	All Saints' Day
December	25	Christmas Day
-	26	Boxing Day

Iceland

General holidays

January	1	New Year's Day
April	1	Maundy Thursday
-	2	Good Friday
-	4	Easter Sunday
-	5	Easter Monday
-	22	First Day of Summer
May	1	Labour Day
-	13	Ascension Day
-	23	Whit Sunday
-	24	Whit Monday
June	17	Independence Day
August	2	August Holiday
December	24[1]	Christmas Eve
-	25	Christmas Day
-	26	Second day of Christmas
-	31[1]	New Years Eve

[1] Half day. Work stops at 13.00 on 24 December (Christmas Eve) and 31 December (New Year's Eve).
All Sundays are holidays

India

General holidays

The holiday information for Indian ports was not available at the time of printing. BIMCO will provide a Holiday Calendar supplement in early 2021 with this information included. Use the QR code below to get the supplement

Alternatively use the URL https://www.bimco.org/web/Indian-Holiday-Supplement

Indonesia

General holidays

January	1	New Year's Day
February	12	Chinese New Year
March	11[1]	Isra Mikraj
-	14	Holy Nyepi Day
April	2	Good Friday
May	1	Labour Day
-	13	Ascension of Jesus Christ
-	13-14[1]	Eid al-Fitr
-	26	Vesak Day
June	1	Birth of Pancasila Day
July	20[1]	Eid al-Adha
August	10[1]	Islamic New Year
-	17	Independence Day
October	19[1]	Birth of Prophet Muhammad
December	25	Christmas Day

[1] Fixed by decree

Iran

General holidays

January	17[1]	Martyrdom of Fatima
February	10	Revolution Day
-	25[1]	Birthday of Imam Ali
March	1	Islamic Republic Day
-	19	Oil Nationalization Day
-	21	Nowruz
-	29[1]	Imam Mahdi's birthday
April	2	Nature Day
May	4	Martyrdom of Imam Ali
-	11	Labor Day
-	13-14[1]	Eid-e-Fetr
June	3	Martyrdom of Imam Khommeini
-	5	Khordad Revolt
-	6[1]	Martyrdom of Imam Sadegh
July	20[1]	Eid-e-Ghorban
-	28[1]	Eid-e-Ghadir
August	18[1]	Tasua
-	19[1]	Ashoura
September	27[1]	Arbaieen Of Ashoora
October	6[1]	Demise of Prophet Muhammad and Martyrdom of Imam Hassan
-	7[1]	Martyrdom of Imam Reza
-	15[1]	Martyrdom of Imam Hassan Askari
-	19[1]	Birthday of Prophet Mohammad & Imam Sadiq

[1] Exact date(s) subject to sighting of the moon.
Friday is the weekly day of rest.

Bandar Imam Khomeini
Working hours:
Saturdays - Thursdays: 07:00-12:00, 13:00-18:00 and 19:00-02:00.
Friday: 07:00-12:00, 13:00-18:00 and 19:00-22:00.
Holidays: Most workable at same hours as above.

Bushire
Working hours:
Saturdays - Thursdays: 07:00-12:00, 13:00-18:00 and 19:00-02:00.
Friday: 07:00-12:00, 13:00-18:00 and 19:00-22:00.
Holidays: Most workable at same hours as above.

Iraq

General holidays

January	1	New Year's Day
-	6	Iraqi Army Day
March	21	Eid Norooz
May	1	Labour Day
-	13-15[1]	Eid al-Fitr
July	14	Republic Day
-	20[1]	Eid al-Adha
August	10[1]	Islamic New Year
-	20[1]	Ashura
October	3	Independence Day
-	19[1]	Mawlid al-Nabi
December	10	Victory Day
-	25	Christmas Day

[1] Exact date(s) subject to sighting of the moon.

Ireland

General holidays

January	1	New Year's Day
March	17	St. Patrick's Day
April	5	Easter Monday
May	3	May Bank Holiday
June	7	June Bank Holiday
August	2	August Bank Holiday
October	25	October Bank Holiday
December	25	Christmas Day
-	26	St. Stephen's Day

Cork
Working hours:
Monday - Friday: 08:00-17:00. Meal break from 13:00-14:00.
Overtime is flexible and as required. On Friday overtime commences at 17:00.
Saturday, Sunday and holidays: 08:00-17:00 at overtime rates. Meal break 13:00-14:00.
Work to be ordered by 14:00 on Friday or day before a holiday.

Dublin
Working hours:
Monday - Friday: 08:00-17:00. Overtime 17:00-08:00 by request
Saturday, Sunday and holidays overtime by request.

Galway
Working hours:
Monday - Friday: 08:00-17:00. Break from 10:00-10:30. Meal break 13:00-14:00.
Saturday: Overtime 07:00-21:00. Meal break 13:00-14:00.
Sunday and holidays: Overtime 08:00-17:00. Meal break 13:00-14:00.

Israel

General holidays

March	28	Passover (Pessah) 1st day
April	3	Passover (Pessah) 7th day
-	15	Independence Day
May	17	Pentecost (Shavuot)
September	7	New Year (Rosh Hashana) 1st Day
-	8	New Year (Rosh Hashana) 2nd Day
-	16	Day of Atonement (Yom Kippur)
-	21	Sukkot
-	28	Feast of the Law (Simchat Torah)

Italy

General holidays

January	1	New Year's Day
January	6	Epiphany
April	5	Easter Monday
April	25	Liberation Day
May	1	Labour Day
June	2	Republic Day
August	15	Assumption of Mary
November	1	All Saints' Day
December	8	Immaculate Conception
December	25	Christmas Day
December	26	Saint Stephen's Day

All Sundays are holidays

Local holidays

Ancona and Falconara
Working hours:
Monday - Saturday: First shift 06:30-13:00 and second shift 13:00-19:30 at 10% extra.
Monday - Friday: Third shift 19:30-02:00 at 50% extra.
Saturday: Third shift 19:30-02:00 at 70% extra.
Monday - Saturday: Fourth shift 00:00-06:00 only in case of consecutive shifts of 6 hours each at 100% extra.
Holidays: First shift 06:30-13:00 at 52% extra. Second shift 13:00-19:30 at 100% extra.

Augusta
Working hours:
Monday - Friday: 08:00-12:00 and 13:00-17:00.
Saturday: 08:00-20:00 at 50% extra and 20:00-06:00 at 70% extra.
Sunday and holidays: 08:00-20:00 at 100% extra and 20:00-06:00 at 70% extra.

Bari
Working hours:
Monday - Friday: 06:30-19:30, 19:30-06:30 with no meal breaks. Overtime possible on request subject to availability of gangs.
Saturday: Overtime 06:30-19:30.
Sunday and holidays: Overtime on request.

Brindisi
Working hours:
Monday - Saturday: First shift 07:00-13:00, second shift 13:30-20:00 and third shift 21:00-02:30.
Sunday and holidays: Work is available 07:00-13:30.

Cagliari
Working hours:
Cagliari
Monday - Saturday: 07:00-13:00 and 13:00-19:00. Overtime: 19:00-01:00.
Sunday and holidays: Work to be agreed with stevedoring companies.
Cagliari container terminal and Assemini Contivecchi chemical terminal
Work 24 hours per day 365 days per year.

Chioggia
Working hours:
Monday - Friday: 08:00-12:00 and 14:00-18:00. Meal break 12:00-14:00.
Shift times: Monday - Friday 18:00-20:00 or 20:00-00:00.

Civitavecchia
Working hours:
Monday - Saturday: 06:00-12:30 and 12:30-19:00. Night shift at 50% extra 19:00-00:30.
Sunday and holidays: 06:00-12:30 and 13:00-19:00 at 70% extra. Night shift 19:00-00:30 at 100% extra.

Crotone

Working hours:

Monday - Friday: 07:00-12:00 and 12:30-16:30. Ordinary working hours.

Overtime on request.

Monday - Friday shifts: First shift 07:00-13:30 at 10% extra, second shift 13:30-20:00 at 10% extra, third shift 20:00-01:30 at 50% extra and fourth shift 01:30-07:00 at 70% extra.

Saturday shifts: Same shifts as above but first and second shift at 10% extra, third shift at 150% extra and fourth shift at 170% extra.

Sunday and holiday shifts: Same shift times as Monday - Friday but first shift at 63% extra, second shift at 100% extra, third shift at 50% extra and fourth shift at 70% extra.

Gaeta

Working hours:

Monday - Friday: 07:00-13:30 and 13:30-20:00.

Saturday: 07:00-13:30.

Gela

Working hours:

Monday - Saturday: 07:00-13:30 and 14:30-21:30.

Sunday and holidays: No work.

Genoa

Working hours:

Containers and general cargo

Genoa Port terminal: 06:30-13:00, 13:00-19:30 and 19:30-01:00. 01:00-06:00 subject to agreement with terminal.

San Giorgio terminal: 07:00-13:00, 13:00-19:00 and 19:00-01:00. 01:00-07:00 subject to agreement with terminal.

Full containers

Voltri Terminal Europa: 06:00-12:00, 12:00-18:00, 18:00-00:00, 00:00-06:00.

Southern European Container Hub: 07:00-13:00, 13:00-19:00, 19:00-01:00, 01:00-07:00.

Bulk cargo

Coal: Monday - Friday: 06:00-14:00, 14:00-22:00, 22:00-06:00.

Other bulk products: Monday - Friday: 06:30-12:30 and 13:00-19:30.

Imperia

Working hours:

Monday - Friday: 08:00-12:00 and 14:00-18:00.

La Spezia

Working hours:

Monday - Friday: 07:00-13:00, 13:00-19:00. Overtime 19:00-01:00, 01:00-07:00 to be agreed.

Saturday: 07:00-13:00. Overtime 13:00-19:00, 19:00-01:00, 01:00-07:00 to be agreed.

Sunday: Overtime all day to be agreed.

Livorno (Leghorn)

Working hours:

Monday - Saturday: 08:00-12:00 and 14:00-18:00. 18:00-20:00 for completion only.

Running shifts: 07:30-13:30. 13:30-19:30 at extra rates which vary according to commodity plus 45 minutes extension for completion only.

Night shift: 19:30-01:30 and 01:30-07:30 at extra rates which vary according to commodity plus 45 minutes extension for completion only. 01:30-07:30 shift at 50% overtime.

Sunday and holidays: Running shift 07:30-13:30 plus 45 minutes extension for completion only. 13:30-19:30 overtime by request.

Holidays: There is no work on 1 May (Labour Day) and 25 December (Christmas Day). There is no work on 1 January (New Year's Day) until 13:30. On 31 December (New Year's Eve), work stops at 19:30.

Marsala

Working hours:

Monday - Friday: 08:00-12:00 and 13:00-17:00. Meal break 12:00-13:00.

Monday - Friday: Overtime 17:00-08:00.

Overtime work possible at extra cost, including Saturday and Sunday.

Messina

Working hours:

Monday - Friday: 08:00-12:00 and 13:00-17:00. Meal break 12:00-13:00. Overtime 06:00-08:00 and 17:00-20:00. Night time 20:00-00:00 and 01:00-06:00 with meal break 00:00-01:00.

Saturday: 08:00-14:30 at 10% extra. After 14:30, 50% extra.

Sunday: 08:00-14:30 at 103% extra, 14:30-21:00 at 100% extra and 21:00-03:30 at 250%extra.

Madonna della Lettera, Patron Saint of the City 00:00-00:00 overtime 150%.

Monfalcone

Working hours:

Portorosega Quay

Monday - Saturday: First shift 07:30-13:30, second shift 14:00-20:00.
Meal breaks 10:00-10:30 and 17:00-17:30.

Overtime: Monday - Saturday third shift 20:30-02:30 at 50% extra.

Sunday and holidays: First shift 07:30-13:30 plus extra charge, second shift 14:00-20:00 plus extra charge, third shift 20:30-02:30 plus extra charge.

Silos de Francischi Quay

Monday - Friday: 06:00-22:00. No meal breaks.

Saturday: Work sometimes available.

Power Plant

Monday - Sunday: 06:30-21:30. No meal breaks.

Naples

Working hours:

Monday - Friday: 08:00-12:00 and 13:00-17:00. The times are approximate as regular working hours vary from terminal to terminal.

Palermo

Working hours:

Monday - Friday: 08:00-12:00 and 13:00-17:00. For completion only 17:00-19:00 at 25% extra and 12:00-13:00 workable at 50% extra.

Continuous shifts: 27% extra 08:00-14:30 and 14:30-21:00, 74% extra 21:00-02:30 and 130% extra 02:30-08:00.

Saturday: Continuous shifts, 27% extra 08:00-14:30 and 14:30-21:00 and 96% extra 21:00-02:30.

Sunday and holidays: Continuous shifts, 77% extra 08:00-14:30 and 130% extra 14:30-21:00.

Port of Gallipoli

Bulk cargoes 00:00-00:00. Other cargoes 07:00-13:00 and 13:00-18:00.

Porto Torres

Working hours:
New Commercial Harbour
Monday - Friday: 08:00-12:00 and 13:30-17:30.
Saturday: 07:00-13:30
Oil, chemicals and gas products
24 hours per day, 365 days per year.

Porto Vesme

Working hours:
Monday - Friday: 08:00-12:00 and 13:00-17:00.
Overtime: Workable at extra cost and to be agreed.
Running shifts: First shift 06:00-12:30, second shift 12:30-19:00, third shift 19:00-00:30 and fourth shift 00:30-06:00.
Saturday: Running shifts only.
Sunday and holidays: Workable and cost to be agreed.

Pozzallo

Working hours:
Monday - Friday: Summer time 07:00-12:00 and 14:00-18:00. Winter time 07:00-12:00 and 13:30-17:30.
Saturday: 07:00-13:00 at 25% extra and 13:00-20:00 at 50% extra.
Sunday and holidays: No work.
Saint John, work is available for 07:00-12:00 at ordinary rates.

Ravenna

Working hours:

Monday - Friday: 08:00-12:00 and 14:00-18:00.

Saturday: 06:30-13:00.

Monday - Friday shifts: Double shift 06:30-13:00 and 13:30-19:30 at 10% extra. Third shift 19:30-02:00 at 50% extra.

Saturday shifts: Double shift 06:30-13:00 at 10% extra and 13:00-19:30 at 22% extra. Third shift 19:30-02:00 at 70% extra.

Sunday and holidays shifts: 06:30-13:00 at 53% extra. 13:00-19:30 at 100% extra. 19:30-02:00 at 135% extra.

Holidays falling on Sunday: 06:30-13:00 at 153% extra. 13:00-19:30 at 200% extra.

Additional 100 %-points are added to working hours for holidays observed on a Sunday.

Reggio Calabria

Working hours:

Monday - Friday shifts: 06:00-12:00 and 13:00-17:00. Meal break 12:00-13:00.

Saturday: Work available at 50% extra.

Sunday and holidays: Work available at 75% extra.

Sant Antioco

Working hours:

Monday - Friday: 08:00-12:00 and 13:00-17:00. Overtime for completion only 17:00-19:00 at 25% extra. Shift work: First and second shifts at 10% extra, third shift at 50% extra and fourth shift at 100% extra.

Running shifts: First shift 06:00-12:30, second shift 12:30-19:00, third shift 19:00-00:30 and fourth shift 00:30-06:00.

Saturday: Only running shifts worked; first and second shifts at 10% extra, third shift at 70% extra and fourth shift at 100% extra.

Sunday: Only running shifts worked; first shift at 53% extra and second shift at 100% extra.

Holidays: Only running shifts worked; first shift at 143% extra, second and third shifts at 170% extra.

Sarroch

Working hours:

Monday - Sunday: 24 hours per day, 365 days per year.

Savona

Working hours:

Monday - Friday: Normal shift 07:00-13:00 and 14:00-20:00. Overtime: Possible night shift 20:00-02:00.

Saturday: Normal shift 07:00-13:00. Overtime: Work possible 14:00-20:00 and 20:00-02:00.

Taranto

Working hours:

ENI Refinery - CBM and jetty

Monday - Sunday: First shift 06:00-14:00, second shift 14:00-22:00, third shift 22:00-06:00, including holidays. Work carried out by ENI's personnel on their account for their own cargoes at their own handling cost.

ILVA Piers

Monday - Sunday: First shift 07:00-15:00, second shift 15:00-23:00, third shift 23:00-07:00, including holidays. Work carried out by ILVA's personnel on their account for their own cargoes at their own handling cost.

Merchant port: It is possible to work as follows (option to be declared on calling first gang and not changeable afterwards):

Shift work: Monday - Saturday: First shift: 07:00-13:30, second shift 13:30-20:00 at 10% extra. Third shift 20:00-02:30, if no Customs control needed, at 35% extra. Sunday first shift at 35% extra, second shift at 70% extra on top of the tariff applicable for first shift.

Trapani

Working hours:

Conventional cargo: Monday - Friday: 07:00-19:00.

Saturday: 07:00-14:00. Overtime 14:00-00:00 at 30% extra.

Sunday and holidays: Overtime at 50% extra.

Trieste
Working hours:
Containers Terminal
Monday - Saturday: First shift 07:00-14:00, second shift 14:00-21:00, third shift 21:00-04:00. Fourth shift 04:00-07:00 overtime by request.
Sunday and holidays: First shift 07:00-14:00 and second shift 14:00-21:00 only.
Commercial Port
Monday - Saturday: First shift 07:30-14:00, second shift 14:00-20:30 and third shift 20:30-03:00.
Sunday and holidays: First shift 07:30-14:00 and second shift 14:00-20:30 only.
Holidays: There is no work on 1 January (New Year's Day), 1 May (Labour Day), 15 August (Assumption), 8 December (Immaculate Conception) and 25 December (Christmas).

Vado Ligure
Working hours:
Bulk: 24 hours per day SHINC.
Reefer terminal: First shift 07:00-13:00, second shift 14:00-20:00, third shift 20:00-02:00 SHINC.

Venice
Working hours:
Monday - Friday: 08:00-12:00 and 13:00-17:00. Meal break 12:00-13:00. Evening shift 17:00-23:30. Bulk cargoes usually at ordinary rates. General cargoes, rates to be agreed. Overtime 23:30-05:30 by request only.
Saturday: 08:00-14:30. Overtime 14:30-21:00 by request only. No meals.
Sunday: Overtime 08:00-14:00. 14:00-20:00 on request only. No meals.
On 24 December (Christmas Eve) and 31 December (New Year's Eve), there is work only 08:00-14:00 at overtime rates. No meal breaks.

Viareggio
Working hours:
Monday - Sunday: 08:00-12:00 and 13:00-17:00.
Saturday: Overtime 13:00-17:00.
Sunday: Overtime 08:00-12:00 and 13:00-17:00.

Ivory Coast

General holidays

January	1	New Year's Day
April	5	Easter Monday
May	1	Labor Day
-	10[1]	Relelation of the Qur'an
-	13	Ascension Day
-	13[1]	Korite
-	24	Whit Monday
July	20[1]	Tabaksi
August	7	Independence Day
-	15	Assumption
October	19[1]	Birth of the Prophet
November	1	All Saints Day
-	15	National Peace Day
December	25	Christmas Day

[1] Exact date(s) subject to sighting of the moon.
If any of the following holidays falls on a Sunday, the following Monday will be also public holiday:
Eid al-Fitr
Eid al-Adha
Christmas Day
National Day
Labour Day.

Abidjan

Working hours:
Monday - Friday: 07:30-12:00 and 13:30-16:30.
00:00-7:30, 12:00-13:30, 16:30-7:30 overtime by request.
Saturday: Day of rest but some private companies can work 07:30-12:00, thereafter overtime.
Sunday: Day of rest. Overtime work possible.
Holidays: Overtime round the clock without stoppage possible but output poor. On 1 January (New Year's Day) and 25 December (Christmas Day), no work in the port 19:00-07:30.
Working hours during Ramadan:
Normal working hours during Ramadan month 07:30-17:30
Overtime only permitted 19:30-07:30

Jamaica

General holidays

January	1	New Year's Day
February	17	Ash Wednesday
April	5	Easter Monday
May	23	Labour Day
August	1	Emancipation Day
-	6	Independence Day
October	18	National Heroes' Day
December	25	Christmas Day
-	26	Boxing Day

If the any of the following holidays fall on a Sunday, it will be observed the following Monday:
New Year's Day
National Labour Day - will also shift from Saturday to Monday
Emancipation Day
Independence Day
Christmas Day - the following day will also be a public holiday.

Bustamante-Kingston
Working hours:
Monday - Sunday: First shift 07:00-15:00 and second shift 15:00-23:00. Flexible shift system on first two shifts within a 4-hour window. Third shift 23:00-07:00 at night shift premium rates. Meal breaks 11:00-12:00, 19:00-20:00 and 03:00-04:00.

Gangs for working ships are available on all shifts prior to notation from agent before ship arrival.

Overtime: Work available at overtime rates on holidays and an extension of a shift.
The port of Kingston works 24 hours per day, 365 days per year.

Montego Bay
Working hours:
Public Wharf
Monday - Friday: 07:00-14:00 and 14:00-21:00 at normal rates. Overtime 22:00-06:00 at time and a half.

Saturday and Sunday: Normal working days.

Holidays: Work available on 24 hour on request of overtime costs.

Ocho Rios
Working hours:
Monday - Sunday and holiday: 00:00-00:00.

Port Esquivel
Working hours:
Monday - Sunday and holiday: 00:00-00:00.

Port Rhoades
Working hours:
Discovery Bay
Monday - Sunday and holiday: 00:00-00:00.
Privately owned by Noranda Bauxite Limited

Rocky Point
Working hours:
Rocky Point Clarendon
Monday - Sunday and holiday: 00:00-00:00.
Privately owned by Alcoa.

Japan

General holidays

January	1	New Year's Day
-	11	Adult Day
February	11	National Foundation Day
-	23	The Emperor's Birthday
March	20	Vernal Equinox Day
April	29	Showa Day
May	3	Constitution Day
-	4	Green Day
-	5	Children's Day
July	19	Marine Day
August	11	Mountain Day
September	20	Respect for the Aged Day
-	23	Autumnal Equinox Day
October	11	Health-Sports Day
November	3	Culture Day
-	23	Labour Thanksgiving Day

Kobe

Working hours:

Day shift 08:30-16:30 and night shifts 16:30-21:30 at extra 60% and 21:30-04:00 at extra 130%.

Meal breaks 12:00-13:00, 16:30-17:30 and 23:00-00:00.

Holiday 100% overtime by request. No work on New year day.

Matsuyama

Working hours:

Monday - Sunday: 24 hours operation.

All holiday overtime by request. No work on New year.

Moji

Working hours:

Day shift 08:30-16:30 and night shifts 16:30-21:30 at extra 60% and 21:30-05:00 at extra 120%.

Meal breaks 12:00-13:00, 17:00-18:00 and 00:00-01:00.

All holiday overtime by request. No work on New year.

Nagoya
Working hours:
Day shift 08:30-16:30 and night shifts 16:30-21:30 at extra 60% and 21:30-04:30 at extra 130%.
Meal breaks 12:00-13:00, 16:30-17:30 and 23:30-00:30.
All holiday overtime by request. No work on New year.

Osaka
Working hours:
Day shift 08:30-16:30 and night shifts 16:30-21:30 at extra 60% and 21:30-04:00 at extra 130%.
Meal breaks 12:00-13:00, 17:00-18:00 and 23:00-00:00.
All holiday overtime by request. No work on New year.

Sasebo
Working hours:
24 hours operation.
No Work: New Year's Day.

Tokyo
Working hours:
Day shift 08:30-16:30 and night shifts 16:30-21:30 at extra 60% and 21:30-04:30 at extra 130%.
Meal breaks 12:00-13:00, 18:00-19:00 and 00:00-01:00.
All holiday overtime by request. No work on New year.

Yokohama
Working hours:
Day shift 08:30-16:30, night shifts 16:30-21:30 at extra 60% and 21:30-04:00 at extra 130%.
Meal breaks 12:00-13:00, 17:30-19:00 and 00:00-01:00.
All holiday overtime by request. No work on New year.

Jordan

General holidays

January	1	New Year
April	28	Easter Sunday (Orthodox)
May	1	Labour Day
-	12[1]	Eid El-Fitr
-	25	Independence Day
July	19[1]	Arafat Day
-	20[1]	Eid El-Adha
August	9[1]	Hijri New Year
October	18[1]	Prophet's Birthday
December	25	Christmas Day

[1] Exact date(s) subject to sighting of the moon.
The weekly holiday is Friday.

Aqaba

Working hours:
Day shift 07:00-19:00. Night shift 19:00-07:00. Both at ordinary flat rates.
Shift work in Ramadan: 08:00 - 17:00 and 21:00 - 07:00

Kazakhstan

General holidays

January	1-2	New Year Holiday
-	7	Christmas
March	8	Women's Day
-	21-23	Nowruz
May	1	Labours' Day
-	7	Defender's Day
-	9	Victory Day
July	6	Capital Day
August	30	Constitution Day
December	1	President Day
-	16-17	Independence Day

Kenya

General holidays

January	1	New Year's Day
April	2	Good Friday
-	5	Easter Monday
May	1	Labour Day
-	13[1]	Idd-ul-Fitr
June	1	Madaraka Day
October	10	Moi Day
-	20	Kenyatta Day
December	12	Independence Day
-	25	Christmas Day
-	26	Boxing Day

[1] Confirmed by special gazette.
Holidays falling on a Sunday will be observed the following workday.
General elections are public holidays.
Unless otherwise specified, the following holidays are not general holidays:
Diwali - Hindu only
Idd-ul-Azha - Muslim only

Lamu
Working hours:
Monday - Sunday: From 08:00-12:00 and from 14:00-17:00.

Mombasa
Working hours:
Monday - Sunday: First shift 07:00-15:00, lunch break 12:00 to 12:30.
Second shift 15:00 to 23:00, dinner break 20:30-21:00 and third shift 23:00-07:00.

Korea, D.P.R. of

General holidays

January	1	New Year's Day
-	12	Korean New Year
February	16	Birth Day of Kim Jong Il
	26	Cheongwoldaeboreum
March	8	International Women's Day
April	5	Chungmyung Day
-	15	Birth Day of Kim Il Sung
-	25	Military Foundation Day
May	1	Labour Day
June	6	Children's Union Foundation Day
July	27	Day of Victory
August	15	National Liberation Day
-	25	Day of Songun
September	9	National Day
-	21	Han'gawi
October	10	Party Foundation Day
November	16	Mothers' Day
December	27	Constitution Day

Korea, Republic of

General holidays

January	1(B)	New Year's Day
February	11-13(B)	Lunar New Year
March	1(AB)	March 1st Movement
May	5(B)	Children's Day
-	19(B)	Buddha's Birthday
June	6(B)	Memorial Day
July	17(A)	Constitution Day
August	15(AB)	Liberation Day
September	20-22(B)	Chuseok Days
October	3(AB)	National Foundation Day
-	9(AB)	Hangul Day
December	25(B)	Christmas Day

Korea operates two holiday schedules:
National holidays (A)
Government holidays (B)

Additionally on schedule B:
Sundays are considered holidays
Election days are considered holidays
If any day of Lunar New Year or Chuseok coincide with a Sunday or another holiday, the following non-statutory holiday will be observed as a statutory holiday
If Children's Day falls coincide with a Saturday, Sunday or another holiday, the following non-statutory holiday will be observed as a statutory holiday

Kuwait

General holidays

January	1	New Year's Day
February	25	National Day
-	26	Liberation Day
March	11[1]	Isra Wal Miraj
May	13-15[1]	Eid Al Fitr
July	19[1]	Arafat day
-	20-22[1]	Eid Al Adha
August	10[1]	Hijri New Year
October	19[1]	Birthday of Prophet Muhammed

[1] Exact date(s) subject to sighting of the moon.

Shuaiba
Working hours:
24 hours round the clock, including weekends and holidays.

Shuwaikh
Working hours:
Sunday - Thursday: 06:30-13:30 and 14:30-21:30.
Saturday: 06:30-13:00 and 13:30-19:30.
Friday weekend: 06:30-16:30 and 20:00-02:00, both shifts on an overtime basis.
Working hours during Ramadan:
06:30 - 16:00 at normal rate
20:00 - 02:00 at overtime rate.

Latvia

General holidays

January	1	New Year's Day
April	2	Good Friday
-	4	Easter Day
-	5	Easter Monday
May	1	Labour Day
-	4	Independence Day
-	9	Mother's Day
-	23	Whit Sunday
June	23	Midsummer's Eve
-	24	Midsummer's Day
July	12[1]	The closing day of the General Latvian Song and Dance Festival
November	18	Proclamation Day
December	24	Christmas Eve
-	25	Christmas Day
-	26	Boxing Day
-	31	New Year's Eve

[1] TBC

Riga
Working hours:
24 hours per day, 7 days a week.

Ventspils
Working hours:
24 hours per day, 7 days a week.

Lebanon

General holidays

January	1	New Year's Day
-	6	Armenian Orthodox Christmas Day
February	9	Saint Maroun's Day
-	14	Rafik Hariri Memorial Day
-	25	Feast of the Annunciation
April	2	Good Friday (Western)
-	30	Good Friday (Eastern)
May	1	Labour Day
-	2	Martyrs' Day
-	9	Liberation Day
-	13-14[1]	Eid Al-Fitr
July	20-21[1]	Eid Al-Adha
August	9[1]	Islamic New Year
-	15	Assumption Day
-	18[1]	Ashoura
October	18[1]	Prophet's Birthday
November	22	Independence Day
December	25	Christmas Day

[1] Exact date(s) subject to sighting of the moon.

Beirut
Working hours:
Monday - Sunday: 00:00-00:00. Saturday, Sunday and holidays: overtime by request.
Working hours during Ramadan:
Work stops one hour before sunset and can be resumed two hours after sunset.

Jiyeh
Working hours:
Monday - Saturday: 08:00-12:00 and 13:00-16:00.
Sunday and holidays: overtime by request.

Port of Tripoli
Working hours:
Monday - Sunday: 07:00-15:00. After 15:00 overtime possible on request.

Selaata Free Zone
Working hours:
Customs
Monday - Thursday and Saturday: 08:00-14:00.
Friday: 08:00-11:00.
Sunday: Overtime by request.

Liberia

General holidays

January	1	New Year's Day
February	11	Armed Forces Day
March	10	Decoration Day
-	15	President J. J. Roberts' Birthday
April	9	Fast and Prayer Day
May	14	National Unification Day
July	26	Independence Day
August	24	Flag Day
November	4	Thanksgiving
-	29	President William V. S. Tubman's Birthday
December	25	Christmas

Libya

General holidays

February	17	Revolution Day
May	1	Labour Day
-	13-15[1]	Eid El Fitr
July	19[1]	Arafat Day
-	20-22[1]	Eid Al Adha
August	9[1]	Hijri New Year
September	16	Martyrs' Day
October	19[1]	Birthday of Prophet Mohamed
-	23	Liberation Day
December	24	Independence Day

[1] Exact date(s) subject to sighting of the moon.

Misurata
Working hours:
Monday - Sunday: 00:00-00:00.

Ras Lanuf
Working hours:
Monday - Sunday: 00:00-00:00.

Tobruk
Working hours:
Summer time: Monday - Sunday: 08:00-13:00 and 14:00 -19:30. Break 13:00-14:00.
Winter time: Monday - Sunday: 08:00-13:00 and 14:00-18:00. Break: 13:00-14:00

Lithuania

General holidays

January	1	New Year's Day
February	16	Independence Day
March	11	Independence Restoration Day
April	4	Easter Sunday
-	5	Easter Monday
May	1	Labour Day
-	2	Mother's Day
June	6	Father's Day
-	24	St. John's Day
July	6	State Day
August	15	Assumption B.V. Mary
November	1	All Saints' Day
-	2	All Souls' day
December	24	Christmas Eve
-	25	Christmas Day
-	26	Second Christmas Day

Klaipeda
Working hours:
Monday - Sunday: 08:00-20:00 and 20:00-08:00.
Holidays: Overtime by request.

Madagascar

General holidays

March	8	Womens Day
-	29	Martyrs Day
April	4	Easter Sunday
-	5	Easter Monday
May	1	Labour Day
-	13	Eid al-Fitr
-	13	Ascension Day
-	23	Whit Sunday
-	24	Whit Monday
June	26	Independence Day
July	20	Eid Al Adha
August	15	Assumption Day
November	1	All Saints' Day
December	25	Christmas Day

Manakara
Working hours:
Monday - Sunday and Holidays: 07:00-17:00.
Easter Sunday, Ascension Day, Whit Sunday and Womens Day: 00:00-00:00.
Night time work not possible.

Port Saint Louis
Working hours:
Monday- Sunday: 00:00-00:00.

Toamasina
Working hours:
Monday - Friday: First shift 06:00-14:00 and second shift 14:00-22:00.
Third shift 22:00-06:00 at overtime by request.
Breaks 13:00-14:00, 21:00-22:00, 05:00-06:00.
Saturday and Sunday: All shifts at overtime by request.
Holidays: No work on New Year's Day, Labour Day, Independence Day, Christmas Day.
All other holidays can be worked at overtime rates.

Malaysia

General holidays

February	12	Chinese New Year
-	13[1]	Chinese New Year (Second day)
May	1	Labour Day
-	13-14[2]	Hari Raya Pausa
-	26	Wesak Day
June	7	Birthday of Yang di Pertuan Agong
July	20	Hari Raya Haji
-	21[3]	Hari Raya Haji (Second day)
August	10[2]	Awal Muharram
-	31	National Day
September	16	Malaysia Day
October	19[4]	Birthday of the Prophet Muhammad
November	4[5]	Deepavali
December	25	Christmas Day

[1] Doesn't apply in Kelantan and Terengganu.
[2] Exact date(s) subject to sighting of the moon.
[3] Only applies in Kelantan and Terengganu. Exact date(s) subject to sighting of the moon.
[4] Fixed by decree.
[5] Doesn't apply in Sarawak. Exact date(s) subject to sighting of the moon.

Local holidays

Johor

January	28	Thaipusam Day
March	23	Birthday of Sultan Johor
April	13[1]	Awal Ramadan
September	13	Hol Almarhum Sultan Johor Day

[1] Exact date(s) subject to sighting of the moon.

Johor

Working hours:
Monday - Sunday: First shift 07:00-15:00, second shift 15:00-23:00 and third shift 23:00-07:00. Breaks 11:00-12:00, 19:00-20:00 and 03:00-04:00.

Kedah

March	11	Israk and Mikraj
April	13[1]	Awal Ramadan
June	20	Birthday of Sultan Kedah
July	21[1]	Second day of Hari Raya Haji (Quban)

[1] Exact date(s) subject to sighting of the moon.

Kelantan

February	13	Chinese New Year (Second day)
April	29	Nuzul Al-Quran
November	11-12	Birthday of Sultan Kelantan

Kuala Lumpur Federal Territory

January	1	New Year's Day
February	1	Federal Territory Day
-	8	Thaipusam Day
May	10	Nuzul Al-Quran

Labuan Federal Territory

January	1	New Year's Day
February	1	Federal Territory Day
April	29	Nuzul Al-Quran
May	30-31	Harvest Festival

Labuan
Working hours:
Liberty Wharf- Governmental Jetty and Private Jetty:
Monday - Thursday: 08:00-17:00 and 18:00-22:00. Break 12:00-13:00. Overtime by request 22:00-00:00.
Friday: 08:00-12:00, 13:30-17:00 and 18:00-22:00. Overtime by request 22:00-00:00.
Saturday: 08:00-12:00. Overtime by request 12:00-17:00.
Amsteel Mills Jetty, Petronas Methanol Jetty, Asian Supply Base Jetty, Sabah Flour & Feed Mills Jetty:
Monday - Sunday: 00:00-00:00.

Malacca

January	1	New Year's Day
April	13[1]	Awal Ramadan
-	15	Malacca Historical Day
October	8	Birthday of the President of Melaka

[1] Exact date(s) subject to sighting of the moon

Malacca
Working hours:
Monday - Sunday: 00:00-00:00.
Petronas Terminal
Monday - Sunday: 00:00-00:00.
TG Bruas Jetty
Monday - Sunday: First shift 08:00-16:00, second shift 16:00-00:00 and third shift 00:00-08:00.

Negeri Sembilan

January	1	New Year's Day
-	14	Anniversary of the Majesty
-	28	Thaipusam Day
March	11	Israk and Mikraj

Pahang

January	1	New Year's Day
April	29	Nuzul Al-Quran
May	22	Hari Hol
July	30	Anniversary of the Sultan of Pahang

Kuantan
Working hours:
Monday - Sunday: First shift 07:30-15:30, second shift 15:30-23:30 and third shift 23:30-07:30.
Breaks 11:30-12:30, 19:30-20:30 and 03:30-04:30.

Perak

January	1	New Year's Day
-	28	Thaipusam Day
April	29	Nuzul Al-Quran
November	5	Birthday of Sultan of Perak

Port of Lumut
Working hours:
Monday - Sunday: First shift 08:00-16:00, second shift 16:00-00:00 and third shift 00:00-08:00.
Meal breaks 11:00-12:00, 19:00-20:00 and 03:00-04:00.
Friday: Break 12:00-15:00.

Perlis

March	11	Israk and Mikraj
April	29	Nuzul Al-Quran
July	17	Anniversary of the King of Perlis
-	21[1]	Hari Raya Haji (Second day)

[1] Exact date(s) subject to sighting of the moon

Pulau Pinang

January	1	New Year's Day
-	28	Thaipusam Day
April	29	Nuzul Al-Quran
July	7	World Heritage Day
-	10	Birthday of the President

Penang
Working hours:
Monday - Friday: First shift 07:30-15:30, second shift 15:30-23:30 and third shift 23:30-07:30.
Saturday and Sunday: Overtime by request at 100% extra.
Holidays: Overtime by request.

Putrajaya Federal Territory

January	1	New Year's Day
-	28	Thaipusam
February	1	Federal Territory Day
April	29	Nuzul Al-Quran

Sabah

January	1	New Year's Day
April	2	Good Friday
May	30	Harvest Festival
October	2	Birthday of the President
December	24	Christmas Eve

Kota Kinabalu
Working hours:
Monday - Sunday: First shift 07:30-11:30, second shift 13:00-17:00 and third shift 18:00-22:00 at normal rates. Fourth shift 22:00-07:30 workable at overtime rates.
Breaks 11:30-13:00 and 17:00-18:00.
Breaks workable at overtime rate.

Lahad Datu
Working hours:
Monday - Sunday: First shift 07:30-11:30, second shift 13:00-17:00 and third shift 18:00-22:00 at normal rates. Fourth shift 22:00-07:30 workable at overtime rates.
Breaks 11:30-13:00 and 17:00-18:00.
Breaks workable at overtime rate.

Sandakan
Working hours:
Monday - Sunday: First shift 07:30-11:30, second shift 13:00-17:00 and third shift 18:00-22:00 at normal rates. Fourth shift 22:00-07:30 workable at overtime rates.
Breaks 11:30-13:00 and 17:00-18:00.
Breaks workable at overtime rate.

Tawau
Working hours:
Monday - Sunday: First shift 07:30-11:30, second shift 13:00-17:00 and third shift
18:00-22:00 at normal rates. Fourth shift 22:00-07:30 workable at overtime rates.
Breaks 11:30-13:00 and 17:00-18:00.
Breaks workable at overtime rate.

Sarawak

January	1	New Year's Day
April	2	Good Friday
June	1-2	Hari Gaway Dayak
July	22	Sarawak Day
October	9	Birthday of the President

Bintulu
Working hours:
Monday - Sunday: First shift 07:00-15:00, second shift 15:00-23:00 and third shift
23:00-07:00.
Breaks 11:00-12:00, 19:00-20:00 and 03:00-04:00.

Kuching
Working hours:
Monday - Sunday: First shift 07:30-15:30, second shift 15:30-23:00 and third shift
23:30-06:00.
Breaks 10:00-10:30, 12:00-13:00, 17:00-17:30, 20:00-20:15 and 03:00-03:30.

Rajang
Working hours:
Monday - Sunday: First shift 07:30-15:30 and second shift 15:30-23:00.
Breaks 10:00-10:30, 12:00-13:00, 17:00-17:30 and 21:00-21:30.

Sibu
Working hours:
Monday - Sunday: First shift 07:30-15:30 and second shift 15:30-23:00.
Breaks 10:00-10:30, 12:00-13:00, 17:00-17:30 and 21:00-21:30.

Selangor

January	1	New Year's Day
-	28	Thaipusam Day
April	29	Nuzul Al-Quran
December	11	Birthday of Sultan of Selangor

Port Klang
Working hours:
Monday - Sunday: First shift 08:00-16:00, second shift 16:00-00:00 and third shift 00:00-08:00.
Breaks 12:00-13:00, 20:00-21:00 and 04:00-05:00.

Terengganu

February	13	Chinese New Year (Second Day)
March	4	Coronation of Sultan of Terengganu
-	11	Israk dan Mikraj
April	26	Day for Sultan of Terengganu
-	29	Nuzul Al-Quran
July	19[1]	Arafat Day

[1] Exact date(s) subject to sighting of the moon

Kemaman
Working hours:
Monday - Thursday: First shift 08:00-16:00, second shift 16:00-00:00 and third shift 00:00-08:00.
Breaks 12:00-13:00, 19:00-20:00 and 03:00-04:00.
Friday and holidays: Same shifts as above but at overtime rates.

Maldives, Republic of

General holidays

April	14	First of Ramzan
May	1	Labour Day
-	14-16[1]	Eid al-Fitr
July	20[1]	Hajj Day
-	21-23[1]	Eid al-Adha
-	26	Independence Day
August	10[1]	Islamic New Year
October	8	Qaumee Dhuvas
-	19[1]	Birth of the Prophet
November	3	Victory Day
-	11	Republic Day
-	17	The Day Maldives Embraced Islam
December	31	New Year

[1] Exact date(s) subject to sighting of the moon.

Male

Working hours:

Monday - Sunday: 23:30-07:30 Overtime. Shift times: 07:30-15:30 and 15:30-23:30. Breaks 12:00-13:00 and 19:00-20:00.

Malta

General holidays

January	1	New Year's Day
February	10	St Paul's Shipwreck
March	19	Feast of St Joseph
-	31	Freedom Day
April	2	Good Friday
May	1	Workers' Day
June	7	Sette Giugno
-	29	Feast of St Peter & St Paul
August	15	Feast of the Assumption
September	8	Victory Day
-	21	Independence Day
December	8	Immaculate Conception
-	13	Republic Day
-	25	Christmas Day

All Sundays are public holidays

Marsaxlokk

Working hours:

Malta Freeport Terminal

Monday - Friday: 00:00-08:00, 08:00-16:00, 16:00-00:00. Breaks 04:00-04:30, 12:00-12:30, 20:00-20:30.

Saturday - Sunday: Work on overtime by request

No work from 08:00 to 08:00 next day on 1 May and 15 August.

No work from 12:00 on 24 December to 08:00 on 26 December.

No work from 16:00 on 31 December to 08:00 on 2 January.

Marshall Islands

General holidays

January	1	New Year's Day
March	1	Nuclear Victims' Remembrance Day
April	2	Good Friday
May	1	Constitution Day
July	2	Fisherman's Day
September	3	Dri-Jerbal Day
-	24	Manit Day
November	17	President's Day
December	3	Gospel Day
-	25	Christmas Day

If a holiday coincides with a Saturday, the preceding Friday will be a public holiday.
If a holiday coincides with a Sunday, the following Monday will be a public holiday.

Martinique

General holidays

January	1	New Year's Day
April	5	Easter Monday
May	1	Labour Day
-	8	Victoria Day
-	13	Ascension Day
-	22	Abolition Day
-	24	Whit Monday
July	14	National Day
August	15	Assumption
November	1	All Saints' Day
-	11	Armistice Day
December	25	Christmas Day

Local holidays

Fort de France

Working hours:
Monday - Friday: First shift 07:00-14:00. Second shift 14:00-21:00. Third shift 21:00-04:00.
Saturday: First shift 07:00-14:00. 14:00-00:00 overtime by request.
Sunday: 00:00-00:00 overtime by request.

Mauritania

General holidays

January	1	New Year's Day
May	1	Labour Day
-	14[1]	Eid Al Fitr
-	25	Africa Day
July	21[1]	Eid Al-Adha
August	10[1]	Awal Muharram
October	19[1]	Mouloud

[1] Exact date(s) subject to sighting of the moon.

As from 1 October 2014, the weekend in Mauritania is from Friday 12.00 until Monday 08.00.

Nouadhibou
Working hours:
Monday - Friday: 08:00-16:00. Meal break 13:45-16:30.
Overtime: 16:00-22:00 at 25% extra. 22:00-00:00 at 50% extra.
Holidays: Overtime at 100% extra

Nouakchott
Working hours:
Monday - Thursday: First shift 08:00-16:00. Second shift 16:30-04:00 at 100% extra.
Saturday & Sunday: First shift 08:00-16:00 at 100% extra. Second shift 16:30-04:00 at 150% extra.
Mouloud, Awal Muharram, Eid AL-Adha and Eid AL Fitr: 16:30-04:00.
No work 08:00-16:00 on 1 May (Labor Day).

Mauritius

General holidays

January	1-2	New Year's Days
-	28	Thaipoosam Cavadee
February	1	Abolition of Slavery
-	12	Chinese Spring Festival
March	11	Maha Shivratree
-	12	Independence and Republic Day
April	13	Ugaadi
May	1	Labour Day
-	14[1]	Eid Ul Fitr
September	11	Ganesh Chaturthi
November	1	All Saints' Day
-	2	Arrival of Indentured Labourers
-	4	Divali
December	25	Christmas Day

[1] Exact date(s) subject to sighting of the moon.

Mathurin
Working hours:
Monday - Friday: Monday - Friday: 07:00-15:00. Overtime by request 15:00-21:00 at 100% extra. 21:00-07:00 at 200% extra.
Breaks: 11:00-12:00, 18:00-18:30.
Saturday: 07:00-11:00. 12:00-18:00 overtime by request at 50% extra. 18:30-07:00 at 100% extra.
Sunday and Holidays: 07:00-16:00 overtime by request at 100% extra. 16:00-21:00 overtime by request at 200% extra.

Port Louis

Working hours:

Multi-purpose terminals I & II

General and conventional cargo: Monday - Friday: 07:00-15:00, 15:00-23:00. Saturday: 07:00-18:00. 18:00-23:00 overtime by request.

Containers: Monday - Friday: 07:00-15:00, 15:00-23:00. Overtime by request 23:00-07:00. Saturday, Sunday and holidays: 07:00-15:00. Overtime by request 15:00-23:00 and 23:00-07:00.

Liquid bulk cargo: Monday - Sunday: 00:00-00:00.

Dry bulk cargo: Monday - Saturday: 00:00-00:00. Sunday and Holidays: 00:00-15:00.

Mauritius bulk sugar terminal: Monday - Saturday: 07:00-22:00. 22:00-0:00:00 overtime by request. Sunday and Holidays: No work

Mauritius container terminal

Monday - Sunday: First shift 07:00-15:00, second shift 15:00-23:00, third shift 23:00-07:00.

No work during Class 3 cyclone warnings.

There is no work on 1-2 January (New Year's Days), 1 May (Labour Day) and 25 December (Christmas Day).

Mexico

General holidays

January	1	New Year's Day
February	1	Constitution Day
March	15	Anniversary of Benito Juarez
May	1	Labour Day
September	16	Independence Day
November	15	Revolution Day
December	25	Christmas Day

Election days are mandatory days of rest

Cayo Arcas
Working hours:
Monday - Sunday: 00:00-00:00.
No work on New Year's Day, Constitution Day, Anniversary of Benito Juarez, Labour Day, Independence Day, Revolution Day and Christmas Day.
Easter week and All Saint's Day: 00:00-00:00.
Work stops following hurricane alerts.

Coatzacoalcos
Working hours:
Monday - Saturday: 08:00-16:00, 16:00-00:00 and 00:00-08:00.
Sunday and holidays: Overtime at 40% extra.
No work on New Year's Day, Constitution Day, Anniversary of Benito Juarez, Labour Day, Independence Day, Revolution Day and Christmas Day.

Guaymas
Working hours:
Monday - Sunday: 08:00-23:00.
No work on New Year's Day, Constitution Day, Anniversary of Benito Juarez, Labour Day, Independence Day, Revolution Day and Christmas Day.

Lazaro Cardenas
Working hours:
Monday - Saturday: 08:00-16:00, 16:00-00:00 and 00:00-08:00.
Sunday and holidays: Overtime at 40% extra.
No work on New Year's Day, Anniversary of Benito Juarez, Labour Day, Independence Day, Revolution Day and Christmas Day.

Manzanillo
Working hours:
Monday - Saturday: 08:00-16:00, 16:00-00:00 and 00:00-08:00.
Sunday and holidays: Overtime at 40% extra.
No work on New Year's Day, Constitution Day, Anniversary of Benito Juarez, Labour Day, Independence Day, Revolution Day and Christmas Day.

San Carlos
Working hours:
Monday - Friday: 08:00-15:30. Saturdays 08:00-13:00.
No work on New Year's Day, Constitution Day, Anniversary of Benito Juarez, Labour Day, Independence Day, Revolution Day and Christmas Day.

Santa Rosalia
Working hours:
Monday - Friday: 08:00-15:30. Saturdays 08:00-13:00.
No work on New Year's Day, Constitution Day, Anniversary of Benito Juarez, Labour Day, Independence Day, Revolution Day and Christmas Day.

Tampico
Working hours:
Monday - Saturday: 08:00-16:00, 16:00-00:00 and 00:00-08:00.
Sunday and holidays: Overtime at 40% extra.
No work on New Year's Day, Constitution Day, Anniversary of Benito Juarez, Labour Day, Independence Day, Revolution Day and Christmas Day.

Vera Cruz
Working hours:
Monday - Saturday: 08:00-16:00, 16:00-00:00 and 00:00-08:00.
Sunday and holidays: Overtime at 40% extra.
No work on New Year's Day, Constitution Day, Anniversary of Benito Juarez, Labour Day, Independence Day, Revolution Day and Christmas Day.

Moldova

General holidays

January	1	New Year's Day
-	7-8	Orthodox Christmas
March	8	Women's Day
May	1	Labour Day
-	2	Orthodox Easter Day
-	3	Orthodox Easter Monday
-	9	Victory Day
-	10	Blajinor Easter
June	1[1]	Children's Day
August	27	Independence Day
-	31	National Language Holiday
December	25	Christmas

[1] Subject to public announcement

Monaco

General holidays

January	1	New Year's Day
-	27	Saint Devote's Day
April	5	Easter Monday
May	1	Labour Day
-	13	Ascension Day
-	24	Whit Monday
June	3	Corpus Christi
August	15	Assumption Day
November	1	All Saints' Day
-	19	H.S.H. the Sovereign Prince's Day
December	8	Immaculate Conception Day
-	25	Christmas Day

If any of the following holidays falls on a Sunday, the following Monday will be observed as a legal holiday:
The Sovereign Prince's Day
New Year's Day
Labour Day
Assumption Day
All Saints' Day
Christmas Day.

Montenegro

General holidays

January	1-2	New Year's Days
May	1	Labour Days
-	21	Independence Day
July	13-14	Sovereignty Day of Montenegro Holiday

If the first day of a holiday falls on a Saturday, the following Monday is a national holiday.
If the first day of a holiday falls on a Sunday, the following Monday and Tuesday are national holidays.
Religious holidays are not general holidays, but applies only to observers of the applicable religion.

Bar

Working hours:

Monday - Friday: 07:00-21:00.

Saturday: 07:00-14:00.

Sunday: 00:00-00:00 overtime on request at 100% extra.

Orthodox Christmas, Orthodox Good Friday and Orthodox Easter Day: overtime on request at 150% extra.

New Year's Days, Labour Days, Independence Day and Sovereignty Day of Montenegro Holiday: 00:00-05:00 overtime on request at 150% extra.

Kotor

Working hours:

Monday - Friday: 08:00-18:00. Overtime 06:00-08:00 and 18:00-23:00 at 50% extra. Night shift 23:00-06:00 at 75% extra.

Saturday: Overtime. First shift 06:00-14:00 at 50% extra. Second shift 14:00-22:00 at 75% extra. Third shift 22:00-06:00 at 100% extra.

Sunday: 00:00-00:00 overtime on request at 100% extra.

Holidays: 00:00-00:00 overtime on request at 150% extra.

Montserrat

General holidays

January	1	New Year's Day
March	17	Saint Patrick's Day
April	2	Good Friday
-	5	Easter Monday
May	3	Labour Day
-	24	Whit Monday
June	14	Queen's Birthday
August	2	Emancipation Day
December	25	Christmas Day
-	26	Boxing Day
-	31	Festival Day

If a public holiday coincides with a Saturday, Sunday or another public holiday, the following day not being a Sautday, Sunday or public holiday will be a public holiday.

Morocco

General holidays

January	1	New Year's Day
-	11	Proclamation of Independence
May	1	Labour Day
-	13-14[1]	Eid al-Fitr
July	20-21[1]	Eid al-Adha
-	30	Enthronement
August	10[1]	Muharram
-	14	Oued Eddahab / Liberation Day
-	20	Revolution Day
-	21	Youth Day
October	19-20[1]	Eid Al Mawled
November	6	Green March Day
-	18	Independence Day

[1] Exact date(s) subject to sighting of the moon.

Mozambique

General holidays

January	1	New Year's Day
February	3	Heroes' Day
April	7	Women's Day
May	1	Worker's Day
June	25	Independence Day
September	7	Victory Day
-	25	Revolution Day
October	5	Day of Peace and Reconciliation
December	25	Family Day

Local holidays

Beira
Working hours:
Monday - Friday: First shift 07:00-19:00, second shift 19:00-07:00.
Break: 12:30-13:00.
Saturday - Sunday and holidays: Overtime by request at 15% extra.
No work from 15:00 on 24 December until 07:00 on 26 December and from 15:00 on 31 December until 07:00 on 2 January.

Maputo
Working hours:
Monday - Saturday 00:00-00:00.
Meal breaks 13:00-13:30 and 23:00-23:30.
Shift work for bulk cargo: 07:00-19:00 and 19:00-07:00.
Shift work for general cargo: 07:00-15:00, 15:00-23:00, 23:00-07:00.
Sunday and holidays: Work available with on Overtime By Request.
Holidays: No work available from 15:00 on 24 December to 07:00 on 26 December (Family Day), and from 15:00 on 31 December to 07:00 on 2 January.

Pemba
Working hours:
Monday - Sunday: 7:00-15:00, 15:00-23:00 and 23:00-07:00.

Quelimane

Working hours:

Monday - Friday: Shift work: First shift 07:30-15:00, second shift 15:30-23:00 and third shift 23:00-07:00. Meal break 12:00-13:30. Half-hour meal break at mid shift.

Saturday, Sunday and holidays: Work available at 10% extra. First shift 07:30-15:00, second shift 15:30-23:00, third shift 23:30-07:00.

Myanmar, Republic of the Union of

General holidays

January	1	New Year's Day
-	4	Independence Day
-	13	Kayin New Year
February	12	Union Day
March	26	Armed Forces Day
-	26	Full Moon Day of Tabaung
April	13	Burmese New Year
-	30	Labour Day
May	25	Full Moon Day of Kasong
July	19	Martyr's Day
-	23	Full Moon Day of Waso
October	19	Thadingyut Festival
November	17	Full Moon Day of Tazaungdaing
-	28	National Day
December	24	Christmas Days
	31	New Years Eve

Yangon
Working hours:
Monday - Friday: Day shifts 08:00-16:00 at normal rates and 16:00-20:00 at overtime rates. Meal break 11:20-12:00. Night shifts 20:00-04:00 at normal rates and 04:00-08:00 at overtime rates. Meal break 23:20-00:00.
Saturday and Sunday: Workable as above.
Holidays: Work available at double cost.

Namibia

General holidays

January	1	New Year's Day
March	21	Independence Day
April	2	Good Friday
-	5	Easter Monday
May	1	Workers' Day
-	4	Cassinga Day
-	13	Ascension Day
-	25	Africa Day
August	26	Heroes' Day
December	10	International Human Rights Day
-	25	Christmas Day
-	26	Day of Goodwill

If a holiday falls on a Sunday, the following Monday will also be a holiday.

Unless otherwise declared in the national gazette, the following days are not public holidays:

Constitution Day

Day of the African Child

Day of the Namibian Child

United Nation Day

Luderitz
Working hours:
Monday - Friday: 07:00-12:00 and 13:00-17:00.
Sunday and holidays: 08:00-12:00 and 13:00-17:00.

Walvis Bay
Working hours:
Monday - Friday: 07:00-12:00 and 13:00-17:00. Overtime by request 17:00-07:00.
Sunday and holidays: 08:00-12:00 and 13:00-17:00.
Sunday: Overtime by request 17:00-08:00 on request.

Nauru

General holidays

January	1	New Year's Day
-	31	Independence Day
February	1	February 1st
April	2	Good Friday
-	5	Easter Monday
-	6	Easter Tuesday
May	17	Constitution Day
October	26	Angam Day
December	25	Christmas Day
-	26	Boxing Day

If a holiday falls on a weekend, the following Monday will be observed as a holiday, with the following exemptions:

Independence Day

Christmas Day

If any of the above mentioned exemptions falls on a weekend, the following Monday and Tuesday will be observed as holidays.

Netherlands

General holidays

January	1	New Year's Day
April	2	Good Friday
-	5	Easter Monday
-	27	King's Birthday
May	5	Liberation Day
-	13	Ascension Day
-	24	Whit Monday
December	25	Christmas Day
-	26	Boxing Day

Local holidays

Amsterdam
Normal working hours
Monday - Sunday: First shift 07:30-16:00,16:30-00:45. Overtime by request 22:45-07:00.
Breaks: 11:45-12:30,20:45-21:15 and 03:00-03:30.
ACT
Monday - Sunday: 00:00-00:00.
IGMA B.V.
Monday - Friday: 07:30-16:00,16:00-00:00 and 00:00-07:30.
Breaks: 11:45-12:30,20:00-20:30 and 05:00-05:30.
Saturday: 07:30-16:00. Break 11:45-12:30. Overtime by request 00:00-07:30,
16:00-00:00.
Sunday: Overtime by request 00:00-07:30, 16:00-00:00 and 07:30-16:00.

Amsterdam continued on the next page

OBA - Bulk Terminal
Monday - Friday: 07:30-15:15,15:15-23:15 and 23:15-07:15.
Breaks: 03:30-04:00,11:30-12:00 and 19:30-20:00.
Saturday: 07:15-15:15. Break 03:30-04:00. Overtime by request 15:30-00:00.
Sunday: Overtime by request 00:00-00:00.
Rietlanden Stevedores B.V.
Monday - Friday: 07:00-15:30,15:30-23:30 and 23:30-07:00.
Breaks: 03:30-04:00,11:30-12:15 and 19:30-20:00.
Saturday: 07:00-15:30. Break 11:30-12:15. Overtime by request 15:30-00:00.
Sunday: Overtime by request 00:00-00:00
United Stevedores Amsterdam (Ter Haak Groep)
Monday - Sunday: 00:00-00:00.
Oiltanking Amsterdam B.V.
Monday - Sunday: 00:00-00:00.

Delfzijl
Working hours:
Monday - Friday: First shift 06:00-14:00, second shift 14:00-22:00 and third shift 22:00-06:00. Monday overtime by request 00:00-06:00.
Saturday: First shift 06:00-14:00. Overtime by request 18:00-00:00.
Sunday overtime by request 00:00-00:00.
Shifts extendable for one and a half hour.

Dordrecht

Working hours:

Mallegat Zuid

VSM/TV: Monday - Sunday: 07:30-16:15.

Standic: Monday - Friday: 07:45-15:45. Overtime by request 15:45-07:45.

Saturday -Sunday: 00:00-00:00 overtime by request.

Centrale Geul

Trans Terminal Dordrecht (TTD): Monday - Friday: 07:30-17:00. Overtime by request 06:00-07:30, 17:00-22:00. Saturday: 06:00-14:00 overtime by request at 50% extra.

Eurogrit: Monday - Friday: 06:30-17:00. Overtime by request 06:00-22:00.

Valvoline: Monday - Friday: First shift 06:00-14:00 and second shift 14:00-22:00. Overtime by request 22:00-00:00. Saturday: 06:00-12:00.

Julianahaven

Standic: Monday - Friday: 07:45-15:45. 15:45-07:45 overtime by request.

Saturday - Sunday: Overtime by request 00:00-00:00.

Silo Dordrecht: Monday - Friday: 07:30-16:30.

Trans National Blenders (TNB): 06:00-21:00. Overtime by request 21:00-06:00.

Saturday - Sunday: Overtime by request 00:00-00:00.

Trans Terminal Dordrecht (TTD): Monday - Friday: 07:30-17:00. Overtime by request 06:00-07:30 and 17:00-22:00. Saturday: 06:00-14:00 overtime by request at 50% extra.

Wilheminahaven

B.V. Zeehavenbedrijf Dordrecht (ZHD): Monday - Friday: 00:00-00:00.

Saturday - Sunday: Overtime by request 00:00-00:00.

Mallegat Noord

B.V. Zeehavenbedrijf Dordrecht (ZHD): Monday - Friday: 00:00-00:00.

Saturday - Sunday: Overtime by request 00:00-00:00.

Eemshaven

Working hours:

Monday - Friday: First shift 06:00-14:00, Second shift 14:00-22:00, third shift 22:00-06:00.

Monday overtime by request 00:00-06:00.

Saturday: First shift 06:00-14:00. Overtime by request 18:00-00:00.

Sunday and Holidays: Overtime by request 00:00-00:00.

Shifts extendable for one and a half hour.

Flushing
Working hours:
Verbrugge Terminals
Monday - Friday: First shift 07:30-15:30 second shift 15:30-23:30. Breaks 9:30-9:45, 12:00-12:30 and 19:30-20:00. 23:30-07:30 overtime.
Saturday, Sunday and holidays: Overtime by request 07:30-15-30, 15:30-23:30 and 23:30-07:30. Breaks 09:30-09:45, 12:00-12:30 and 19:30-20:00.
Vopak Terminals
Monday - Sunday: 00:00-00:00.
Ovet B.V. Terminal
Monday - Friday shifts: 06:00-09:30, 10:00-14:00, 14:00-17:30, 18:30-22:00 and 22:00-01:30. Monday overtime 02:00-06:00.
Saturday - Sunday: Overtime by request on same above shift time.
Holidays: 18:00-06:00 on overtime by request.

Harlingen
Working hours:
Harlingen Seaport operating hours:
Monday - Sunday and holidays: 00:00-00:00.
Kuhlman Repko Shipping:
Monday - Sunday and holidays: 00:00-00:00.
Nesta Shipping:
Monday - Sunday and holidays: 00:00-00:00.

Ijmuiden
Working hours:
Tata steel works
Monday - Sunday: 00:00-00:00.
Velserkom
Monday - Friday: First shift 06:00-14:00, second shift 14:00-22:00. Breaks 10:00-10:30 and 18:00-18:30. Overtime 22:00-06:00. Monday overtime by request 00:00-06:00.
Saturday: 06:00-14:00. Overtime by request from 14.00-00:00.
Sunday: Overtime by request 00:00-00:00.

Moerdijk

Working hours:

Roode Vaart Dock

Overslagsbedrijf Moerdijk: Monday - Saturday: 07:00-17:00. Overtime by request 17:00-00:00, 00:00-07:00.

Sunday: Overtime by request 00:00-00:00.

Tref: Monday - Friday: 07:30-16:15. Overtime by request 16:15-00:00, 00:00-07:30.

Saturday - Sunday: Overtime by request 00:00-00:00.

Bolsius: Monday - Friday: 07:30-16:00. Overtime by request 16:00-00:00, 00:07:30.

Saturday - Sunday: Overtime by request 00:00-00:00.

Noordelijke Insteekhaven

Overslagsbedrijf Moerdijk: Monday - Saturday: 07:00-17:00. Overtime by request 17:00-00:00, 00:00-07:00.

Sunday: Overtime by request 00:00-00:00.

Shell: Monday - Sunday: 00:00-00:00.

Afvalstoffen Terminal Moerdijk: Monday - Sunday: 00:00-00:00.

Centrale Insteekhaven

Combined Cargo Terminals B.V.: Monday - Friday: 07:00-15:30. Overtime by request 15:30-00:00, 00:00-07:00.

Saturday - Sunday: Overtime by request 00:00-00:00.

Omya: 00:00-00:00.

Delta Marine Terminal: Monday - Friday: 07:30-16:00. Overtime by request 16:00-00:00, 00:00-07:30.

Saturday - Sunday: Overtime by request 00:00-00:00.

B.V. Zeehavenbedrijf Dordrecht: Monday - Friday: 07:30-23:30. Overtime by request 23:30-07:30. Monday overtime by request 00:00-07:30.

Saturday - Sunday: Overtime by request 00:00-00:00.

Cronimet: Monday - Thursday: 07:30-15:00. Overtime by request 15:00-00:00, 00:00-07:30.

Friday: 07:30-13:00. Overtime by request 13:00-00:00, 00:00-07:30.

Saturday - Sunday: Overtime by request 00:00-00:00.

B S Natuursteen B.V.: Monday - Friday: 07:00-17:30. Overtime by request 17:30-00:00, 00:00-07:00.

Saturday - Sunday: No work.

van der Vlist: Monday - Friday: 07:30-16:15. Overtime by request 16:15-00:00, 00:00-07:30.

Saturday: Overtime by request 00:00-00:00. Sunday no work.

Van Dalen: Monday - Friday: 07:30-17:00. Overtime by request 17:00-00:00, 00:00-07:30.

Saturday - Sunday: Overtime by request 00:00-00:00.

Delta Marine Terminal: Monday - Friday: 07:30-16:00. Overtime by request 16:00-00:00, 00:00-07:30.

Saturday - Sunday: Overtime by request 00:00-00:00.

Overslagsbedrijf Moerdijk: Monday - Saturday: 07:00-17:00. Overtime by request 17:00-00:00, 00:00-07:00.
Sunday: Overtime by request 00:00-00:00.
Den Hartogh: Monday - Friday: 08:00-17:00. Overtime by request 17:00-00:00, 00:00-08:00.
Saturday - Sunday: Overtime by request 00:00-00:00.

Rotterdam
Working hours:
Bulk Cargoes, other than agri-bulk
EMO - Europees Massagoed-Overslagbedrijf: Monday - Sunday: 00:00-00:00.
Erts-en Kolen Overslagbedrijf: Monday - Sunday: 00:00-00:00.
EBS - European Bulk Services (mineral bulk)
Monday - Sunday: Three shifts: 07:15-15:30, 15:15-23:30 and 23:15-07:30. Breaks 11:15-11:45, 19:15-19:45 and 03:15-03:45. Holidays: 15:30-00:00 overtime by request.
Containers
ECT - Europe Container Terminals:
Monday - Sunday: 07:15-15:30, 15:15-23:30 and 23:15-07:30. Breaks 11:30-12:00, 19:15-19:45 and 03:15-03:45.
Work stops at 15:30 on 24 December (Christmas Eve) and 31 December (New Year's Eve - work to resume at 15:15 on 1 January). There is no work on 25 December (Christmas Day - work to resume at 07:15 on 26 December).
Oil Terminals
Monday - Sunday: 00:00-00:00.

Scheveningen
Working hours:
Monday - Sunday: 00:00-00:00.

Schiedam
Working hours:
Monday - Sunday: 00:00-00:00.

Terneuzen

Working hours:

Verbrugge Terminals B.V.

Monday - Friday: First shift 07:45-16:00 and Second shift 16:00-00:00. Meals 09:30-09:45, 12:00-12:30 and 20:00-20:30. Overtime by request 00:00-07:45. Saturday, Overtime by request as per above shift time.

Holiday: Overtime by request 00:00-00:00.

Ovet B.V. (Terneuzen Terminal) Bulk Cargoes

Monday - Friday: First shift 06:00-14:00, second shift 14:00-22:00 and third shift 22:00-06:00. Breaks 09:30-10:00, 17:30-18:00 and 01:30-02:00.

Saturday - Sunday: Overtime by request as per above shift time.

Holidays: 18:00-06:00.

Vlaardingen

Working hours:

Municipal harbour

Koningin Wilhelminahaven: Monday - Sunday: 00:00-00:00.

Hooymeijer Port Terminal: Monday - Saturday 07:00-16:30.

Zevenmanshaven (private)

Monday - Sunday: 00:00-00:00.

Vopak Tank Terminal B.V.

Monday - Sunday: 00:00-00:00.

Vulcaanhaven (private)

Monday - Sunday: 00:00-00:00.

Zaandam

Working hours:

Monday - Friday: 06:00-14:00 and 14:00-22:00.

Saturday: 06:00-10:30 Overtime by request.

New Caledonia

General holidays

January	1	New Year's Day
April	5	Easter Monday
May	1	Labour Day
-	8	VE Day
-	13	Ascension Day
-	24	Whit Monday
July	14	French National Holiday
August	15	Assumption Day
September	24	New Caledonia Day
November	1	All Saints' Day
-	11	Armistice Day
December	25	Christmas Day

Noumea

Working hours:

Monday - Friday: 07:00-14:30 and 14:30-22:00. Overtime by request at 200% extra 22:00-00:00 and at 300% extra 00:00-06:00.

Saturday: 07:00-14:30 and 14:30-22:00. Overtime by request at 300% extra 22:00-00:00, 00:00-06:00.

Sunday and holidays: 00:00-00:00. Overtime by request at 300% extra.

New Zealand

General holidays

January	1	New Year's Holidays
-	2	Day after New Year's Day
February	6	Waitangi Day
April	2	Good Friday
-	5	Easter Monday
-	25	Anzac Day
June	7	Queen's Birthday
October	25	Labour Day
December	25	Christmas Day
-	26	Boxing Day

Local holidays

Auckland

February	1	Auckland Anniversary Day

Gisborne

February	1	Auckland Anniversary Day

Lyttelton

November	12	Canterbury Anniversary Day

Marsden Point

February	1	Northland Anniversary Day

Napier

October	22	Hawkes Bay Anniversary Day

Nelson

February	1	Nelson Anniversary Day

Onehunga

February	1	Auckland Anniversary Day

Otago Harbour

March	22	Otago Anniversary Day

Port Marlborough

November	1	Marlborough Anniversary Day

South Point

April	6	Southland Anniversary Day

Taranaki

March	8	Taranaki Anniversary Day

Tauranga

February	1	Auckland Anniversary Day

Working hours:
Monday - Sunday and Holidays: 00:00-00:00.
Christmas Day: 00:00-00:00 Overtime by request.

Timaru

September	27	Canterbury (South) Anniversary Day

Westport

February	1	Buller Anniversary Day

Nicaragua

General holidays

January	1	New Year's Day
April	1	Holy Thursday
-	2	Good Friday
May	1	Labour Day
July	19	The Sandinista Revolution Day
September	14	Battle of San Jacinto
-	15	Independence Day
December	8	Immaculate Conception Day
-	25	Christmas Day

Local holidays

Corinto

May	3	Day of the Holi Cross

Puerto Cabezas

Working hours:

Monday - Friday: 07:00-12:00, 13:00-18:00 and 19:00-22:00. Overtime by request 22:00-00:00. Breaks 12:00-13:00 and 18:00-19:00.

Saturday: 07:00-12:00 and 13:00-18:00. Overtime by request 18:00-00:00.

Holidays: 00:00-00:00 Overtime by request at 100% extra.

Nigeria

General holidays

January	1	New Year's Day
April	2	Good Friday
-	5	Easter Monday
May	1	Worker's Day
-	13[1]	Eid el Fitr
June	12	Democracy Day
July	20[1]	Id el Kabir
October	1	Independence Day
December	25	Christmas Day
-	26	Boxing Day

1 Exact date(s) subject to sighting of the moon.

Brass Oil Terminal
Working hours:
Monday - Friday: 07:30-19:30. Overtime 19:30-06:30.
Saturday, Sunday and holidays: Overtime 07:30-15:30 and 15:30-23:30.

Calabar
Working hours:
Monday - Friday: 07:30-19:30. Overtime 19:30-06:30.
Saturday, Sunday and holidays: Overtime 07:30-15:30 and 15:30-23:30.

Lagos
Working hours:
Monday - Friday: 07:30-15:30 and 15:30-22:30. Overtime 22:30-06:30.
Saturday, Sunday and holidays: Overtime 07:30-15:30 and 15:30-22:30.

Okrika
Working hours:
Monday - Friday: 07:30-19:30. Overtime 19:30-06:30.
Saturday, Sunday and holidays: Overtime 07:30-15:30 and 15:30-23:30.

Port Harcourt
Working hours:
Monday - Friday: 07:30-19:30. Overtime 19:30-06:30.
Saturday, Sunday and holidays: Overtime 07:30-15:30 and 15:30-23:30.

Sapele
Working hours:
Monday - Friday: 07:30-15:30, 15:30-22:30 and 22:30-06:30.
Saturday, Sunday and holidays: 08:00-12:00.

Warri
Working hours:
Monday - Friday: 07:30-15:30, 15:30-22:30 and 22:30-06:30.
Saturday and Sunday: 08:00-12:00.
Holidays: 08:00-12:00 at normal and 12:00-00:00 overtime by request.

Norway

General holidays

January	1	New Year's Day
April	1	Maundy Thursday
-	2	Good Friday
-	4	Easter Sunday
-	5	Easter Monday
May	13	Ascension Day
-	23	Whit Sunday
-	24	Whit Monday
December	25	Christmas Day
-	26	Labour Day

All Sunday are public holidays.
1 May and 17 May are not public holidays, but considered equal to Sundays

Bergen
Working hours:
Monday - Friday: 07:30-15:00. Break 11:30-12:00. Overtime by request 15:00-21:00 at 50%, 21:00-00:00 at 100% extra.
Saturday: 07:30-13:00 at 50%, 13:00-00:00 100% extra. Break 11:30-12:00.
Sunday and holidays: 00:00-00:00 Overtime by request 100% extra. No work Good Friday, Easter Sunday, Constitution Day, Whit Sunday, 25 December (Christmas Day). Labour Day overtime at planned.
Work stops at 13:00 on 24 December (Christmas Eve) and 31 December (New Year's Eve).

Bodo
Working hours:
Monday - Sunday: 00:00-00:00.

Fredrikstad

Working hours:

Monday - Friday: 06:00-14:00, 14:00-22:00, 22:00-06:00.

Ordinary working hours: Monday - Friday: 07:00-15:30. Break 09:00-09:30.

Saturday and Sunday: 06:00-14:00, 14:00-22:00, 22:00-06:00 at 100% extra.

Holidays: No work available.

Work stops at 12.30 on Easter Eve, 24 December (Christmas Eve) and 31 December (New Year's Eve).

Halden

Working hours:

Monday - Friday: 06:30-14:30. Break 11:00-11:30. Overtime by request 14:30-21:00 at 50%, 21:00-00:00 at 100% extra.

Saturday: 06:30-12:00 at 50% extra. Break 09:00-09:30.

12:00-00:00 at 100% extra.

Sunday and holidays: No work.

Haugesund

Working hours:

Monday - Friday: 07:30-15:30. Overtime by request 15:30-21:00 at 50% extra. 21:00-07:30 at 100% extra.

Saturday, Sunday and holidays: Overtime by request 00:00-00:00.

No work 24 and 31 December.

Port Authority opening hours:
Monday - Friday: 06:30 - 22:00
Saturday and Sunday: 10:00 - 18:00.

Heroya

Working hours:

Monday - Friday: 06:30-14:30, 14:30-22:30, 22:30-06:30. Breaks 11:00-11:30, 19:00-19:30, 03:00-03:30.

Saturday and Sunday: 06:30-18:30, 18:30-06:30 Breaks 11:30-12:00, 23:30-00:00.

No work 14:30-22:30 on 24 December (Christmas Eve).

Karmsund
Working hours:
Monday - Sunday and Holidays: 00:00-00:00.

Krageroe
Working hours:
Monday - Friday: Ordinary working hours 07:00-15:00. Breaks at 11:30-12:00.
Saturday, Sunday and holidays: Overtime by request 00:00-00:00.
Holidays: No work on 1 January, Good Friday, Easter Sunday, 1 May, Constitution Day and 25 December (Christmas Day).

Kristiansand S
Working hours:
Monday - Friday: First shift 06:00-14:00, Second shift 14:00-22:00. Third shift 22:00-06:00 at 100% extra overtime by request. Breaks 11:30-12:00, 15:00-16:00, 21:00-22:00 and 01:00-02:00.
Saturday: Overtime by request 07:30-12:00 at 50% extra, 12:00-00:00 at 100% extra.
Sunday and holidays: Overtime by request 00:00-00:00 at 100% extra. No work holidays New Year's Day, Good Friday, Easter Sunday, Labour Day, Constitution Day, Whit Sunday and Christmas Day.

Larvik
Working hours:
Monday - Friday: 07:00-15:00, 15:00-23:00 and 23:00-07:00.
Breaks: 10:30-11:00.
Saturday - Sunday and Holidays: 00:00-00:00 Overtime by request.

Menstad
Norsk Hydro (private)
Working hours:
Monday - Friday: 07:15-15:15. Overtime by request 15:15-21:00 at 50% extra.
Breaks: 11:00-11:30, 15:15-15:45, 18:00-18:30.
Saturday, Sunday and holidays: No work.

Narvik
Working hours:
Monday - Sunday and Holidays: 00:00-00:00.
24 December (Christmas Eve) until 06:00 on 25 December (Christmas Day).
No overtime charges apply for stevedoring work.

Oslo
Working hours:
Monday - Friday: 07:00-15:00. Breaks 09:00-09:30 and 12:30-13:00. Overtime 15:00-07:00.
Saturday, Sunday and holidays: 00:00-00:00 overtime by request. Constitution Day and 24 December (Christmas Eve), when there is no work.

Porsgrunn
Working hours:
Crane quay
Monday - Friday: 07:00-15:00. Breaks from 09:00-09:15 and 12:15-12:30. Overtime 15:00-21:00 at 50% extra.
Saturday, Sunday and holidays: No work.
Deepwater Quay
Bulk cargo discharge only.
Monday - Friday: Breaks from 11:00-11:30, 19:00-19:30 and 03:00-03:30.
Saturday, Sunday and holidays: 00:00-00:00 overtime by request.
Elkem Mangan
Loading
Monday - Thursday: 07:00-15:00. Friday: 07:00-14:00. Break 10:00-10:30.
Discharging
Monday - Thursday: 06:00-21:30. Friday: 06:00-20:00. Breaks 18:00-18:30.
Saturday, Sunday and holidays: No work.

Skien
Working hours:
Monday - Friday: 07:00-15:00. Overtime 15:00-21:00 at 50% extra.
Saturday: Overtime 07:00-12:00 at 50% extra.
Sunday and holidays: No work.
Work stops at 12:00 on 24 December (Christmas Eve) and 31 December (New Year's Eve).

Stavanger
Working hours:
Monday - Friday: 07:30-15:00. Overtime 15:00-21:00 and 06:00-7:30 at 50% extra and 21:00-06:00 at 100% extra.
Saturday and Sunday: Overtime at 100% extra.
Holidays: Overtime at 133% extra.

Toensberg
Working hours:
Monday - Friday: Overtime 15:00-07:000 and 00:00-007:00 at 60% extra.
Saturday: Overtime 07:00-00:00 at 60% extra.
Sunday: Overtime 00:00-00:00 at 60% extra.

Trondheim
Working hours:
Monday - Friday: 07:00-15:00. Breaks 09:00-09:30 and 11:00-11:30.
Overtime 15:00-21:00 at 50% extra and 21:00-07:00 at 100% extra.
Saturday and Sunday: Overtime 00:00-00:00 at 100% extra.
Holidays: No work. Work can be arranged on Constitution Day and Whit Monday. Work stops at 12:00 on 24 December (Christmas Eve) and 31 December (New Year's Eve).

Oman

General holidays

March	11[1]	Isra'a Wal Miraj
May	11[1]	Eid-al-Fitr (Holiday)
July	19[1]	Eid- al-Adha (Holiday)
August	10[1]	Hijri New Year
October	19[1]	Mawlid
November	18	Oman National Day

[1] Exact date(s) subject to sighting of the moon.
Friday will be substituted if it coincides with the first day of either Eid holiday.
Any or both days of the weekend will be compensated by one day, should they coincide with other holidays.

Mina al Fahal
Working hours:
Monday - Sunday: 07:00-18:00 and 18:00-07:00.

Mina Sultan Qaboos
Working hours:
Monday - Sunday: 07:00-16:00.
Overtime: 00:00-07:00 and 16:00-00:00.

Salalah
Working hours:
Saturday - Thursday: 08:00-23:00. Break 13:00-14:00.
Overtime: 23:00-08:00.
Friday and holidays: 00:00-00:00 overtime by request.

Pakistan

General holidays

February	5	Kashmir Day
March	23	Pakistan Day
May	1	Labour Day
-	15-17[1]	Eid ul-Fitr
July	21-23[1]	Eid ul-Azha
August	14	Independence Day
-	19-20[1]	Ashoora
October	20[1]	Eid Milad-un-Nabi
December	25	Christmas Day / Quaid-e-Azam Day

[1] Exact date(s) subject to sighting of the moon.

Gwadar

Working hours:

Monday - Saturday: 07:00-19:00 and 19:00-07:00. Breaks 11:30-12:30 and 23:00-23:30.
Sunday and Holiday: 07:00-19:00 and 19:00-07:00 overtime by request. Breaks 11:30-12:30 and 23:00-23:30.

Karachi

September	21	Urs

Working hours:

Sunday - Thursday: 07:30-11:30, 12:30-16:30, 19:00-23:00 and 23:30-03:30. Breaks 11:30-12:30 and 23:00-23:30.

Overtime: 16:30-18:30, 23:00-23:30, 03:30-06:30 and 11:30-12:30.

Friday: 07:30-12:30, 14:00-16:30, 19:00-23:00 and 23:30-03:30. Breaks 12:30-14:00 and 23:00-23:00.

Overtime: 16:30-18:30, 23:00-23:30 and 03:30-06:30

Saturday: 07:30-11:30, 12:30-16:00, 19:00-23:00 and 23:00-00:35. Breaks 11:30-12:30 and 23:00-23:30.

Overtime: 11:30-12:30, 16:00-18:00, 23:00-23:30 and 03:30-06:30.

Sunday: 12:30-16:30, 19:00-23:00, 23:30-03:30 overtime by request and 07:30-11:30, 11:30-12:30, 16:30-18:30, 23:00-23:30, 03:30-06:30 at 100% extra.

Breaks 11:30-12:30 and 23:00-23:30.

Holidays: 7:30-12:30, 12:30-18:30, 18:30-23:30, 23:30-06:30 and breaks 11:30-12:30, 23:00-23:30 overtime at 100% extra. Ashoora break 11:30-12:30 and 23:00-23:30.

Muhammad Bin Qasim

Working hours:

Monday - Thursday: 08:00-16:00, 16:00-00:00, 00:00-08:00. Breaks 13:00-14:00 and 14:00-19:00.

Friday: 08:00-16:00, 16:00-00:00, 00:00-08:00. Breaks 13:00-15:00 and 14:00-19:00.

Saturday: 08:00-16:00, 16:00-00:00, 00:00-08:00. Breaks 13:00-14:00 and 14:00-19:00.

Sunday: 08:00-16:00, 16:00-00:00, 00:00-08:00 overtime at 100% extra. Breaks 13:00-14:00 and 14:00-19:00.

Holiday: 08:00-16:00, 16:00-00:00, 00:00-08:00 and breaks 13:00-14:00, 18:00-19:00 overtime at 100% extra.

Panama

General holidays

January	1	New Year's Day
-	9	Day of Martyrs
February	16	Mardi Gras
April	2	Good Friday
May	1	Labour Day
November	3	Separation Day
-	5	Colon Day
-	10	Los Santos Uprising Day
-	28	Independence Day
December	8	Panama Mother's Day
-	25	Christmas Day

Balboa
Working hours:
Monday - Saturday: 00:00-00:00.
Sunday and holidays: 00:00-00:00 overtime at 25% extra.

Cristobal
Working hours:
Monday - Sunday: 00:00-00:00.
Sunday: Overtime at 25% extra.
Holiday: 00:00-23:55 overtime at 25% extra.

Papua New Guinea

General holidays

January	1	New Year's Day
April	2	Good Friday
-	3	Easter Saturday
-	4	Easter Sunday
-	5	Easter Monday
June	14	Queen's Birthday
July	23	National Remembrance Day
August	26	National Repentance Day
September	16	Independence Day
December	25	Christmas Day
-	26	Boxing Day

If a holiday falls on a Sunday, the following Monday shall be a public holiday.
If Christmas Day falls on a Sunday, the following Tuesday shall be a public holiday.

Port Moresby

Working hours:
Monday - Sunday: 08:00-22:00 and 22:00-08:00. Breaks 10:00-10:15, 12:00-13:00,
15:00-15:15, 17:00-18:00, 20:00-20:15.

Ordinary working hours
Monday - Thursday: 08:00-16:30 and overtime at 50% extra on 16:30-08:00.
Friday: 08:00-16:00 and 16:00-08:00 overtime at 50% extra.
Saturday - Sunday: 8:00-16:00 and 16:00-08:00 overtime at 100% extra.
Holiday: 00:00-00:00 overtime at 50% extra.
No work on Good Friday and Christmas Day.

Paraguay

General holidays

January	1	New Year's Day
March	1	Day of Heroes
April	1	Holy Thursday
-	2	Good Friday
May	1	International Labour Day
-	14	Independence Days
June	12	Peace of Chaco
August	15	Founding of Asuncion
September	29	Boqueron Battle Victory Day
December	8	Victory of Caacupe
-	25	Christmas Day

Asuncion
Working hours:
Monday - Friday: 07:00-16:00. Overtime 16:00-00:00.
Saturday, Sunday and holidays: 00:00-00:00 overtime by request.

Peru

General holidays

January	1	New Year's Day
April	1	Maundy Thursday
-	2	Good Friday
May	1	Labour Day
June	29	Saint Peter and Saint Paul's Day
July	28-29	National Holidays
August	30	Saint Rose Day
October	8	Battle of Angamos
November	1	All Saints' Day
December	8	Immaculate Virgin Day
-	25	Christmas Day

Callao

Working hours:

Monday - Sunday: 07:00-14:00, 14:00-21:00 and 22:00-07:00.
Sunday and holidays: Overtime by request.

Philippines

General holidays

January	1	New Year's Day
April	1	Maundy Thursday
-	2	Good Friday
-	9	Araw ng Kagitingan
May	1	Labour Day
-	13[1]	Eid'l Fitr
June	12	Independence Day
July	20[1]	Eidul Adha
August	30	National Heroes' Day
November	30	Bonifacio Day
December	25	Christmas Day
-	30	Rizal Day

[1] Exact date(s) subject to sighting of the moon.

Beside national holidays, the Philippines observes special (non-working) days.
According to the Philippine Labor Code, both schedules impose overtime payment as per below:
National holidays: 200%
Non-working days: 130%

Iloilo
Working hours:
Monday - Sunday: 07:00-18:00 and 19:00-06:00.
Breaks 06:00-07:00, 12:00-13:00, 18:00-19:00.
Holidays: There is no work on Eidul Adha, Good Fridayand on New Year's Eve from 19:00
31 December to 19:00 on 1 January.
Sunday and holidays: Overtime by request.

Manila
Working hours:
Monday - Sunday: 07:00-18:00 and 19:00-06:00.
Breaks 06:00-07:00, 12:00-13:00, 18:00-19:00.
Sunday and holidays: Overtime by request.
Holidays: There is no work on Eidul Adha, Good Friday and on New Year's Eve from 19:00
31 December to 19:00 on 1 January.

Poland

General holidays

January	1	New Year's Day
-	6	Epiphany
April	4	Easter Sunday
-	5	Easter Monday
May	1	National Day
-	3	Third May National Day
-	23	Pentecost Sunday
June	3	Corpus Christi
-	15	Assumption B.V. Mary
November	1	All Saints' Day
-	11	Independence Day
December	25	Christmas Day
-	26	St. Stephen's Day

All Sundays are holidays

Darlowo
Working hours:
Monday - Sunday: First shift 07:00-15:00, second shift 15:00-23:00 and third shift 23:00-07:00.
Saturday: Overtime planned.
Sunday and Holiday: Overtime by request.

Gdansk
Working hours:
Monday - Sunday: First shift 07:00-15:00, second shift 15:00-23:00 and third shift 23:00-07:00.
Saturday, Sunday and holidays: Overtime by request.

Gdynia
Working hours:
Monday - Sunday: First shift 07:00-15:00, second shift 15:00-23:00 and third shift 23:00-07:00.
Saturday, Sunday and holidays: Overtime by request.

Kolobrzeg
Working hours:
Monday - Sunday: First shift 06:00-14:00 and second shift 14:00-22:00.
Breaks 10:00-10:30 and 18:00-18:30.
Saturday: 80% extra applies.
Sunday: 100% extra applies.
Holidays: Overtime by request. Work usually stops at 14:00 on 11 June Corpus Christi and 24 December (Christmas Eve).

Szczecin+Swinoujscie
Working hours:
Swinoujscie:
Monday - Friday: First shift 07:00-15:00, second shift 15:00-23:00, third shift 23:00-07:00. Breaks 11:00-11:30, 19:00-19:30, 03:00-03:30.
Saturday, Sunday and holidays are days off.
Szczecin:
Monday - Friday: First shift 06:00-14:00, second shift 14:00-22:00, third shift 22:00-06:00. Breaks 10:00-10:30, 18:00-18:30, 02:00-02:30.
Saturday, Sunday and holidays are days off.

Ustka
Working hours:
On the following holidays, work available at 50% extra: New Years Day, Easter Monday, and St. Stephen's Day.
Working hours:
General cargo
Monday - Saturday: First shift 07:00-15:00, second shift 15:00-23:00 and third shift 23:00-07:00. Breaks 11:00-11:30, 19:00-19:30 and 03:00-03:30.
Sunday: No work.
Timber
Monday - Saturday: First shift 07:00-15:00 and second shift 15:00-23:00.
Breaks 11:00-11:30 and 19:00-19:30.
Sunday: No work.
Coal
Monday - Sunday: First shift 07:00-15:00, second shift 15:00-23:00 and third shift 23:00-07:00.
Breaks 10:30-11:30, 18:30-19:30 and 02:30-03:30. 50% extra: National Day.

Portugal

General holidays

January	1	New Year's Day
April	2[1]	Good Friday
-	4	Easter Sunday
-	25	Freedom Day
May	1	Labour Day
June	3	Corpus Christi
-	10	Portugal Day
August	15	Assumption Day
October	5	Republic Day
November	1	All Saints' Day
December	1	Restoration of Independence
-	8	Immaculate Conception
-	25	Christmas Day

[1] Local observation may deviate

Local holidays

Aveiro

Working hours:

Monday - Friday: First shift 08:00-17:00, second shift 17:00-00:00 and third shift 00:00-07:00. Second and third shifts are at overtime rates.
Breaks 12:00-13:00, 20:00-21:00 and 03:00-04:00.
Saturday and Holiday: Overtime at 75% extra.

There is no work on 1 January (New Year's Day), Good Friday, Easter Sunday, Republic Day, Labour Day and 25 December (Christmas Day).

Faro

Working hours:

Monday - Sunday: 08:00-17:00. Break 12:00-13:00. Overtime 17:00-00:00. Break 20:00-21:00.
Saturday, Sunday and holidays: Overtime by request.

There is no work on 1 January (New Year's Day), Good Friday, Republic Day, Easter Sunday and 25 December (Christmas Day).

Figueira da Foz
Working hours:
Monday - Sunday: 08:00-17:00. Break 12:00-13:00. Overtime 17:00-00:00.
Break 20:00-21:00.
Saturday, Sunday and holidays: Overtime by request.
There is no work on 1 January (New Year's Day), Good Friday, Republic Day,
Easter Sunday.

Funchal
Working hours:
Monday - Sunday: First shift 08:00-17:00, second shift 17:00-00:00.
Breaks 12:00-13:00 and 20:00-21:00.
Saturday, Sunday and holidays: Workable at 75% extra.
There is no work on New Year's Day, Good Friday, Easter Sunday.

Lisbon
Working hours:
Monday - Friday: First shift 08:00-17:00 and second shift 17:00-00:00. Breaks
12:00-13:00 and 20:00-21:00. Third shift 00:00-08:00 at overtime.
Saturday, Sunday and holidays: First shift 08:00-17:00 and second shift 17:00-00:00 and
third shift 00:00-08:00 at overtime. Breaks 12:00-13:00 and 20:00-21:00.
There is no work on 1 January (New Year's Day), Good Friday, Easter Sunday and
25 December (Christmas Day).

Portimao
Working hours:
Monday - Friday: First shift 08:00-17:00 and second shift 17:00-00:00. Breaks
12:00-13:00 and 20:00-21:00. Second shift is at overtime planned.
Saturday, Sunday and holidays: Overtime by request.
There is no work on Good Friday, Easter Sunday and 25 December (Christmas Day).

Setubal
Working hours:
Monday - Friday: First shift 08:00-17:00 and second shift 17:00-01:00.
Breaks 12:00-13:00 and 20:00-21:00. Third shift 01:00-08:00 at overtime planned.
Saturday, Sunday and holidays: Same hours as Monday-Friday, but all at overtime by
request.
Work stops at 17:00 on 24 December (Christmas Eve) and 31 December (New Year's Eve).
There is no work on Good Friday and Easter Sunday.

Sines

Working hours:

Monday - Friday: First shift 07:00-13:00, second shift 13:00-19:00 and third shift 19:00-01:00. Overtime 01:00-07:00.

Saturday, Sunday and holidays: First shift 07:00-13:00, second shift 13:00-19:00, third shift 19:00-01:00 and fourth shift 01:00-07:00 overtime by request.

There is no work on 1 January (New Year's Day), Good Friday, Easter Sunday and 25 December (Christmas Day).

Viana do Castelo

Working hours:

Monday - Friday: 08:00-00:00. Breaks 12:00-13:00 and 20:00-21:00.

Saturday and Sunday: Overtime by request.

Puerto Rico

General holidays

January	1	New Year's Day
-	18	Martin Luther King Day
February	15	Presidents Day
March	22	Emancipation Day
April	2	Holy Friday
May	30	Memorial Days
July	4	Independence Day
September	6	Labour Day
October	11	Columbus Day
November	11	Veterans Day
-	25	Thanksgiving Day
December	25	Christmas Day

If a holiday coincides with a Sunday, the following Monday will be a public holiday.

San Juan

Working hours:

Monday - Friday: 07:00-12:00 and 13:00-16:00. Overtime 16:00-18:00, 19:00-23:00, 00:00-06:00. Breaks 12:00-13:00, 18:00-19:00, 03:00-04:00, 06:00-07:00 and 23:00-00:00.

Saturday, Sunday and Holiday: 07:00-12:00, 13:00-16:00, 16:00-18:00, 19:00-23:00 and 00:00-06:00 overtime by request. Breaks 12:00-13:00, 18:00-19:00, 03:00-04:00, 06:00-07:00 and 23:00-00:00.

Container ships

Monday - Sunday: 07:00-00:00.

Saturday, Sunday and holidays: Overtime by request.

Qatar

General holidays

February	9	National Sports Day
May	11-16[1]	Eid al-Fitr Holiday
	13-15[2]	Eid al-Fitr Holiday
July	19-23[1]	Eid al-Adha Holiday
	20-22[2]	Eid al-Adha Holiday
December	18	National Day

[1] Public sector. Exact date(s) subject to sighting of the moon.
[2] Private sector. Exact date(s) subject to sighting of the moon.

Mesaieed
Working hours:
Saturday - Thursday: 06:00-20:00. Break 13:00-14:00. Overtime 20:00-06:00.
Friday and Holiday: 00:00-00:00 overtime by request.
During Ramadan month ordinary working hours are subject to changes.

Ras Laffan
Working hours:
Saturday - Thursday: 07:00-20:00. Break 12:00-13:00. Overtime 20:00-07:00.
Friday and Holiday: 00:00-00:00 overtime by request.
Sunday to Thursday 07.30-15.30 (excluding Public Holidays).
During Ramadan month ordinary working hours are subject to changes.

Reunion

General holidays

January	1	New Year's Day
April	5	Easter Monday
May	1	Labour Day
-	8	Victory Day
-	13	Ascension Day
May	24	Whit Monday
July	14	National Day
August	15	Assumption Day
November	1	All Saints' Day
-	11	Armistice Day
December	20	Abolition Day
-	25	Christmas Day

Port Reunion

Working hours:
Monday - Saturday: 07:00-14:00, 14:00-21:00 and 14:00-17:00, 21:00-23:00, 21:00-04:00 overtime by request.
Sunday: Work 07:00-21:00 at overtime by request.
Break 12:00-13:00. Holiday: 00:00-00:00 overtime by request.
There is no work on 1 January (New Year's Day), 1 May (Labour Day), 20 December (Slavery Abolition Day) and 25 December (Christmas Day).

Romania

General holidays

January	1-2	New Year's Days
-	24	Union Day
April	30	Good Friday
May	1	Labour Day
-	2	Orthodox Easter Day
-	3	Orthodox Easter Monday
June	1	Children's Day
-	20-21	Orthodox Pentecost
August	15	St. Mary
November	30	St. Andrew
December	1	National Day
-	25	Christmas Day
-	26	Second Christmas Day

Constantza
Working hours:
Monday - Friday: First shift 07:00-19:00 and second shift 19:00-07:00. Breaks 12:00-13:00 and 00:00-01:00.
Saturday and Sunday: 00:00-00:00 overtime by request.
Working hours depend on stevedoring company.

Russia

General holidays

January	1-6[1]	New Year Holidays
-	7	Christmas (Russian Orthodox)
February	23	Fatherland Defenders Day
March	8	International Women's Day
May	1	Day of Spring and Labour
-	9	Victory Day
June	12	Russia Day
November	4	National Unity Day

[1] 1 - 6 and 8 January.

Holiday falling on a Sunday will be observed the following Monday

The following weekend day are rescheduled:

Saturday 2 January to 5 November

Sunday 3 January to 31 December

Saturday 20 February to 22 February

Archangel
Working hours:
Monday - Sunday: 00:00-08:00, 08:00-16:00 and 16:00-00:00.

Kaliningrad
Working hours:
Commercial port terminal
Monday - Friday: 08:00-17:00. Overtime 17:00-08:00
Saturday and Sunday: 00:00-00:00 overtime by request.
Holiday: 00:00-00:05 overtime by request.
There is a no work 20:00 on 31 December until 20:00 on 1 January.
Fishing port terminal
Monday - Friday: 08:00-17:00. Overtime 17:00-08:00.
Saturday, Sunday Holiday: 00:00-00:00 overtime by request.
There is a no break 20:00 on 31 December until 00:00 on 1 January.

Kholmsk

Working hours:

Cargo handling and auxiliary operations around the clock, seven days a week including holidays.

Monday - Sunday: 08:00-17:00 and 17:00-00:00. Break 12:00-13:00.

Monday - Sunday 00:00-08:00 overtime by request.

Holiday: 00:00-00:00.

Port Authority working hours:

Monday - Thursday: 08.30-17.15

Friday: 08.30-14.30

Korsakov

Working hours:

Monday - Sunday and Holiday: 00:00-00:00.

Monday - Friday: 08:30-17:30 excluding holidays.

Murmansk

Working hours:

Monday - Sunday and Holiday: 00:00-00:00.

Terminal JSC "Murmansk Commercial Sea Port"

Monday - Friday: 08:00-17:00.

Novorossiysk

Working hours:

Monday - Friday: 08:00-16:00. Overtime 16:00-08:00.

Saturday, Sunday and holidays: 00:00-00:00 overtime by request.

Trade port

Monday - Sunday: 07:00-19:00 and 19:00-07:00. Breaks 12:00-13:00 and 00:00-01:00.

Timber port

Monday - Sunday: 07:00-19:00 and 19:00-07:00. Breaks 11:00-12:00 and 23:00-00:00.

Work performed 24 hours per day, subject to individual agreements/contracts.

St Petersburg

Working hours:

Monday - Sunday and Holiday: 00:00-00:00.

There is a no work 20:00 on 31 December until 00:00 on 1 January.

Monday - Friday 08.30-17.00, excluding holidays.

Taganrog
Working hours:
Monday - Friday: 08:00-20:00 and 20:00-08:00.
Monday - Thursday 08.00-17.00 excluding holiday

Tuapse
Working hours:
Monday - Friday: 08:00-20:00 and 20:00-08:00.
Holiday: 00:00-00:00.
08.00-17.00 excluding holidays.

Samoa

General holidays

January	1	New Year's Day
-	2[1]	Day after New Year's Day
April	2	Good Friday
-	3	Easter Saturday
-	5	Easter Monday
May	10	Mother's Day
June	01	Independence Day
August	9	Father's Day
October	11	Lotu a Tamaiti
December	25[2]	Christmas Day
	26[3]	Boxing Day

[1] Observed 4 January
[2] Observed 27 December
[3] Observed 28 December

The Monday immediately after will be a holiday, if any of the following holidays coincides with a Sunday:
Christmas Day
Boxing Day
New Year's Day
2 January

The Tuesday immediately after will be a holiday, if any of the following holidays coincides with a Sunday:
Christmas Day
New Year's Day

Election Day and the day before are public holidays.

Apia
Working hours:
Monday - Friday: 08:00-12:00 and 13:00-16:30. Break 12:00-13:00. Overtime 16:30-00:00 and 00:00-08:00.
Saturday: 00:00-00:00 overtime by request.
Sunday: 21:00-00:00 overtime by request.

Samoa, American

General holidays

January	1	New Year's Day
February	22	Washington's Birthday
April	2	Good Friday
-	17	Flag Day
May	30	Memorial Day
July	4	Independence Day
-	16	Manu'a Cession Day
September	6	Labour Day
November	11	Veterans' Day
-	25	Thanksgiving Day
December	25	Christmas Day

Sao Tome

General holidays

January	1	New Year's Day
February	3	Martyr's Day
May	1	Labour Day
July	12	Independence Day
September	6	Armed Forces Day
-	30	Agricultural Reform Day
December	21	Sao Tome Day
-	25	Christmas Day

Saudi Arabia

General holidays

May	8-17[1]	Eid al Fitr
July	15-25[1]	Eid-ul-Adha
September	23	National Day of Saudi Arabia

[1] Exact date(s) subject to sighting of the moon.

Dammam
Working hours:
Monday - Sunday: First shift 07:00-18:00 and second shift 19:00-06:00. Breaks 12:00-13:00 and 00:00-01:00.
Holidays: No holidays; only breaks of 12:00-13:00 and 00:00-01:00 on Eid-ul-Fitr (Ramadan Feast), National Day of Saudi Arabia and Eid-ul-Adha (Haj Pilgrimage)

Jeddah
Working hours:
Monday - Sunday: First shift 07:00-19:00 and second shift 19:00-07:00. Breaks 12:00-13:00 and 00:00-01:00.
Holidays: No holidays; only breaks of 12:00-13:00 and 00:00-01:00 on Eid-ul-Fitr (Ramadan Feast), National Day of Saudi Arabia and Eid-ul-Adha (Haj Pilgrimage).

Jubail
Working hours:
Monday - Sunday: First shift 07:00-19:00 and second shift 20:00-06:00. Breaks 12:00-13:00 and 00:00-01:00.
Holidays: No holidays; only breaks of 12:00-13:00 and 00:00-01:00 on Eid-ul-Fitr (Ramadan Feast), National Day of Saudi Arabia and Eid-ul-Adha (Haj Pilgrimage)

Ras Tanura Terminal
Working hours:
Monday - Sunday: 00:00-00:00 per day in three shifts.
Holidays: Shift work available.

Yanbu

Working hours:

Monday - Sunday: First shift 07:00-19:00 and second shift 19:00-07:00. Breaks 12:00-13:00 and 00:00-01:00.

Holidays: No holidays; only breaks of 12:00-13:00 and 00:00-01:00 on Eid-ul-Fitr (Ramadan Feast), National Day of Saudi Arabia and Eid-ul-Adha (Haj Pilgrimage).

Senegal

General holidays

January	1	New Year's Day
April	4	Independence Day
-	5	Easter Monday
May	1	Labour Day
-	13	Ascension Day
-	13[1]	Korite
-	24	Whit Monday
July	20[1]	Tabaski
August	15	Assumption Day
-	19[1]	Tamkarit
September	25	Grand Magal of Touba
October	19[1]	Prophet Monhammmed's Birthday
November	1	All Saints' Day
December	25	Christmas Day

[1] Exact date(s) subject to sighting of the moon.
If Korite or Tabaksi falls on a Sunday, the following Monday is a holiday.

Seychelles

General holidays

January	1-2	New Year's Days
April	2	Good Friday
-	3	Holy Saturday
-	5	Easter Monday
May	1	Labour Day
June	3	Corpus Christi
-	18	Constitution Day
-	29	Independence Day
August	15	Assumption Day
November	1	All Saints' Day
December	8	Immaculate Conception
-	25	Christmas Day

All Sundays are holidays.

Where any Public Holiday except Sunday falls on a Sunday, the next following day, not being itself a Public Holiday, shall be a Public Holiday.

Port Victoria

Working hours:

Monday - Saturday: 00:00-00:00 per day.

Sunday and holidays: Overtime at a 50% extra.

Port Authorities work 24/7.

Sierra Leone

General holidays

January	1	New Year's Day
February	18	Armed Forces Day
March	8	International Women's Day
April	2	Good Friday
-	5	Easter Monday
-	27	Independence Day
May	15[1]	Eid Al Fitri
July	21[1]	Eid Al Adha
October	19[1]	Maulid-un-Nabi
December	25	Christmas Day
-	26	Boxing Day

[1] Exact date(s) subject to sighting of the moon.

Freetown
Working hours:

Monday - Friday: First shift 08:00-19:00, second shift 19:00-08:00.

Saturday and Sunday: Overtime available 08:00-19:00 and 19:00-08:00.

Holidays: Work on overtime available, except for the following: There is no work on Good Friday and Christmas Day.

Singapore

General holidays

January	1	New Year's Day
February	12	Chinese New Year
April	2	Good Friday
May	1	Labour Day
-	13[1]	Hari Raya Puasa
-	26	Vesak Day
July	20[1]	Hari Raya Haji
August	9	National Day
November	4	Deepavali
December	25	Christmas Day

[1] Exact date(s) subject to sighting of the moon
If a holiday falls on a Sunday, then the following Monday is declared a public holiday.

Singapore
Working hours:
SA corporation wharves/terminals
Monday - Sunday: 07:00-11:00, 12:00-15:00, 15:00-18:30, 19:30-23:00 and 23:00-06:00.
Jurong Port
Monday - Sunday: 07:00-11:00, 12:00-15:00, 15:00-18:30, 19:30-23:00 and 23:00-06:00.

Slovenia

General holidays

January	1-2	New Year's Days
February	8	Culture Day (Preseren's Day)
April	27	Day of Uprising Against Occupation
May	1-2	Labour Days
June	8	Primoz Trubar Day
-	25	Statehood Day
August	17	Unification Day
September	15	Return of Primorska
-	23	Slovenian Sports Day
October	25	Sovereignty Day
November	1	Remembrance Day
-	23	Rudolf Maister Day
December	26	Independence Day

The following are not holidays:
Easter Sunday and Monday
Pentecost Sunday
August 15, Assumption of Mary
October 31, Reformation Day
December 25, Christmas

Solomon Islands

General holidays

January	1	New Year's Day
April	2	Good Friday
-	3	Easter Saturday
-	5	Easter Monday
May	24	Whit Monday
June	13	Queen's Birthday
July	7	Independence Day
December	25	Christmas Day
-	26	National Day of Thanksgiving

If a holiday falls on a Sunday, the following day will be a public holiday.
If a holiday falls on a Saturday, it will usually be observed the preceding Friday.
If 26 December is a Monday, the following day shall be a public holiday.

Local holidays

Central

June	29	Provincial holiday

Choiseul

February	25	Provincial holiday

Guadalcanal

August	1	Provincial Holiday

Honiara
Working hours:
Monday - Sunday: 00:00-00:00 normal. Breaks 11:30-13:00, 16:00-16:30 and 23:30-01:00.
Holidays: Workable at additional cost.

Isabel

June	2	Provincial holiday

Makira & Ulawa

August	3	Provincial holiday

Malaita

August	15	Provincial holiday

Rennell and Bellona

July	20	Provincial holiday

Temotu

June	8	Provincial holiday

Western

December	7	Provincial holiday

Somalia

General holidays

January	1	New Year's Day
March	11	Isra and Mi'raj
May	1	Labour Day
-	13-14[1]	Eid-ul-Fitr
-	18-19	Public holidays
June	6	Public holiday
July	20-21[1]	Eid Al Adha
August	10[1]	Islamic New Year
October	19[1]	Mawlid Nabo

[1] Exact date(s) subject to sighting of the moon.
All Fridays are considered public holidays.

South Africa

General holidays

January	1	New Year's Day
March	21	Human Rights Day
April	2	Good Friday
-	5	Family Day
-	27	Freedom Day
May	1	Workers' Day
June	16	Youth Day
August	9	National Women's Day
September	24	Heritage Day
December	16	Day of Reconciliation
-	25	Christmas Day
-	26	Day of Goodwill

If a holiday falls on a Sunday, the following Monday will be a public holiday.

Cape Town
Working hours:
Agri Ro-Ro Terminal
Monday - Sunday: 00:00-00:00 normal working. All holidays is normal working.
Terminal closed from 24 December 18:00 - 26 December 06:00.
Terminal closed from 31 December 18:00 - 2 January 06:00.
Fresh Produce Terminal (FPT)
Monday - Sunday: First shift 06:30-14:30 and second shift 14:30-22:30. Breaks 10:30-11:00 and 18:30-19:00.
Monday - Sunday: Overtime is available on request depending on labour availability at overtime rates 22:30 to 06:30.
Closed Christmas Day and New Year's Day.
Container Terminal
Monday - Sunday: 00:00-00:00 normal working.
Closed on Christmas Day and New Year's Day.

Durban

Supplied by barge on public holidays.

Working hours:

Break-bulk, Combi, City and Maydon Wharf Terminal

There is no work on 25 December (Christmas Day).

There is only one shift available from 06:00-14:00 on 1 January (New Year's Day).

Monday - Friday: First shift 06:00-14:00, second shift 14:00-22:00 and third shift 22:00-06:00.

Saturday, Sunday and holidays: 00:00-00:00 overtime by request.

Maydon Wharf Leasehold Berths

There is no work on 25 December (Christmas Day) and 1 January (New Year's Day). On 24 and 31 December (Christmas Eve and New Year's Eve) terminals work only 06:00-14:00, with work by volunteers until 18:00 for completion.

Monday - Friday: First shift 06:00-14:00, second shift 14:00-22:00 and third shift 22:00-06:00.

Saturday - Sunday: First shift 6:00-18:00, second shift 18:00-06:00.

Holidays: First shift 06:00-18:00 and second shift 18:00-06:00. Holiday work at overtime rates.

Container Terminal

There is no work on 25 December (Christmas Day) and 1 January (New Year's Day).

Monday - Friday: First shift 06:00-14:00, second shift 14:00-22:00 and third shift 22:00-06:00.

Saturday, Sunday and holidays: 00:00-00:00 overtime by request.

Bulk Appliance Berth

There is no work on 25 December (Christmas Day) and 1 January (New Year's Day).

Monday - Sunday: 00:00-00:00 normal working.

Holidays: 00:00-00:00 overtime by request.

Maydon Wharf 2

Monday - Friday: 00:00-00:00 normal working.

Saturday, Sunday and Holidays: 00:00-00:00 overtime by request.

Bunker berths

Monday - Sunday: 00:00-00:00 normal working.

East London

Working hours:
General Cargo/Combi Terminal
Monday - Friday: First shift from 07:00-19:00 and second shift 19:00-06:00.
Saturday, Sunday: 07:00-19:00, 19:-06:00 overtime by request.
All holidays: 07:00-15:00 overtime by request.
No work New Year's Day and Christmas Day 15:00-00:00.
Grain Elevator (Import/Export)
Monday - Sunday: 00:00-00:00 normal working.
All holidays: 00:00-00:00 overtime by request.
No work New Year's Day and Christmas Day 15:00-00:00.

Port Elizabeth

Monday - Sunday: First shift 06:00-14:00, second shift 14:00-22:00 and third shift 22:00-06:00. Breaks 10:00-10:30, 18:00-18:30 and 02:00-02:30.
Working hours:
Ore Berth
Monday - Sunday: First shift 06:00-14:00 and second shift 14:00-22:00.
Third shift 22:00-06:00.
Container Terminal
Monday - Friday: First shift 06:00-14:00, second shift 14:00-22:00 and third shift 22:00-06:00.
Saturday and Sunday: First shift 06:00-18:00 and second shift 18:00-06:00. No meal breaks.

Richards Bay

Working hours:

Coal terminal

Monday - Sunday: 00:00-00:00 normal working.

The terminal is closed only for Christmas, from 14:00 on 24 December (Christmas Eve) until 06:00 on 26 December (Day of Goodwill).

Richards Bay bulk terminals

First shift 06:00-18:00, second shift 18:00-06:00. Breaks 10:00-10:30, 14:30-15:00, 02:30-03:00.

The terminal is closed on 30 April to 2 May (Workers' Day), 24-26 December (Christmas Day) and 31 December to 2 January, (New Year's Day). The period of closure on all three days is from 14:00 the previous day until 06:00.

Multi purpose terminal

Monday - Friday: First shift 06:00-14:00, second shift 14:00-22:00 and third shift 22:00-06:00. Breaks 10:00-10:30, 17:30-18:00, 02:00-02:30.

Saturday and Sunday: First shift 06:00-18:00 and second shift 18:00-06:00. Breaks 10:00-10:30, 14:30-15:00, 02:30-03:00.

The terminal is closed on 30 April to 2 May (Workers' Day), 24-26 December (Christmas Day) and 31 December to 2 January, (New Year's Day). The period of closure on all three days is from 14:00 the previous day until 06:00.

Saldanha Bay Harbour

Working hours:

Monday - Thursday: First shift 07:00-15:00, second shift 15:00-23:00, third shift 23:00-07:00.

Friday -Sunday: First shift 07:00-19:00 and second shift 19:00-07:00.

All holidays 07:00-19:00 and 19:00-07:00 normal working.

Holidays: There is no work on 30 April to 2 May (Worker's Day), 24-26 December (Christmas Day) and 31 December to 2 January, (New Year's Day).

Iron ore terminal

Monday - Sunday and holidays: 00:00-00:00 normal working.

Spain

General holidays

January	1	New Year's Day
April	2	Good Friday
May	1	Labour Day
August	15	Assumption of the Virgin
October	12	National Day
November	1	All Saints' Day
December	6	Constitution Day
December	8	Immaculate Conception Say
-	25	Christmas Day

Holidays falling on a Sunday will either be observed the following Monday or the shift to Monday may be altered by the local administrations declaring a day of local importance as a holiday.

Autonomous region and local holidays

Andalucia

January	6	Epiphany
February	28[1]	Andalucia Day
April	1	Maundy Thursday

[1] Observed 1 March.

Algeciras

June	23	Miércoles de Feria
July	16	Festividad Nuestra Señora del Carmen

Almeria

June	24	San Juan
August	28	Virgen del Mar

Working hours:
Monday - Friday: 08:00-18:00. Break 12:00-14:00. Overtime 18:00-20:00
Saturday, Sunday and holidays: Overtime charges applicable 08:00-14:00, 14:00-20:00, 20:00-02:00, and 02:00-08:00.

Cadiz Bay Port

February	15	Carnival Monday
October	7	Our Lady of Rosary

Working hours:

Monday - Friday: 08:00-20:00 at normal working. Overtime 20:00-00:00 by request.
Saturday: 08:00-14:00 at normal working. Overtime 14:00-00:00 by request.
Sunday and holidays: 00:00-00:00 overtime by request.
Holidays: There is no work on New Year's Day, Labour Day.

Huelva

August	3	Huelva City Fair
September	8	Our Lady of la Cinta (Patron of the Town)

Working hours:

Monday - Friday: First shifts 08:30-14:30 and second shift 14:30-20:30. Overtime 20:30-02:30 and 02:30-08:30 by request.
Saturday, Sunday and holidays: Overtime 00:00-00:00 by request.

Malaga

August	19	Incorporation of Malaga to the Crown of Castilla
September	8	Our Lady of Victory (Patroness Day)

Working hours:

Monday - Friday: First shift 08:00-12:00, 14:00-18:00 and 18:00-00:00. Intensive shifts 08:00-14:00, 14:00-20:00, 20:00-02:00 and 02:00-08:00.
Saturday: 08:00-14:00 at 100% extra. Work after 14:00 only possible to complete ship in intensive shifts, and gangs to be ordered previous working day.
Sunday and holidays: Overtime by request at 100% extra.
Shifts after Saturday 14:00 is only for completion of ship.

Motril

May	3	Dia de la Cruz
June	24	San Juan

Sevilla

April	21	Miercoles de Feria
June	3	Corpus Christi

Working hours:
Monday - Sunday: First shift 08:00-14:00 second shift 15:00-21:00. Overtime 21:00-08:00 by request.
No work on Our Lady of Carmen.

Asturias

January	6	Epiphany
April	1	Maundy Thursday
September	8	Asturias Day

Aviles

April	5	Easter Monday
August	28	San Augustin

Working hours:
Monday - Friday: 08:00-17:00. Break 12:00-13:00. Overtime is arrangeable 17:00-23:00 and 23:00-05:00.
Saturday, Sunday, holidays: 08:00-14:00, 15:00-21:00, 22:00-04:00 at overtime rates.
On 31 December working hours are from 08:00-14:00. Labours start to work again on 2 January at 08:00.

Gijon

February	16	Carnival
June	29	San Pedro

Working hours:
Commercial berths
Monday - Friday: 08:00-17:00. Break 12:00-13:00. Overtime 17:00-23:00 and 23:00-06:00.
Saturday, Sunday and holidays: Work possible on overtime 08:00-14:00, 15:00-21:00 and 22:00-04:00.
EBHI Terminal
Monday -Sunday: First shift 06:00-14:00, second shift 14:00-22:00, third shift 22:00-06:00.
On 31 December working hours are from 08:00-14:00. Labours start to work again on 2 January at 08:00.
Asturias Day and Maundy Thursday workable at overtime.

Balearic Islands

January	6	Epiphany
March	1	Day of the Balearic Islands
April	1	Maundy Thursday
-	5	Easter Monday

La Savina

August	5	Santa María
December	3	San Francisco Javier

Palma de Mallorca

January	20	St. Sebastian
June	24	San Juan

Working hours:
Monday - Sunday: 08:00-12:00 and 12:00-18:00.
Monday - Sunday: 20:00-02:00 and 02:00-08:00 overtime by request.
Holidays: Workable at same hours as above but overtime by request.

Puerto de Alcudia

June	29	San Pedro
July	2	Virgen de la Victoria

Working hours:
Ordinary shifts Monday - Friday: 08:00-12:00 and 14:00-18:00.
Intensive shifts Monday - Sunday: 08:00-14:00 or 14:00-20:00.
Intensive shifts Monday - Sunday: 20:00-02:00 and 02:00-08:00 overtime by request.
Holidays: Overtime by request 08:00-14:00, 14:00-20:00, 20:00-02:00 and 02:00-08:00.

Puerto de Ibiza

May	7	Local holiday
August	5	Our Lady of the Snows

Working hours:
Monday - Sunday: 08:00-14:00 and 14:00-18:00.
Monday - Sunday: 20:00-02:00 and 02:00-08:00 overtime by request. Saturday
08:00-14:00 at 150% and 14:00-20:00 at 200% extra.
Holidays: Workable at same hours as above.

Puerto de Mahon

September	8	Virgen de Gracia
-	9	Virgen de Gracia (Second day)

Working hours:
Monday - Friday: 08:00-12:00 and 14:00-18:00.

Basque Country

January	6	Epiphany
April	1	Maundy Thursday
-	5	Easter Monday

Bilbao

July	31	San Ignacio
August	27	Semana Grande (Friday)

Working hours:

Monday - Friday: 08:00-18:00. Break 12:00-14:00. Intensive shifts 08:00-14:00 and 14:00-20:00. Overtime 20:00-02:00 and 02:00-08:00 by request.

Saturday, Sunday and holidays: 08:00-14:00, 14:00-20:00, 20:00-02:00 and 02:00-08:00 overtime by request.

There is no work on 1 January (New Year's Day), 1 May (Labour Day), 31 July (San Ignacio).

Pasajes

June	24[1]	San Juan
July	7[2]	San Fermín
-	16[3]	Virgen del Carmen
-	31	St. Ignatius
September	14[4]	Virgen del Carmen

[1] Donibane, North section
[2] Antxo, South section
[3] Trintxerpe, West section
[4] Lezo, East section

Working hours:

Monday - Friday: First shift 07:00-14:00 and second shift 14:00-21:00.
Saturday and Sunday: Overtime 08:00-14:00 by request.

Canary Islands

January	6	Epiphany
April	1	Maundy Thursday

Arrecife

February	16	Martes de Carnaval
August	25	San Ginés
September	19	Nuestra Señora de Los Volcanes

La Salineta

June	24	San Juan Bautista
September	8	Nuestra Señora del Pino
November	17	San Gregorio Taumaturgo

Las Palmas

February	16	Carnival Tuesday
June	24	San Juan Bautista
August	9	Nuestra Señora del Pino

Working hours:
Monday - Friday: First shift 08:00-14:00, second shift 14:00-20:00, third shifts 20:00-02:00 at 30% extra and fourth shift 02:00-08:00 at 65% extra.
Saturday: First shift 08:00-14:00 at 15% extra, second shift 14:00-20:00 at 30% extra, third shift 20:00-02:00 at 70% extra and fourth shift 02:00-08:00 at 80% extra.
Sunday and holidays: First shift 08:00-14:00, second shift 14:00-20:00 at 30% extra, third shift 20:00-02:00 at 70% extra and fourth shift 02:00-08:00 at 80% extra.

Puerto del Rosario

February	16	Carnival Tuesday
September	17	Nuestra Señora de la Peña
October	7	Nuestra Señora del Rosario

Santa Cruz de la Palma

May	3	City foundation
July	5	Second day of the pilgrimage for Nuestra Señora de las Nieves
August	5	Nuestra Señora de las Nieves

Santa Cruz de Tenerife

February	2	Virgen de la Candelaria
May	3	Día de la Cruz
July	16	Virgen del Carmen

Working hours:

Monday - Friday: First shift 08:00-14:00 and second shift 14:00-20:00 at normal rates. Third shift 20:00-02:00 at 50% extra. Fourth shift 02:00-08:00 at 90% extra.

Saturday: 08:00-14:00 at 13% extra. 14:00-20:00 at 40% extra. 20:00-02:00 at 90% extra. 02:00-08:00 at 140% extra.

Sunday and holidays: 08:00-14:00 and 14:00-20:00 at 40% extra. 20:00-02:00 at 90% extra. 02:00-08:00 at 110% extra.

In holidays Maundy Thursday, Canarian's Autonomy Day and Festividad de la Bajada de la Virgen del Socorro 08:00-14:00 and 14:00-20:00 30% extra. 20:00-02:00 70% extra and 02:00-08:00 80% extra.

Cantabria

January	6	Epiphany
April	1	Holy Thursday
July	28	Day of the Institutions
September	15	La Bien Aparecida

Santander

May	24	Virgen del Mar
August	30	Santos Mártires

Working hours:
Monday - Sunday: 08:00-14:00, 14:00-20:00 and 00:00-06:00. 20:00-00:00 and 06:00-08:00 completion hours at overtime by request.
Holidays: 06:00-08:00 and 20:00-00:00 overtime by request.
No work on 1 January (New Year's Day), 1 May (Labour day).

Catalonia

January	6	Epiphany
April	5	Easter Monday
June	24	St. John
September	11	Catalonian Day

Alcanar - Alfaques

May	15	Festivitat de Sant Isidre
October	9	Festes d'Octubre

Barcelona

May	24	Whit Monday
September	24	Mare de Déu de la Mercè

Working hours:

Monday - Friday: 08:00-12:00 and 14:00-18:00. Break 12:00-14:00.

08:00-14:00 at 35% extra, 14:00-20:00 at 35% extra, 20:00-02:00 at 100% extra and 02:00-08:00 at 150% extra intensive shifts at overtime by request.

Saturday: 08:00-14:00 at 50% extra, 14:00-20:00 at 200% extra, 20:00-02:00 at 200% extra and 02:00-08:00 at 200% extra intensive shifts at overtime by request.

Sunday and holidays: 08:00-14:00 at 200% extra overtime by request. No work on New Year's Day, Good Friday and Labour Day.

Palamos

May	24-25	Festa Major

Tarragona

August	19	St. Magí
September	23	St. Tecla

Working hours:

Monday - Friday: 08:00-12:00 and 14:00-18:00. 18:00-20:00, 20:00-02:00 and 02:00-04:00, 12:00-14:00 overtime by request.

Saturday: 08:00-14:00 (port cranes), 14:00-20:00 (Ship's gear/mobile cranes) and 20:00-02:00 (ship's gear/mobile cranes) at overtime by request.

Sunday: 08:00-14:00 and 02:00-08:00 overtime by request.

Holidays: 00:00-00:00.

Vilanova i la Geltru

February	15	Dilluns de carnaval
August	5	Festa Major

Ceuta

January	6	Epiphany
April	1	Maundy Thursday
July	20	Eid al-Adha
September	2	Day of Ceuta

Ceuta

June	14	San Antonio
August	5	Nuestra Señora de África

Working hours:
Monday - Sunday: 00:00-00:00.
Holidays: 00:00-00:00. 19:00-07:00 no work on New Year's Day.

Galicia

January	6	Epiphany
March	19	San José
April	1	Maundy Thursday
June	17	Día de las Letras Gallegas

A Coruna
La Coruna

February	16	Shrove Thursday
June	24	San Xoán

Working hours:
Monday - Friday: 08:00-12:00 and 14:00-18:00.
Saturday, Sunday and Holidays: 00:00-00:00 overtime by request.
Bulk Terminal
Monday - Friday: 08:00-14:00 and 14:00-20:00.
Saturday, Sunday and Holidays: 00:00-00:00 overtime by request.

Ferrol

January	7	St. Julian
April	5	Easter Monday

Working hours:
Monday - Friday: 08:00-17:30. Break 12:00-13:30. 17:30-23:30 overtime by request.
08:00-14:00, 14:00-20:00, 20:00-02:00 and 02:00-08:00 intensive shifts at overtime by request.
Saturday and Sunday: Shift times 08:00-14:00,
14:00-20:00, 20:00-02:00 and 02:00-08:00 overtime by request.

Marin

July	16	Virgen del Carmen
September	8	Virgen del Puerto

Working hours:
Monday - Friday: 08:00-13:00 and 15:00-18:00. 08:00-14:00 intensive shift. 15:00-21:00, 22:00-03:00 and 04:00-08:00 intensive shift at overtime by request.
Saturday and Sunday: 00:00-00:00 overtime by request.

Ribadeo

August	16	Día de San Roque
September	8	Día da Patroa

Vigo

February	16	Shrove Tuesday
August	16	San Roque

Working hours:

General cargo

Monday - Friday: 08:00-12:00 and 14:00-18:00. 12:00-13:00 and 18:00-19:00 extension hours at overtime by request. 08:00-14:00, 14:00-20:00, 20:00-02:00 and 02:00-08:00 intensive shifts. 20:00-21:00 extension hour.

Saturday: 08:00-14:00 and 14:00-20:00 overtime by request. 20:00-00:00 extension hour at overtime by request. 08:00-14:00 overtime by request.

Sunday and Holidays: 08:00-14:00 and 14:00-00:00 overtime by request.

On 31 December (New Year's Day) work is available only 08:00-14:00, until 18:00 for perishable goods.

Vilagarcia de Arousa

February	16	Shrove Tuesday
May	22	Santa Rita

Melilla

January	6	Epiphany
March	13	Día de la autonomía
April	1	Maundy Thursday
July	21	Eid al-Adha

Port of Melilla

September	8	Virgin of the Victory
-	17	Dia de Melilla

Working hours:
Monday - Friday: 08:00-14:00, 14:00-20:00 and 20:00-02:00.
Saturday, Sunday and holidays: 00:00-00:00 overtime by request.

Murcia

January	6	Epiphany
March	19	San Joseph's Day
April	1	Maundy Thursday
June	9	Murcia Regional Day

Port of Cartagena

March	26	Viernes de Dolores
September	24	Fiesta de Cartagineses y Romanos

Working hours:
Monday - Friday: 08:00-12:00 and 13:30-17:30.
Saturday, Sunday and Holidays: 08:00-14:00.

Valencia Community

January	6	Epiphany
March	19	San José
April	5	Easter Monday
June	24	San Juan
October	9	Día de la Comunitat Valenciana

Alicante

April	15	Santa Faz
June	23	Fogueres

Working hours:
Monday - Friday: 08:00-14:00 and 14:00-20:00. 20:00-02:00 and 02:00-08:00 overtime by request.
Saturday and sunday: 08:00-14:00, 14:00-20:00, 20:00-02:00 and 02:00-08:00 overtime by request.

Castellon

March	8	Monday of Fiestas de la Magdalena
June	29	San Pedro

Working hours:
Monday - Friday: 08:00-13:00 and 14:00-17:00. 20:00-02:00 and 02:00-08:00 overtime by request. Break 13:00-14:00. 08:00-14:00 and 14:00-20:00 Intensive shifts.
Saturday, Sunday and holidays: 08:00-14:00 at 100% extra overtime by request.

Gandia

April	12	San Vicent Ferrer
October	4	Día de Sant Francesc de Borja

Sagunto

April	12	San Vicente Ferrer
July	30	Saints Abdon and Senen

Working hours:
Monday - Friday: 08:00-14:00 and 15:00-20:00. 20:00-08:00 overtime by request. Break 14:00-15:00.
Saturday, Sunday and holidays: 00:00-00:00 overtime by request.

Torrevieja

April	12	San Vicente Ferrer
July	16	Virgen del Carmen

Working hours:

Monday - Friday: 06:00-14:00 and 14:00-22:00.
Saturday, Sunday and holidays: No work.

Valencia

January	22	Sant Vicent Màrtir
April	12	Sant Vicent Ferrer

Working hours:

Monday - Friday: 08:00-14:00 and 14:00-20:00. 20:00-02:00 and 02:00-08:00 overtime by request.
Saturday: 08:00-14:00. 14:00-20:00, 20:00-02:00 and 02:00-08:00 overtime by request.
Sunday and holidays: 00:00-00:00 overtime by request.
No work on 1 January (New Year's Day) and 1 May (Labour Day).

Sri Lanka

General holidays

January	14	Tamil Thai Pongal Day
-	28	Duruthu Full Moon Poya Day
February	4	Independence Day
-	26	Nawam Full Moon Poya Day
March	11	Mahasivarathri Day
-	28	Madin Full Moon Poya Day
April	2	Good Friday
-	13-14	Sinhala and Tamil New Year Days
-	26	Bak Full Moon Poya Day
May	1	May Day
-	14	Id-Ul-Fitr (Ramazan Festival Day)
-	26-27	Vesak Full Moon Poya Days
June	24	Poson Full Moon Poya Day
July	21	Id-Ul-Alha (Hadji Festival Day)
-	23	Esala Full Moon Poya Day
August	22	Nikini Full Moon Poya Day
September	20	Binara Full Moon Poya Day
October	19	Milad-Un-Nabi
-	20	Vap Full Moon Poya Day
November	4	Deepavali Festival Day
-	18	Ill Full Moon Poya Day
December	18	Unduvap Full Moon Poya Day
-	25	Christmas Day

Colombo
Working hours:
Jaye Container Terminal
Monday - Sunday: 07:00-18:00 and 18:00-07:00. Break 21:00-21:30.
Conventional Berths
Monday - Friday: 07:30-16:30, 16:30-00:30, 00:30-04:00 and 04:00-06:30. Breaks 12:00-13:00 and 21:00-22:00.
Saturday: 07:30-13:30, 13:30-16:30, 16:30-21:30, 21:30-00:30, 03:00-04:00 and 04:00-06:30.
Private Terminals
Monday - Sunday: 00:00-00:00.

Galle
Working hours:
Monday - Friday: 07:30-16:30, 16:30-00:30, 00:30-04:00 and 04:00-06:30.
Saturday: 07:30-13:30, 13:30-16:30, 16:30-21:30, 21:30-00:30, 03:00-04:00 and 04:00-06:30.

Trincomalee
Working hours:
Monday - Friday: 07:30-16:30, 16:30-00:30, 00:30-04:00 and 04:00-06:30.
Saturday: 07:30-13:30, 13:30-16:30, 16:30-21:30, 21:30-00:30, 03:00-04:00 and 04:00-06:30.

St Eustatius

General holidays

January	1	New Year's Day
April	2	Good Friday
-	4	Easter Sunday
-	5	Easter Monday
-	27	King's Birthday
May	1	Labour Day
-	13	Ascension Day
November	16	Statia Day
December	15	Kingdom Day
-	25	Christmas Day
-	26	2nd Christmas Day

St Helena

General holidays

April	2	Good Friday
-	5	Easter Monday
May	21	St. Helena Day
June	21	H.M. the Queen's Official Birthday
December	25	Christmas Day
-	26	Boxing Day

Other holidays than Christmas Day falling on a Saturday or Sunday will be observed either the preceding Friday or the following Monday.

If Christmas Day fall on a Saturday or Sunday, it will be observed the following Tuesday.

Jamestown
Working hours:
Monday - Friday: 06:00-18:00. 18:00-06:00 overtime by request.
Saturday: 06:00-18:00 at 25% extra for overtime planned. 18:00-06:00 overtime by request.
Sunday: 06:00-18:00 at 100% extra. 18:00-06:00 overtime by request.
Holidays: 18:00-06:00 at 100% extra overtime by request.

St Kitts and Nevis

General holidays

January	1	New Year's Day
-	2	Carnival Day
April	2	Good Friday
-	5	Easter Monday
May	3	Labour Day
July	22	Culturama Day
August	3	Emancipation Day
September	16	Nation Heroes Day
-	19	Independence Day
December	25	Christmas Day
-	26	Boxing Day

St Lucia

General holidays

January	1	New Year's Day
-	2	Day after New Year's Day
February	22	Indenpendence Day
April	2	Good Friday
-	5	Easter Monday
May	1	Labour Day
-	24	Whit Monday
June	3	Corpus Christi
August	1	Emancipation Day
October	4	Thanksgiving Day
December	13	National Day
-	25	Christmas Day
-	26	Boxing Day

St Maarten

General holidays

January	1	New Year's Day
April	2	Good Friday
-	5	Easter Monday
-	27	King's Day
-	30	Carnival
May	1	Labour Day
-	13	Ascension Day
July	1	Emancipation Day
October	11	Constitution Day
November	11	Sint Marteen Day
December	25	Christmas Day
-	26	St. Stephen's Day

St Pierre-Miquel

General holidays

January	1	New Year's Day
April	5	Easter Monday
May	1	First of May
-	8	1945 Armistice Day
-	13	Ascension Day
-	24	Whit Monday
July	14	National Holiday
August	15	Assumption B.V. Mary
November	1	All Saints' Day
-	11	1918 Armistice Day
December	25	Christmas Day

Saint Pierre

Working hours:

Monday - Friday: 07:30-16:00. 16:00-00:00 at 100% extra and 00:00-07:30 at 200% extra overtime by request. Breaks 12:00-13:30 and 19:00-20:00.

Saturday: 07:30-12:00. 16:00-00:00 at 100% extra and 00:00-07:30 at 200% extra overtime by request. Thereafter at double-time rates, with triple-time rates for night work.

Sunday: 16:00-00:00 at 100% extra, 00:00-07:30 at 200% extra and 07:30-16:00 at 100% extra overtime by request.

Holidays: 07:30-00:00 at 100% extra, 00:00-07:30 at 200% extra. No work on New Year's Day, Christmas Day.

St Vincent and the Grenadines

General holidays

January	1	New Year's Day
March	14	Easter Monday
April	2	Good Friday
-	5	Easter Monday
May	1	National Worker's Day
-	24	Whit Monday
July	5	Carnival
August	1	Emancipation Day
October	27	Independence Day
December	25	Christmas Day
-	26	Boxing Day

Holidays falling on a Sunday will be observed the following Monday.

Sudan

General holidays

January	1	Independence Day
-	7	Orthodox Christmas
May	13[1]	Eid el-Fitr
July	20[1]	Eid al-Adha
August	10[1]	Islamic New Year
October	19[1]	Birth of Prophet Mohammed

[1] Exact date(s) subject to sighting of the moon.

Port Sudan

Working hours:

Saturday - Thursday: 07:30-14:30 and 15:30-22:30. 23:30-05:30 overtime by request.
Friday and holidays: 07:30-12:00, 15:30-22:30 and 23:30-05:30 overtime by request.
00:00-00:00 No work on Eid el-Fitr and Eid al-Adha.

Suriname

General holidays

January	1	New Year's Day
February	25	Day of Liberaton and Innovation
March	29	Holi Phagwah
April	2	Good Friday
-	5	Easter Monday
May	1	Labour Day
-	13[1]	Idul Fitr
July	1	Keti Koti Day
-	20[1]	Idul Adha
August	9	Indigenous People' Day
October	10	Maroons Day
November	4	Deepavali Day
-	25	Independence Day
December	25	Christmas Day
-	26	Second Christmas Day

[1] Exact date(s) subject to sighting of the moon.

Sweden

General holidays

January	1	New Year's Day
-	6	Epiphany
April	2	Good Friday
-	4	Easter Sunday
-	5	Easter Monday
May	1	Labour Day
-	13	Ascension Day
-	23	Pentecost Sunday
June	6	National Day
-	26	Midsummer Day
November	6	All Saints' Day
December	25	Christmas Day
-	26	Second Day of Christmas

Aahus

Working hours:

Monday - Friday: 07:00-16:00. Breaks 09:00-09:30, 12:00-12:45 and 14:30-14:45.
Saturday, Sunday and holidays: 00:00-00:00 overtime by request.

Falkenberg

Working hours:

Monday: 07:00-16:00. Breaks 09:00-09:15, 12:15-13:00 and 14:30-14:45. 00:00-07:00 and
16:00-07:10 overtime by request.

Tuesday - Thursday: 07:00-16:00. Breaks 09:00-09:15, 12:15-13:00 and 14:30-14:45.
16:00-07:10 overtime by request.

Friday: 07:00-16:00. Breaks 12:15-13:00, 09:00-09:15 and 14:30-14:45. 16:00-00:00
overtime by request.

Saturday and Sunday: 00:00-00:00 overtime by request.

Additional hours possible at overtime rates, subject to labour availability.

Gaevle
Working hours:
Monday - Friday: 07:00-15:30. Breaks 09:30-10:00 and 12:30-13:00.
Saturday and Sunday: 07:00-15:30 overtime by request.

Gothenburg
Working hours:
Container terminal
Monday - Friday: 06:45-15:00, 15:00-23:00 and 23:00-07:00.
Saturday and Sunday: 00:00-00:00 overtime by request.
Car Terminal
Monday - Friday: 07:00-16:00.

Halland
Working hours:
Monday - Friday: 07:00-16:00. Breaks 09:00-09:15 and 11:45-12:30.
16:00-07:00 overtime by request.
Saturday, Sunday and holidays: 00:00-00:00 overtime by request.

Hallstavik
Working hours:
Monday - Friday: 00:00-00:00.
Saturday and Sunday: 06:00-22:00. 00:00-06:00 and 22:00-00:00 overtime by request.
Holidays: No work.

Hargshamn
Working hours:
Monday - Sunday and Holidays: 06:00-14:00, 14:00-22:00 and 22:00-06:00. Breaks
09:00-09:30 and 18:00-18:30.
No work on New Year's Day, Easter Sunday, Easter Monday, Ascension Day, Pentecost
Sunday.

Helsingborg
Working hours:
Monday - Friday: 07:00-16:00. Breaks 09:00-09:30, 11:45-12:30 and 14:30-14:45.
16:00-20:00 overtime by request.
Saturday: 07:00-00:00 overtime by request.
Sunday and Holidays: 07:00-20:00 overtime by request.

Iggesund
Working hours:
Monday - Friday: 07:00-15:45. 15:45-00:15 overtime by request. Breaks 09:00-09:30, 11:30-12:00 and 20:00-20:30.
Holidays: 00:00-00:00 overtime by request. 00:00-00:00 Normal hours on Midsummer Day and All Saints' Day.

Kalmar
Working hours:
Monday - Friday: 07:00-16:00. Breaks 08:30-09:00 and 12:30-13:00. 16:00-07:00 at 100% extra overtime by request.
Saturday: 00:00-00:00 at 100% extra overtime by request.
Sunday: 00:00-00:00 at 150% extra overtime by request.
Holidays: 00:00-00:00 at 200% extra overtime by request.

Karlstad
Working hours:
Monday: 07:00-16:00. Breaks 09:00-09:30, 11:00-11:15 and 13:00-13:30. 16:00-07:00 and 00:00-07:00 overtime by request.
Tuesday - Thursday: 07:00-16:00. Breaks 09:00-09:30, 11:00-11:15 and 13:00-13:30. 16:00-07:00 overtime by request.
Friday: 07:00-16:00. Breaks 09:00-09:30, 11:00-11:15 and 13:00-13:30. 16:00-00:00 overtime by request.
Saturday and Sunday: 00:00-00:00 overtime by request.

Koeping
Working hours:
Monday: 07:00-16:00. Breaks 09:00-09:30 and 13:00-13:30. 16:00-07:00 and 00:00-07:00 overtime by request.
Tuesday - Thursday: 07:00-16:00. Breaks 09:00-09:30 and 13:00-13:30. 16:00-07:00 overtime by request.
Friday: 07:00-16:00. Breaks 09:00-09:30 and 13:00-13:30. 16:00-00:00 overtime by request.
Saturday, Sunday and holidays: 00:00-00:00 overtime by request.

Landskrona
Working hours:
Monday - Friday: 07:00-16:00. Breaks 09:00-09:15 and 11:45-12:30.

Lidkoeping
Working hours:
Monday: 07:00-16:00. Breaks 09:00-09:30 and 13:00-13:30. 16:00-07:00 and 00:00-07:00 overtime by request.
Tuesday - Thursday: 07:00-16:00. Breaks 09:00-09:30 and 13:00-13:30. 16:00-07:00 overtime by request.
Friday: 07:00-16:00. Breaks 09:00-09:30 and 13:00-13:30. 16:00-00:00 overtime by request.
Saturday, Sunday and holidays: 00:00-00:00 overtime by request.

Luleaa
Working hours:
Monday - Friday: Shift work 06:00-14:00 and 14:00-22:00. Breaks 10:00-10:30. 18:30-06:00 overtime by request.
Uddebo oil port
Monday - Sunday: 00:00-00:00
Iron Ore Loading
Monday - Sunday: 06:00-01:00. 01:00-06:00 overtime by request.

Lysekil
Working hours:
Monday: 07:00-16:00. Breaks 09:00-09:15 and 12:00-13:00. 16:00-07:00 and 00:00-07:00 overtime by request.
Tuesday - Thursday: 07:00-16:00. Breaks 09:00-09:15 and 12:00-13:00. 16:00-07:00 overtime by request.
Friday: 07:00-16:00. Breaks 09:00-09:15 and 12:00-13:00. 16:00-00:00 overtime by request.
Saturday and Sunday: 00:00-00:00 overtime by request.

Malmoe
Working hours:
Monday - Friday: 07:00-16:00. 16:30-20:00 at 100% extra and 20:00-07:00 at 200% extra overtime by request.
Saturday: 07:00-13:30 at 100% extra and 13:30-21:00 at 150% extra overtime by request.
Sunday: 00:00-00:00 at 150% extra overtime by request.
Holidays: 00:00-00:00 at 200% extra overtime by request.

Monsteraas
Working hours:
Monday: 06:40-15:25. 15:25-06:40 and 00:00-06:40 overtime by request.
Tuesday - Friday: 06:40-15:25. 15:25-06:40 overtime by request.
Saturday, Sunday and Holidays: 00:00-00:00 overtime by request.

Norrkoeping
Working hours:
Monday - Friday: 07:00-15:30. 16:00-00:00 overtime by request. Breaks 09:00-09:15, 12:00-12:30, 18:30-19:00 and 21:45-22:00.
Ohman terminal:
Monday - Friday: 06:00-18:00.
Pampus terminal:
Monday - Thursday: 06:00-21:30. Friday: 06:00-18:00.

Norrsundet
Working hours:
Monday - Friday: 06:00-14:00. Ordinary working hours: 07:00-16:00.
Breaks 10:30-10:30 and 12:30-13:00. 06:00-14:00, 14:00-22:00 and 22:00-06:00.
Saturday and Sunday: 06:00-18:00 and 18:00-06:00. 00:00-00:00 overtime by request.
Holidays: 00:00-00:00 overtime by request.

Oernskoeldsvik
Working hours:
Monday - Friday: 07:00-16:00. Break 11:00-12:00.
Saturday, Sunday and holidays: 00:00-00:00 overtime by request.

Otterbaecken
Working hours:
Monday - Friday: 07:00-16:00. Breaks 09:00-09:30 and 13:00-13:30.

Oxeloesund

Working hours:

Dry Bulk Terminal

Monday - Thursday: 06:00-14:00, 14:00-22:00 and 22:00-06:00. Breaks 08:30-09:00, 19:00-19:30 and 03:00-03:30.

Friday: 06:00-14:00 and 14:00-22:00. Breaks 08:30-09:00, 19:00-19:30 and 03:00-03:30.

Saturday and Sunday: 06:00-18:00. Breaks 08:30-09:00, 19:00-19:30 and 03:00-03:30. 18:00-06:00 overtime by request.

General Cargo Terminal

Monday - Friday: 06:00-14:00 and 14:00-22:00. Breaks 08:30-09:00, 19:00-19:30. 22:00-06:00 overtime by request.

Saturday and Sunday: 22:00-06:00, 06:00-14:00 and 14:00-22:00 overtime by request. workable at overtime costs.

Oil/Chem Terminal

Monday - Sunday: 00:00-00:00 overtime by request.

Skelleftehamn

Working hours:

Monday - Friday: 06:30-15:00. 15:00-22:30 and 22:30-06:30 overtime by request. Breaks 10:00-10:30, 18:30-19:00 and 02:00-02:30.

Saturday, Sunday and holidays: 00:00-00:00 overtime by request.

Soedertaalje

Working hours:

Monday: 07:00-16:00. Breaks 08:30-09:00, 11:30-12:00 and 14:00-14:15. 16:00-07:00 and 00:00-07:00 overtime by request.

Tuesday - Thursday: 07:00-16:00. Breaks 08:30-09:00, 11:30-12:00 and 14:00-14:15. 16:00-07:00 overtime by request.

Friday: 07:00-16:00. Breaks 08:30-09:00, 11:30-12:00 and 14:00-14:15. 16:00-00:00 overtime by request.

Saturday, Sunday and holidays: 00:00-00:00 overtime by request.

Soelvesborg

Working hours:

Monday - Friday: 07:30-16:00. Breaks 09:00-09:15 and 12:00-12:30.

Saturday, Sunday and holidays: 00:00-00:00 overtime by request.

Stockholm
Working hours:
Monday - Friday: 07:00-16:00. Breaks 09:00-09:30, 11:00-11:15 and 13:30-14:00.
06:00-07:00 and 16:00-20:00 overtime by request.

Sundsvall
Working hours:
Monday - Friday: 07:00-16:00. 16:00-01:00 overtime by request.
Breaks 09:00-09:15, 11:00-11:45, 13:45-14:00, 18:00-18:30 and 22:30-23:00.
Saturday and Sunday: 07:00-16:00 overtime by request.

Trelleborg
Working hours:
Monday - Friday: 07:00-16:00. Breaks 08:30-09:00 and 12:00-12:30.
Saturday: 00:00-00:00 at 100% overtime by request.
Sunday: 00:00-00:00 at 150% overtime by request.
Holidays: 00:00-00:00 overtime by request. 12:00-13:00 no work on New Year's Day,
Pentecost Sunday.

Trollhaettan
Working hours:
Monday - Friday: 07:00-16:00. Breaks 09:00-09:30 and 13:00-13:30.
Saturday: 07:00-14:00 at 100% extra and 14:00-16:00 at 200% extra overtime by request.
Sunday: 07:00-16:00 at 150% extra overtime by request.
Holidays: 00:00-00:00 overtime by request.

Uddevalla
Working hours:
Monday - Friday: 07:00-16:00. Breaks 09:00-09:30 and 13:00-13:30.
16:00-00:30 overtime by request.
Saturday, Sunday and holidays: 07:00-16:00 overtime by request.
No work on New Year's Day, Easter Sunday, Labour Day, Ascension Day.

Umeaa
Working hours:
Monday - Friday: 06:00-15:00. Break from 10:00-11:00.
Saturday, Sunday and Holidays: 00:00-00:00 overtime by request.

Vaenersborg
Working hours:
Monday - Friday: 07:00-16:00. Breaks 09:00-09:30 and 13:00-13:30.
Saturday: 07:00-14:00 at 100% extra and 14:00-16:00 at 200% extra overtime by request.
Sunday: 07:00-16:00 at 150% extra overtime by request.
Holidays: No work.

Varberg
Working hours:
Monday - Friday: 07:00-16:00. Breaks 09:10-09:30 and 11:50-12:30.
Saturday, Sunday and holidays: 00:00-00:00 overtime by request.

Vasteras
Working hours:
Monday - Friday: 07:00-16:00. Breaks 09:00-09:30 and 12:00-12:30. 16:00-07:00 overtime by request.
Saturday, Sunday and holidays: 00:00-00:00 overtime by request.

Vestervik
Working hours:
Monday - Friday: 07:00-16:00. Breaks 09:00-09:30 and 13:00-13:30.

Visby
Working hours:
Monday - Friday: 07:00-16:00. Breaks 09:00-09:30 and 12:00-13:00.

Wallhamn
Working hours:
Monday - Friday: 07:00-16:00. 16:00-00:00 at 100% extra overtime by request.
Breaks 09:00-09:30 and 13:00-13:30.
Saturday: 00:00-00:00 at 100% extra overtime by request.
Sunday: Work available 00:00-00:00 at 150% extra overtime by request.
Holidays: Work available 00:00-00:00 at 200% extra overtime by request.

Ystad
Working hours:
Monday - Friday: 07:00-16:00 and 04:30-23:00.
Breaks 09:00-09:30 and 12:00-12:30.

Syria

General holidays

January	1	New Year
March	8	Revolution Day
-	21	Mother's Day
April	17	Evacuation Day
May	1	Labour Day
-	2	Easter Sunday (Orthodox)
-	6	Martyr's Day
-	13-15[1]	Ramadan Bairam
July	20-23[1]	Adha Bairam
August	10[1]	Islamic New Year
October	6	October Liberation War
-	19[1]	Birth of the Prophet
December	25	Christmas Day

[1] Exact date(s) subject to sighting of the moon.

Banias Oil Terminal
Working hours:
Monday - Sunday: 07:00-15:00. 15:00-07:00 at 25% extra overtime by request.

Lattakia
Working hours:
Monday - Sunday: 00:00-00:00.
Conventional ships: Monday - Sunday: 07:00-15:00, 15:00-23:00 and 23:00-007:00.
Breaks 14:00-15:00, 22:00-23:00 and 06:00-07:00.
Holidays: 00:00-00:00.
Container ships: Monday - Sunday: 07:00-19:00 and 19:00-07:00. Break 14:00-15:00.
Holidays: 00:00-00:00
No work on New Year, Ramadan Bairam and Adha Bairam.

Tartous
Working hours:
Conventional ships: Monday - Sunday: 07:00-15:00, 15:00-23:00 and 23:00-07:00.
Container ships: Monday - Sunday: 00:00-08:00, 08:00-16:00 and 16:00-00:00.

Tahiti

General holidays

January	1	New Year's Day
March	5	Missionary Day
April	2	Good Friday
-	5	Easter Monday
May	8	Victory Day
-	13	Ascension Day
-	24	Whit Monday
June	29	Internal Autonomy Day
July	14	French National Day
August	15	Assumption Day
November	1	All Saints' Day
-	11	Armistice Day
December	25	Christmas Day

Papeete

Working hours:

Monday - Friday shifts: 07:00-11:00 and 13:00-17:00. 18:00-22:00, 11:00-13:00 and 17:00-18:00 at overtime. Breaks 11:00-13:00 and 17:00-18:00.

Saturday shifts: 07:00-11:00, 13:00-17:00, 18:00-22:00, 11:00-13:00 and 17:00-18:00 at overtime.

Sunday: No work.

Holidays: 00:00-00:00 at overtime, except 1 January (New Year's Day), 1 May (Labour Day) and 25 December (Christmas Day). Work stops at 17:00 on 24 December (Christmas Eve) and 31 December (New Year's Eve).

Tanzania

General holidays

January	1	New Year's Day
-	12	Zanzibar Revolution Day
April	2	Good Friday
-	5	Easter Monday
	7	Karume Day
-	26	Union Day
May	1	Labour Day
-	14[1]	Eid ul-Fitr
July	7	Saba Saba Day
-	21[1]	Eid El Haj
August	8	Nane Nane (Farmer's) Day
October	14	Mwalimu Nyerere Day
-	19[1]	Maulid Day
December	9	Independence Day
-	25	Christmas Day
-	26	Boxing Day

[1] Exact date(s) subject to sighting of the moon.
Holidays falling on Saturday or Sunday will be kept on those days.

Dar Es Salaam
Working hours:
Monday - Friday shifts: 07:00-15:00, 15:00-23:00. 23:00-07:00 at overtime.
Saturday, Sunday and holidays: 00:00-00:00 at overtime.

Mtwara
Working hours:
Monday - Friday shifts: 07:00-15:00 and 14:45-22:15.
Saturday, Sunday and holidays: 07:00-12:30 and 12:30-20:30 at overtime.
Working hours during Ramadan: As holidays plus additional break 18.30-19.30.

Tanga

Working hours:

Monday - Friday shifts: 07:00-15:00 and 14:45-22:15.

Saturday, Sunday and holidays: 07:00-12:30 and 12:30-20:30 at overtime.

Working hours during Ramadan: As holidays plus additional break 18.30-19.30.

Zanzibar

Working hours:

Monday - Friday shifts: 07:00-14:30, 15:00-21:30 and 22:00-07:00.

Saturday shift: 00:00-00:00 at overtime.

Sunday shifts: 07:00-14:30, 15:00-21:30 and 22:00-07:00 at overtime.

Holidays: 07:00-14:30, 15:00-21:30 and 22:00-07:00 at overtime.

Eid holidays shifts: 09:00-14:30 and 15:00-21:30 at overtime.

Working hours during Ramadan month: 07.00-14.00.

Overtime may be worked 14.00-17.00 and 22.00-07.00

Thailand

General holidays

January	1	New Year's Days
February	10	Makha Bucha Day
April	6	Chakri Memorial Day
-	13	Songkran Festival
May	1	National Labour Day
-	4	H.M. King's Corrnation
-	6	Visakha Bucha Day
June	3	H.M. The Queen's Birthday
July	6	Asahna Bucha Day
-	28	H.M. The King's Birthday
August	12	H.M. Queen Mother's Birthday
October	13	Memory of King Bhumibol
-	23	Chulalongkorn Memorial Day
December	7	King Bhumibol's Birthday
-	10	Constitution Day
-	31	New Year's Eve

If a holiday falls on a Saturday or Sunday, the following Monday will be considered a holiday.

Timor-Leste Dem. Rep. of

General holidays

January	1	New Year's Day
April	2	Good Friday
May	1	Labour Day
-	13	Idul Fitri
-	20	Independence Restoration Day
June	3	Corpus Christi
July	20	Idul Adha
August	30	Popular Consulation Day
November	1	All Saints' Day
-	2	All Souls' Day
-	12	National Youth Day
-	28	Independence Day
December	7	National Heroes Day
-	8	Immaculate Conception
-	25	Christmas Day

Togo

General holidays

January	1	New Year's Day
April	4	Easter Sunday
-	5	Easter Monday
-	27	Independence Day
May	1	Labour Day
-	13	Ascension Day
-	13[1]	Korite
-	23	Whit Sunday
-	24	Whit Monday
June	21	National Martyrs' Day
July	20[1]	Tabaski
August	15	Assumption Day
September	23	Anniversary of Attack on Lomé
November	1	All Saints' Day
December	25	Christmas Day

[1] Exact date(s) subject to sighting of the moon.

Kpeme
Working hours:
Monday - Saturday shifts: 06:00-18:00. 18:00-06:00 overtime at 50%.
Sunday shifts: 06:00-18:00, 18:00-06:00 overtime at 50%.
Holidays: At 50% overtime.

Lome
Working hours:
Monday - Saturday: 06:00-14:00, 14:00-22:00 and 22:00-06:00.
Sunday and holidays: 06:00-14:00.

Tonga

General holidays

January	1	New Year's Day
April	2	Good Friday
-	5	Easter Monday
-	25	Anzac Day
June	4	Emancipation Day
July	4	Official Birthday of HM King Tupou VI
September	17	Birthday of HRH Crown Prince Tupouto'a 'Ulukalala
November	4	Constitution Day
December	4	Tupou I Day
-	25	Christmas Day
-	26	Boxing Day

If the holiday falls on a Tuesday or Wednesday, it will be celebrated on the Monday before the actual holiday. If, however, the holiday falls on a Thursday, Friday, Saturday or Sunday, then it will be celebrated on the Monday following the actual holiday. This does not apply to New Year's Day, Good Friday, Easter Monday, Anzac Day, Christmas Day or Boxing Day.

7 June, 5 July, 8 November, 6 December and 27 December Observed.

Nukualofa
Working hours:
Monday - Friday: 08:30-12:30 and 12:30-16:30. Break 12:30-13:30.
Saturday: 08:00-12:00. 12:00-23:00 at overtime.
Sunday: No work.
Holidays: 00:00-00:00 at overtime, except Good Friday and Christmas Day.

Trinidad & Tobago

General holidays

January	1	New Year's Day
March	30	Spiritual Baptist Liberation Day
April	2	Good Friday
-	5	Easter Monday
May	13	Eid ul-Fitr
-	30	Indian Arrival Day
June	3	Corpus Christi
-	19	Labour Day
August	1	Emancipation Day
-	31	Independence Day
September	24	Republic Day
November	24	Diwali
December	25	Christmas Day
-	27	Boxing Day

If a holiday falls on a Sunday coincides with another holiday, the next following day that is not a public holiday shall be a public holiday.

Point Lisas
Working hours:
Monday - Sunday shifts: 07:00-15:00, 15:00-23:00 and 23:00-07:00.
Breaks 11:00-11:30, 19:00-19:30 and 03:00-03:30.
Holiday shifts: 7:00-15:00, 15:00-23:00 and 23:00-07:00 at overtime.
On 24-25 December: Overtime.

Port of Spain
Working hours:
Monday - Friday shifts: 07:00-15:00, 15:00-23:00 and 23:00-07:00.
Breaks 11:00-11:30, 19:00-19:30 and 03:00-03:30.
Saturday, Sunday and holidays: 07:00-16:00, 16:00-23:00 and 23:00-06:00.
Breaks 11:00-12:00, and 02:00-03:30.

Tunisia

General holidays

January	1	New Year's Day
-	14	Revolution Day
March	20	Independence Day
April	9	Martyrs' Day
May	1	Labour Day
-	13[1]	Aid El Fitr
July	20[1]	Aid El Kebir
-	25	Republic Day
August	10[1]	Ras el am el Hejri
-	13	Women's Day
October	15	Evacuation Day
-	19[1]	Prophet Mohammed's Birthday

[1] Exact date(s) subject to sighting of the moon.
Saturday: Ordinary working day.
Sunday: Weekly day of rest.

Menzel Bourguiba
Working hours:
Monday - Saturday shifts: 07:00-13:00, 14:00-20:00 and 20:00-04:00.
Holidays: Overtime at 100%.
No work on Republic Day, Evacuation Day and Aid El Fitr.

Port de Gabes
Working hours:
Bulk cargo, dry and liquid
Monday - Sunday and holidays: 00:00-00:00.
General and bagged cargo
Monday - Saturday shifts: 07:00-13:00 and 13:00-19:00. 19:00-01:00 at overtime.
Sunday and holidays: 07:00-13:00, 13:00-19:00 and 19:00-01:00 at overtime.
No work on Republic Day, first day of Aid El Fitr, Evacuation Day and 7:00-13:00 on 1 May (Labour Day).

Sfax
Working hours:
General cargo
Monday - Saturday shifts: 07:00-13:00, 14:00-20:00 and 21:00-03:00.
Sunday and holidays: Overtime.
Bulk cargo
Monday - Sunday and holidays: 00:00-00:00.

Sousse
Working hours:
Monday - Saturday: 07:00-13:00, 14:00-20:00 and 21:00-03:00.
Sunday and holidays: 07:00-13:00, 14:00-20:00 and 21:00-03:00 at overtime.
No work on Evacuation Day.
Working hours during Ramadan: 07.00-17.00 and 21.00-02.00.

Tunis - La Goulette
Working hours:
Monday - Sunday shifts: 07:00-13:00, 14:00-19:00 and 21:00-03:00.
Monday - Sunday shift extensions: 13:00:14:00, 19:00:20:00 and 03:00:04:00 at overtime.
Holidays: 07:00-13:00, 14:00-19:00 and 21:00-03:00 at overtime.
Working hours during Ramadan:
First shift: 07.00-12.30, extension by one hour
Second shift: 13.00-16.15, no extension
Third shift: 21.00-03.00, extension by one hour
Shift extensions allows for completion of ship
No work on Republic Day, first day of Aid El Fitr and Evacuation Day.

Turkey

General holidays

January	1	New Year's Day
April	23	Celebration of National Sovereignty & Children's Holiday
May	1	Labour Day
-	19	Commemoration of Ataturk, Youth and Sports Holiday
-	12[1]	Eve of Sheker Bayram
-	13[2]	Sheker Bayram
July	15	Democracy and National Unity Day
-	20[1]	Eve of Courban Bayram
-	21[2]	Courban Bayram
August	30	Victory Day
October	28[1]	Eve of Republic Day
-	29	Republic Day

[1] From 1 PM. Exact date(s) subject to sighting of the moon.
[2] Exact date(s) subject to sighting of the moon.

Gulluk
Working hours:
Monday - Sunday shifts: 08:00-00 :00, 00:00-08:00.

Iskenderun
Working hours:
Iskenderun - Port: Monday - Sunday shift: 00:00-00:00.
TCDD - Terminal: Monday - Sunday shift: 00:00-00:00.
Sunday and holidays: 00:00-00:00 at overtime.
There is no night mooring at Sasa, Petrolifisi, Delta, Aygaz, BP and Toros terminals.

Turkmenistan

General holidays

January	27	Day of Defenders of the Fatherland
February	18	Day of diplomatic workers of Turkmenistan
-	18	World Health Day
March	27	Holiday "Suw damjasy - altyn danesi"
April	4	Feast of the Turkmen horse
-	7	Day of employees of the internal affairs bodies of Turkmenistan
-	25	Turkmen Carpet Festival
May	29	International Children's Day
-	30	World Environment Day
June	1	Day of textile workers
-	5	Science Day
-	6	Day by the worker of culture and art
-	12	Galla Bayrams
-	27	Day of health workers and the medical industry
July	18	Day of border guards
-	21	Day of the Turkmen melon
August	8	Day of the Ruhnama
-	11	Day of knowledge and students
September	1	Day of workers in the energy industry
-	11	Day of the Naval Forces of Turkmenistan
-	12	International Day of Older Persons
October	1	Harvest Festival
-	9	Holiday of Neighborhood
November	28	Day of workers in the oil and gas industry and geology
December	5	Memorial Day of the first President of Turkmenistan S.A. Niyazova

If a holiday falls on a Saturday or Sunday, the following Monday will be a public holiday.

Tuvalu

General holidays

January	1	New Year's Day
March	8	Commonwealth Day
April	2	Good Friday
-	5	Easter Monday
May	10	Te Aso o te Tala Lei
June	12	Queen's Birthday
August	2	National Children's Day
October	1	Tuvalu Day
November	9	Prince of Wales' Birthday
December	25	Christmas Day
-	26	Boxing Day

If a holiday falls on a Saturday or Sunday, the following Monday will be a public holiday.
If October 2 or December 26 falls on a Sunday, the following Monday and Tuesday will be public holidays. If they fall on a Monday, the following Tuesday will be a public holiday.

Ukraine

General holidays

January	1	New Year's Day
-	7	Orthodox Christmas
March	8	Women's Day
May	1	Labour Day
-	2	Orthodox Easter Day
-	9	Victory Day
June	20	Father's Day
-	28	Constitution Day
August	24	Independence Day
October	14	Day of the Defender
December	25	Christmas Day

If a holiday coincides with a day off, the day off will be carried over to the days following the holiday.

Ilyichevsk
Working hours:
Monday - Sunday shifts: 08:00-19:00 and 20:00-07:00.
Breaks: 00:00-01:00 and 12:00-13:00.
Holidays shift: 00:00-00:00.

Kherson
Working hours:
Monday - Sunday shifts: 00:00-08:00, 08:00-16:00 and 16:00-00:00.
Breaks: 03:20-04:00, 12:00-12:40 and 20:00-20:40.
Holidays: 00:00-00:00.

Nikolayev
Working hours:
Monday - Sunday shifts: 08:00-20:00 and 20:00-08:00.
Break: 12:00-13:00.
Holidays: 00:00-00:00.

Odessa
Working hours:
Monday - Sunday shifts: 08:15-19:45 and 20:15-07:45.
Breaks: 01:00-02:00 and 13:00-14:00.
Holidays: 00:00-00:00. No work from 17:00 on 31 December to 17:00 on 1 January.

Sevastopol
Working hours:
Monday - Sunday shifts: 09:00-20:00 and 21:00-08:00.
Breaks: 01:00-02:00 and 13:00-14:00.
Holidays: 00:00-00:00.

Theodosia
Working hours:
Monday - Sunday shifts: 08:00-16:00, 16:00-23:00 and 23:00-08:00.
Breaks: 11:30-12:00, 19:30-20:00 and 03:30-04:00.
Holidays: 00:00-00:00.

Yuzhny
Working hours:
Monday - Sunday shifts: 08:30-19:30 and 20:30-07:30.
Breaks: 00:00-01:00 and 12:00-13:00.
Holidays: 00:00-00:00.

United Arab Emirates

General holidays

January	1	New Year's Day
May	13-14[1]	Eid Al Fitr
June	19[1]	Afrah Day
-	20-21[1]	Eid Al Adha
August	10[1]	Hijri New Year's Day
October	19[1]	Prophet's Birthday
November	30	Commemoration Day
December	2	National Day

[1] Exact date(s) subject to sighting of the moon.
Friday and Saturday: Weekly days of rest.

Dubai
Working hours:
Jebel Ali
Saturday - Thursday shifts: 07:00-16:00. 16:00-07:00 at overtime.
Breaks 12:00-13:00, 00:00-01:00.
Friday and holidays: 00:00-00:00 at overtime.
Port Rashid
Sunday - Thursday shifts: 07:00-16:00. 16:00-19:00 at overtime.
Break 13:00-14:00
Friday, Saturday: 00:00-00:00 at overtime.
Skeleton staff available on shift basis round the clock.

Fujairah
Working hours:
Monday - Sunday shifts: 07:00-19:00 and 19:00-07:00.
Breaks 12:00-13:00 and 23:00-00:00.

Mina Saqr
Working hours:
Monday - Sunday and holidays: 00:00-00:00.

Mina Zayed
Working hours:
Saturday - Thursday shifts: 07:00-13:30, 13:30-20:30 and 20:30-03:30.
Holidays: 00:00-00:00 at overtime.
Working hours during Ramadan: 07.00-13.00 and 13.00-07.00 at overtime

Sharjah-Port Khalid
Working hours:
Saturday - Thursday shifts: 06:00-14:00 and 14:00-22:00. 22:00-06:00 at overtime.
Friday shifts: 06:00-14:00, 14:00-22:00 and 22:00-06:00 at overtime.
Holidays: 00:00-00:00 at overtime.
Working hours during Ramadan:
First shift 07.00-14.00
Second shift 14.00-22.00
Third shift 22.00-03.00
Break 16.30-18.30

United Kingdom

Channel Islands

There are no uniform holiday legislation covering the entire geographical area refered to as the Channel Islands. Please find holiday information for each Island under the respective port.

Alderney

January	1	New Year's Day
April	5	Easter Monday
May	3	Early May Holiday
-	31	Spring Holiday
August	2	August Holiday
December	26	Boxing Day

If 1 January or 26 December is a Sunday, the following Monday will be a holiday instead.
If 25 December is a Sunday 27 December is a holiday.

Working hours:

Monday - Sunday shifts: 06:00-19:00. 19:00-06:00 at overtime.

Ro/Ro berths

Monday - Sunday: 06:00-00:00. 00:00-06:00 at overtime.

St Helier

January	1	New Year's Day
April	2	Good Friday
-	5	Easter Monday
May	3	Early May Bank Holiday
-	31	Spring Bank Holiday
August	30	Summer Bank Holiday

According to information provided by the Jersey government will Christmas Day and Boxing Day be substituted on the following weekdays, should they coincide with Saturdays and Sundays.

Working hours:

Monday - Sunday shifts: 06:00-19:00. 19:00-06:00 at overtime.

Ro/Ro berths

Monday - Sunday: 06:00-00:00. 00:00-06:00 at overtime.

St Peter Port

January	1	New Year's Day
April	2	Good Friday
-	5	Easter Monday
May	3	May Day Bank Holiday
-	9	Liberation Day
-	31	Spring Bank Holiday
August	30	Summer Bank Holiday
December	25	Christmas Day
-	26	Boxing Day

According to information provided by the Guernsey government will Christmas Day and Boxing Day be substituted on the following weekdays, should they coincide with Saturdays and Sundays.

Working hours:

Monday - Friday shift: 08:00-17:00. Break 12:00-13:00. 17:00-08:00 at overtime.

Saturday, Sunday and holidays: 00:00-00:00 at overtime.

St Sampson

January	1	New Year's Day
April	2	Good Friday
-	5	Easter Monday
May	3	May Day Bank Holiday
-	9	Liberation Day
-	31	Spring Bank Holiday
August	30	Summer Bank Holiday
December	25	Christmas Day
-	26	Boxing Day

According to information provided by the Guernsey government will Christmas Day and Boxing Day be substituted on the following weekdays, should they coincide with Saturdays and Sundays.

Working hours:

Monday - Friday shift: 08:00-17:00. Break 12:00-13:00. 17:00-08:00 at overtime.

Saturday, Sunday and holidays: 00:00-00:00 at overtime.

England-Wales

January	1	New Year's Day
April	2	Good Friday
-	5	Easter Monday
May	3	Early May Bank Holiday
-	31	Spring Bank Holiday
August	30	Summer Bank Holiday
December	25	Christmas Day
-	26	Boxing Day

According to information provided by the UK government will Christmas Day and Boxing Day be substituted on the following weekdays, should they coincide with Saturdays and Sundays.

Bristol
Working hours:
Monday - Sunday: 00:00-00:00.
Holidays: 00:00-00:00 at overtime.
No work on 25 December (Christmas Day) and 26 December (Boxing Day).

Cardiff
Working hours:
Monday - Friday ordinary: 08:00-17:00. Break 13:00-14:00.
Monday - Friday shifts: 06:00-18:00. Breaks 09:00-09:30 and 13:00-14:00.
Saturday, Sunday and holidays: 00:00-00:00 at overtime.

Goole
Working hours:
Monday - Sunday: 08:00-12:00 and 13:00-17:00. 17:00-08:00 at overtime.

Grimsby
Working hours:
Monday - Friday: 06:00-18:00. 18:00-06:00 at overtime.
No work on 1 January (New Year's Day), 25 December (Christmas Day), and 26 December (Boxing Day)

Hull
Working hours:
Monday - Friday: 08:00-18:30. 06:00-08:00 and 18:30-21:30 at overtime.
Breaks 09:30-10:00, 12:00-13:00 and 15:30-16:00.
Saturday and Sunday: At overtime.
Holidays: No work.

Immingham
Working hours:
Monday - Friday: 06:00-18:00. 18:00-06:00 at overtime.
Saturday, Sunday and holidays: At overtime
Humber International Terminal, Immingham: 00:00-00:00.
Holidays: At overtime.
No work on 1 January (New Year's Day), 25 December (Christmas Day), and 26 December (Boxing Day).

Liverpool
Working hours:
General Cargo
Monday - Friday: 07:00-19:00. 19:00-07:00 at overtime.
Saturday and Sunday: 07:00-19:00 and 19:00-07:00 at overtime.
Seaforth Container Terminal
Monday - Friday: 06:00-06:00.
Saturday: 06:00-15:00.
Holidays: 00:00-00:00 at overtime.
Seaforth Grain Terminal
Monday - Friday: 07:00-19:00. 19:00-07:00 at overtime.
Saturday and Sunday: 07:00-13:00, 13:00-19:00 and 19:00-07:00 at overtime.
Seaforth Forest Products Terminal
Monday - Friday: 07:00-19:00. 19:00-07:00 at overtime.
Saturday: 07:00-19:00 and 19:00-07:00 at overtime.
Liverpool Bulk Terminal
Monday - Sunday: 00:00-00:00.
Holidays: At overtime.

Manchester
Working hours:
Ellesmere Port Docks
Monday - Friday: 08:00-17:00. 17:00-08:00 at overtime.
Saturday, Sunday and holidays: 00:00-00:00 at overtime.
EMR Scrap Terminal
Monday - Friday: 07:30-18:00.
Saturday and Sunday: 00:00-00:00 at overtime.
Holidays: No work.

Newport
Working hours:
Monday - Thursday: 08.00-17.00. Breaks 13.00-14.00.
Friday: 08.00-16.00.
Saturday and Sunday shifts: 06.00-14.00 and 14.00-22.00 at overtime.
Holidays: 00:00-00:00 at overtime.
No work on 1 January (New Year's Day), 25 December (Christmas Day) and 26 December (Boxing Day). Work stops at midday on 24 December (Christmas Eve).

Plymouth
Working hours:
Monday - Friday: 08.00-17.00. 00:00-07:00 and 17:00-08:00 at overtime.
Saturday and Sunday: 00:00-00:00 at overtime.
Holidays: Work is available at 00:00-00:05 on overtime.

Port of Tyne
Working hours:
Monday - Sunday: 00:00-00:00.
Holidays: 00:00-00:00.
No work on 25 December (Christmas Day).

Port Talbot
Working hours:
Monday - Sunday and holidays: 00:00-00:00.

Portsmouth

Working hours:

Portsmouth International Port
Monday - Sunday and holidays: 00:00-00:00.

Albert Johnson and Flathouse Quays
Monday - Sunday and holidays: 00:00-00:00. No work on 25 December (Christmas Day).

Ramsgate

Working hours:
Monday - Sunday: 00:00-00:00.

River Tees

Working hours:

Tees Dock
Monday - Friday shifts: 06.00-13.45 and 14.00-21.45. 22.00-05.45 at overtime.
Saturday and Sunday shifts: 06.00-13.45, 14.00-21.45 and 22.00-05.45 at overtime.
Holidays: 00:00-00:00 at overtime. No work on 25 December (Christmas Day).

Private river wharves
Monday - Sunday: 00:00-00:00.

Runcorn

Working hours:
Monday - Friday: 07.00-17.00. 17:00-07:00 at overtime.
Saturday and Sunday: 00:00-00:00 at overtime.
Holidays: 00:00-00:00 at overtime by agreement and subject to labour availability.
Work stops at 12.00 on 24 December (Christmas Eve) and 31 December (New Year's Eve).

Seaham

Working hours:
Monday - Friday: 08.00-12.00 and 12.30-17.00. Break 12.00-12.30.
17:00-08:00 at overtime.
Saturday, Sunday and holidays: 00:00-00:00 at overtime.

Southampton
Working hours:
General Cargo/Ro-Ro vessels
Monday - Thursday: 08:00-17:00. 17:00-23:00 at overtime.
Friday: 08:00-16:00. 16:00-22:00 at overtime.
Container port
Monday - Sunday shifts: 07:00-19:00 and 19:00-07:00.
Dibles Wharf
Monday - Friday: 07:00-16:30. 16:30-19:00 at overtime.
Saturday: 07:00-12:00 at overtime.
Marchwood Wharf
Monday - Saturday: 07:00-22:00.
Sunday: 00:00-00:00 at overtime.
Solent Stevedores berth 106-109 Western Dock
Monday - Friday: 08:00-17:00. 07:00-08:00 and 17:00-19:00 at overtime.
Saturday and Sunday: 00:00-00:00 at overtime.
Holidays: 00:00-00:00 at overtime. No work on 1 January (New Year's Day),
25 December (Christmas Day) and 26 December (Boxing Day).

Sunderland
Working hours:
Monday - Friday: 08:00-16:30. 06:00-08:00 and 16:30-22:00 at overtime.
Saturday, Sunday: 06:00-22:00 at overtime. All holidays 00:00-00:00 at overtime.
No work on 1 January (New Year's Day) and 25 December (Christmas Day).

Swansea
Working hours:
Monday - Thursday: 07:00-16:30 or 06:00-14:00 optional. 16:30-07:00 at overtime.
Friday: 07:00-15:30 or 06:00-13:00 optional, 15:30-07:00.
Saturday or Sunday: 06:00-14:00 and 14:00-22:00 at overtime.
Holidays: 00:00-00:00 at overtime.
Kings Dock (General cargo berths and coal wharfs): No work on 25 December (Christmas Day).

Isle of Man

January	1	New Year's Day
April	2	Good Friday
-	5	Easter Monday
May	3	Early May Bank Holiday
-	31	Late May Bank Holiday
June	11	TT Bank Holiday
July	5	Tynwald Day
August	30	Summer Bank Holiday
December	25	Christmas Day
-	26	Boxing Day

According to information provided by the Isle of Man government will Christmas Day and Boxing Day be substituted on the following weekdays, should they coincide with Saturdays and Sundays.

Northern Ireland

January	1	New Year's Day
March	17	St Patrick's Day
April	2	Good Friday
-	5	Easter Monday
May	3	Early May Bank Holiday
-	31	Spring Bank Holiday
July	12	Battle of the Boyne
August	30	Summer Bank Holiday
December	25	Christmas Day
-	26	Boxing Day

According to information provided by the UK government will Christmas Day and Boxing Day be substituted on the following weekdays, should they coincide with Saturdays and Sundays.

Local holidays

Belfast
Working hours:
Bulk terminals:
Monday - Friday: 08:00-17:00. 17:00-08:00 at overtime.
Saturday, Sunday and holidays: 00:00-00:00 at overtime.

Londonderry
Working hours:
Monday - Friday: 08:00-17:00. Breaks 10:30-11:00 and 13:00-14:00.
17:00-20:00 at overtime.
Saturday and Sunday: 08:00-20:00 at overtime.
No work on 25 December (Christmas Day).

Warrenpoint
Working hours:
Monday - Thursday: 08:00-17:00. 17:00-08:00 at overtime.
Friday: 08:00-16:00. 16:00-08:00 at overtime.
Saturday, Sunday and holidays: 00:00-00:00 at overtime.

Scotland

January	1	New Year's Day
-	2	New Year's Holiday
April	2	Good Friday
May	3	Early May Bank Holiday
-	31	Spring Bank Holiday
August	2	Summer Bank Holiday
November	30	St. Andrew's Day
December	25	Christmas Day
-	26	Boxing Day

According to information provided by the UK government will Christmas Day and Boxing Day be substituted on the following weekdays, should they coincide with Saturdays and Sundays.
Similarily will 2 January - the New Year holiday, be substituted on the first following Monday should it otherwise coincide with a Saturday or Sunday.

Local holidays

Aberdeen

April	19	Spring Holiday
July	12	Midsummer Holiday
September	6	Autumn Holiday

Working hours:
Monday - Friday: 08:00-17:00, 18:00-00:00 and 00:00-06:00
Breaks 12:00-13:00 and 17:00-18:00.
Saturday, Sunday and holidays: 00:00-00:00 at overtime.
No work on 1 January.

Ayr

April	13	Easter Monday
September	17, 20	Ayr Gold Cup

Working hours:
Standard port loading hours
Monday - Thursday: 08:00-17:00. Break 12:00-13:00. 00:00-08:00 and 17:00-08:00 at overtime.
Friday: 08:00-16:00. Break 12:00-13:00. 17:00-00:00 at overtime.
Saturday, Sunday and holidays: 00:00-00:00 at overtime.

Dundee

April	5	Spring Holiday
July	26	Trades Holiday
October	4	Autumn Holiday

Working hours:
Monday - Thursday: 08:00-17:00. Break 12:00-13:00. 17:00-19:00 and 19:00-08:00 at overtime.
Friday: 08:00-16:00. Break 12:00-13:00. 16:00-18:00 and 18:00-00:00 at overtime.
Saturday, Sunday and holidays: 00:00-00:00 at overtime.
No work on 1 January (New Year's Day) and 25 December (Christmas Day).

Glasgow

April	5	Easter Monday
July	17	Glasgow Fair
September	27	Autumn Holiday

Working hours:
Monday - Thursday: 08:00-12:00 and 13:00-17:00. 17:00-08:00 at overtime.
Monday 00:00-08:00 at overtime.
Friday: 08:00-12:00 and 13:00-16:00. 16:00-00:00 at overtime.
Saturday, Sunday and holidays: 00:00-00:00 at overtime.
Overtime to be ordered in periods:
Weekdays: 2 or 4 hours
Weekends: 4, 8 or 12 hours

Grangemouth

April	5	Earl Spring Holiday
September	13	Autumn Holiday

Working hours:
Container compound
Monday - Thursday: 07:00-19:00. Friday: 08:00-16:00.
General cargo
Monday - Thursday: 08:00-17:00. 17:00-08:00 at overtime.
Friday: 08:00-16:00. 16:00-08:00 at overtime.

Greenock

Working hours:

Monday - Friday: 08:00-17:00. 17:00-08:00 at overtime.

Saturday, Sunday and holidays: 00:00-00:00 at overtime.

No work on 1-2 January and 25-26 December.

Invergordon

Working hours:

Monday - Friday 08:00-18:00. Break 12:30-13:00. 18:00-08:00 at overtime.

Saturday, Sunday and holidays: 00:00-00:00 at overtime.

Inverness

Working hours:

Monday - Friday: 07:00-18:00. 18:00-07:00 at overtime.

Breaks: 09:30-10:00, 12:30-13:00, 17:00-17:30.

Saturday, Sunday and holidays: 00:00-00:00 at overtime.

Kirkwall

Working hours:

Monday - Friday: 08:00-17:00. Break 12:00-13:00.

Holidays: 00:00-00:00 at overtime.

No work on 1 January (New Year's Day), 25 December (Christmas Day) and 26 December (Boxing Day).

Overtime is sometimes possible. However, since all overtime is voluntary, owners/charterers should always contact local agent/stevedores beforehand to obtain an indication of possibilities/costs.

Leith

Working hours:

Monday - Thursday: 08:00-12:00 and 13:00-17:00. 17:00-08:00 at overtime.

Friday 08:00-12:00 and 13:00-16:00. 16:00-08:00 at overtime.

Saturday, Sunday and holidays: 00:00-00:00 at overtime.

Lerwick

January	26	Up Helly Aa Festival

Working hours:
Monday - Sunday and holidays: 00:00-00:00.

Montrose
Working hours:
Monday - Sunday: 08:00-17:00. Break 12:00-13:00. 17:00-08:00 at overtime.

Perth
Working hours:
Monday - Friday: 08:00-17:00. Break 12:30-13:00. 17:00-08:00 at overtime.
Saturday, Sunday and holidays: 00:00-00:00 at overtime.

Peterhead
Working hours:
Monday - Friday: 08:00-17:00. 17:00-08:00 at overtime.
Saturday, Sunday and holidays: 00:00-00:00 at overtime.

Uruguay

General holidays

January	1	New Year's Day
-	6	Epiphany
February	15	Carnival Monday
-	16	Carnival Tuesday
April	1	Maundy Thursday
	2	Good Friday
-	19	Landing of the 33 Patriots Day
May	1	Labour Day
-	18	Battle of Las Piedras
June	19	Artigas' Birthday
July	18	Constitution Day
August	25	Independence Day
October	12	Day of the Races
November	2	All Souls' Day
December	25	Christmas Day

If a holiday coincides with a Tuesday or Wednesday it will be observed the preceding Monday.
If a holiday coincides with a Thursday or Friday, it will be observed the following Monday.
The following holidays are exempted from the above provisions:
The days or Carnival and Easter
   1 and 6 January
   1 May
   18 July
   25 August
   25 December

USA

Federal holidays

January	1	New Year's Day
-	18	Martin Luther King
February	15	Presidents' Day
May	31	Memorial Day
July	4	Independence Day
September	6	Labor Day
October	11	Columbus Day
November	11	Veterans Day
-	25	Thanksgiving Day
December	25	Christmas Day

The USA observes no national holidays. Each state follows their own holiday schedule.
The above mentioned federal legal public holidays for 2021 are for guidance only.

State holidays

Alabama

January	1	New Year's Day
-	18	Robert E. Lee & Martin Luther King Jr. Day
February	15	George Washington & Thomas Jefferson's Birthday
April	26	Confederate Memorial Day
May	31	Memorial Day
June	7	Jefferson Davis' Birthday
July	4	Independence Day
September	6	Labor Day
October	11	Columbus Day, Fraternal Day & American Indian Heritage Day
November	11	Veterans' Day
-	25	Thanksgiving Day
December	25	Christmas Day

If a holiday coincides with a Saturday the preceding Friday is a holiday. If a holiday coincides with a Sunday the following Monday is a holiday.

All Sundays are public holidays.

Mobile AL

Working hours:

Monday - Friday - Ordinary working hours : 08:00-12:00 and 13:00-17:00. 17:00-08:00 at overtime.

Monday - Friday - Crane operators: 07:00-12:00 and 12:30-15:30.

Saturday and Sunday: 00:00-00:00 at overtime.

Holidays: 00:00-00:00 at 50% overtime: Victory Day, Confederate Memorial Day, Jefferson Davis' Birthday, Martin Luther King, Presidents' Day, Memorial Day, Columbus Day, Veterans Day, Thanksgiving Day

00:00-00:00 at 100% overtime: New Year's Day, Independence Day, Labor Day, Christmas Day.

Alaska

January	1	New Year's Day
-	18	Martin Luther King Jr. Day
February	15	Presidents' Day
March	29	Seward's Day
May	31	Memorial Day
July	4	Independence Day
September	6	Labor Day
October	18	Alaska Day
November	11	Veterans' Day
-	25	Thanksgiving Day
December	25	Christmas Day

All Sundays are legal holidays.
If a holiday coincides with a Sunday, the following Monday shall be a legal holiday.

Anchorage AK
Working hours:
Monday - Friday: 07:00-00:00,
Holidays: No work on 1 January (New Year's Day), 31 May (Memorial Day), and 25 December (Christmas Day).

Seward AK
Working hours:
Monday - Friday: 07:00-20:00.
Holidays: 00:00-00:00 at overtime. No work on 1 January (New Year's Day), 31 May (Memorial Day), 4 July (Independence Day) and 25 December (Christmas Day).

Valdez AK
Working hours:
Monday - Friday: 07:00-19:00.
Holidays: 00:00-00:00 at overtime. No work on 1 January (New Year's Day), 31 May (Memorial Day), 4 July (Independence Day) and 25 December (Christmas Day).

California

January	1	New Year's Day
-	18	Martin Luther King Jr. Day
February	12	Lincoln Day
-	15	President's Day
March	31	Cesar Chevez Day
April	2[1]	Good Friday
May	31	Memorial Day
July	4	Independence Day
September	6	Labor Day
-	9	Admission Day
-	24	Native American Day
October	11	Columbus Day
November	11	Veterans' Day
-	25	Thanksgiving Day
December	25	Christmas Day

[1] From noon to 3 PM

If any of the following holidays coincides with a Sunday, the following Monday shall be a holiday:

1 January
12 February
31 March
4 July
9 September
11 November
25 December

If 11 November coincides with a Saturday, the preceding Friday shall be a holiday.

All Sundays are holidays.

Local discrepancies may occur.

Humboldt Bay CA

Working hours:

Monday - Sunday shifts: 08:00-17:00, 18:00-03:00 and 03:00-08:00.

Connecticut

January	1	New Year's Day
-	18	Martin Luther King Jr. Day
February	12	Lincoln's Birthday
-	15	Washington's Birthday
April	2	Good Friday
May	31	Memorial Day
July	4	Independence Day
September	6	Labor Day
October	11	Columbus Day
November	11	Veterans' Day
-	25	Thanksgiving Day
December	25	Christmas Day

When a holiday coincides with a Saturday, the preceding Friday shall be a legal holiday. When a holiday coincides with a Sunday, the following Monday shall be a legal holiday.

Delaware

January	1	New Year's Day
-	18	Martin Luther King Jr. Day
April	2	Good Friday
May	31	Memorial Day
July	4	Independence Day
September	6	Labor Day
November	11	Veterans Day
-	25	Thanksgiving Day
-	26	Day after Thanksgiving
December	25	Christmas Day

If a holiday falls on a Saturday, the preceding Friday shall be a legal holiday. If a holiday fall on a Sunday, the following Monday shall be a legal holiday.
All Saturdays are legal holidays.

Wilmington DE

Working hours:

Port employees

Monday - Friday: 07:00-17:00. 17:00-07:00 at overtime. Breaks: 12:00-13:00 and 18:00-19:00.

Saturday and Sunday: 00:00-00:00 at overtime.

Holidays: 00:00-00:00 at overtime on New Year's Day, Martin Luther King's Birthday, Memorial Day, Independence Day, Labour Day, Thanksgiving and Christmas Day.

Deep Sea Union

Monday - Friday: Flexible working hours 07:00-15:00 17:00-19:00. 07:00-18:00 normal. Break 12:00-13:00. Work performed outside of these hours at overtime rates.

Saturday and Sunday: 00:00-00:00 at overtime.

Holidays: 00:00-00:00 at overtime on Martin Luther King's Birthday, Memorial Day and Thanksgiving. No work on New Year's Day, Independence Day, Labor Day and Christmas Day.

Florida

January	1	New Year's Day
-	15	Martin Luther King Jr. Day
-	19	Birthday of Robert E. Lee
February	12	Lincoln's Birthday
-	15	Susan B. Anthony's Birthday
-	15	Washington's Birthday
April	2	Good Friday
-	2	Pascua Florida Day
-	26	Confederate Memorial Day
May	31	Memorial Day
June	3	Birthday of Jefferson Davis
-	14	Flag Day
July	4	Independence Day
September	6	Labor Day
October	11	Columbus Day and Farmers' Day
November	11	Veterans' Day
-	25	Thanksgiving Day
December	25	Christmas Day

If a holiday coincides with a Sunday the following Monday shall be a holiday.
Mardi Gras / Shrove Tuesday may be observed locally as a holiday.

Tampa

January	1	Gasparilla Day

Working hours:
Monday - Friday: 08:00

Georgia

January	1	New Year's Day
-	18	Martin Luther King Jr. Day
April	2[1]	State Holiday
May	31	Memorial Day
July	4[2]	Independence Day
September	6	Labor Day
October	11	Columbus Day
November	11	Veterans Day
-	25	Thanksgiving Day
-	26[3]	State Holiday
December	23[4]	Washington's Brithday
-	25[5]	Christmas Day

All Sundays are holidays
[1] Substitutes 26 April
[2] Observed 5 July
[3] Substitutes 19 January
[4] Substitutes 15 February
[5] Observed 24 December

Brunswick GA
Working hours:
Monday - Friday: 08:00-17:00. 17:00-08:00 at overtime.
Breaks: 06:00-07:00, 12:00-13:00, 18:00-19:00 and 00:00-01:00.
Saturday, Sunday and holidays: 00:00-00:00 at overtime.

Savannah GA
Working hours:
Monday - Friday: 08:00-17:00. 17:00-08:00 at overtime.
Breaks: 06:00-07:00, 12:00-13:00, 18:00-19:00 and 00:00-01:00.
Saturday, Sunday and holidays: 00:00-00:00 at overtime.

Hawaii

January	1	New Year's Day
-	18	Martin Luther King Jr. Day
February	15	President's Day
March	26	Prince Jonah Kuhio Kalanianaole Day
April	2	Good Friday
May	31	Memorial Day
June	11	King Kamehameha I Day
July	4	Independence Day
August	20	Statehood Day
September	6	Labor Day
November	11	Veterans' Day
-	25	Thanksgiving Day
December	25	Christmas Day

If a holiday coincides with a Saturday, the preceding Friday shall be a holiday. If a holiday coincides with a Sunday, the following Monday shall be a holiday.

Illinois

January	1	New Year's Day
-	18	Martin Luther King Jr. Day
February	12	Lincoln's Birthday
-	15	Presidents' Day
March	1	Casimir Pulaski's birthday
April	2	Good Friday
May	31	Memorial Day
July	4	Independence Day
September	6	Labor Day
October	11	Columbus Day
November	11	Veterans' Day
-	25	Thanksgiving Day
December	25	Christmas Day

Chicago IL

Working hours:

Monday - Friday: 08:00-12:00 and 13:00-17:00. Break 12:00-13:00. 17:00-08:00 at overtime.

Saturday and Sunday: 00:00-00:00 at overtime.

Indiana

January	1	New Year's Day
-	12	Lincoln's Birthday
-	18	Martin Luther King Jr. Day
February	15	Washington's Birthday
April	2	Good Friday
May	31	Memorial Day
July	4	Independence Day
September	6	Labor Day
October	11	Columbus Day
November	11	Veterans' Day
-	25	Thanksgiving Day
December	25	Christmas Day

If a holiday falls on a Saturday, the preceding Friday will be a legal holiday instead. If a holiday falls on a Sunday, the following Monday will be a legal holiday instead.
All Sundays are legal holidays

Burns Harbour IN
Working hours:
Monday - Sunday and holidays: 00:00-00:00
Labour rates after hours are not necessarily at overtime rates depending on crews, stevedore and prior arrangements.

Louisiana

January	1	New Year's Day
-	8	Battle of New Orleans
-	18	Martin Luther King Jr. Day
-	19	Robert E. Lee Day
February	15	Washington's Birthday
-	16	Mardi Gras
April	2	Good Friday
May	31	National Memorial Day
June	3	Confederate Memorial Day
July	4	Independence Day
August	30	Huey P. Long Day
September	6	Labor Day
October	11	Christopher Columbus Day
November	1	All Saints' Day
-	11	Veterans' Day
-	25	Thanksgiving Day
December	25	Christmas Day

If any of the following holidays falls on a Sunday, the following day will be a holiday:
  December 25
  January 1
  July 4
Saturdays are half-holiday from noon to midnight.
Mardi Gras is not by default a holiday.

Maine

January	1	New Year's Day
-	18	Martin Luther King Jr. Day
February	15	Presidents' Day
April	19	Patriots' Day
May	31	Memorial Day
July	4	Independence Day
September	6	Labor Day
October	11	Indigenous People Day
November	11	Veterans' Day
-	25	Thanksgiving Day
December	25	Christmas Day

If a holiday coincides with a Sunday, it will be observed the following Monday.

Maryland

Month	Day	Holiday
January	1	New Year's Day
-	18	Martin Luther King Jr. Day
February	12	Lincoln's Birthday
-	15	Washington's Birthday
March	25	Maryland Day
April	2	Good Friday
May	31	Memorial Day
July	4	Independence Day
September	6	Labor Day
-	12	Defenders' Day
October	11	Columbus Day
November	11	Veterans' Day
-	25	Thanksgiving Day
-	26	American Indian Heritage Day
December	25	Christmas Day

If a holiday falls on a Sunday, it is observed on the following Monday.

Baltimore MD
Working hours:
Monday - Sunday: 08:00-17:00. 17:00-08:00 at overtime.

Massachusetts

January	1	New Year's Day
-	18	Martin Luther King Jr. Day
February	15	Washington's Birthday
April	19	Patriot's Day
May	31	Memorial Day
July	4	Independence Day
September	6	Labor Day
October	11	Columbus Day
November	11	Veterans' Day
-	25	Thanksgiving Day
December	25	Christmas Day

If any of the following holidays coincides with a Sunday they will be observed the following Monday:
1 January
4 July
11 November
25 December

Boston MA

March	17	Evacuation Day
June	17	Bunker Hill Day

Working hours:
Monday - Friday: 08:00-12:00 and 13:00-17:00. Break 12:00-13:00, 17:00-18:00.
18:00-22:00 at overtime.
Saturday and Sunday: 08:00-17:00 at overtime.
Holidays: 00:00-00:00 at overtime.

Container handling and perishable cargoes:
Monday - Friday: 08:00-12:00 and 13:00-17:00. 06:00-08:00, 18:00-22:00 at overtime.
Break 12:00-13:00, 17:00-18:00.
Saturday and Sunday: 08:00-17:00 at overtime.
Overtime on Lincoln's Birthday.
No work after 01.00 unless labourers agree except on passenger, bulk, container, LASH, Sea-Bee and Ro/Ro ship and perishable cargo.
Saturday: Work after 17.00 only to finish a ship by 19.00. Passenger, bulk, container, LASH, Sea-Bee, and Ro/Ro ships will be worked Saturday nights.

Michigan

January	1	New Year's Day
-	18	Martin Luther King Jr. Day
February	12	Lincoln's Birthday
-	15	Washington's Birthday
May	31	Memorial Day
July	4	Independence Day
September	6	Labor Day
October	11	Columbus Day
November	11	Veterans' Day
-	25	Thanksgiving Day
December	25	Christmas Day

If any of the following holidays fall on a Sunday, the following Monday will be a public holiday:
  January 1
  Febraury 12
  July 4
  November 11
  December 25
Saturdays from 12 noon are considered legal holidays.

Minnesota

January	1	New Year's Day
-	18	Martin Luther King Jr. Day
February	15	Presidents' Day
May	31	Memorial Day
July	4	Independence Day
September	6	Labor Day
October	12	Christopher Columbus Day
November	11	Veterans' Day
-	25	Thanksgiving Day
December	25	Christmas Day

If any of the following holidays falls on a Saturday, they will be observed the preceding Friday. Should they fall on a Sunday, they will be observed the following Monday:
  New Year's Day
  Independece Day
  Veterans' Day
  Christmas Day

Duluth-Superior MN
Working hours:
General cargo - Lake Superior Warehousing Co., Inc.
Monday - Friday: 08:00-12:00 and 12:30-16:30. 16:30-08:00 on 50% overtime.
Saturday, Sunday and holidays: 00:00-00:00 at 50% overtime.
Grain loading - Ceres Terminals
Monday - Friday: 07:00-15:30 or 08:00-16:30. Break 12:00-12:30. 15:30-00:00 or 16:30-00:00 at overtime.
Monday - Saturday: 100% overtime at 00:00-07:00 or 00:00-08:00.
Saturday: 07:00-00:00 or 08:00-00:00 at 100% overtime.
Sunday: At 100% overtime.

Mississippi

January	1	New Year's Day
-	18	Martin Luther King Jr. Day
February	15	Presidents' Day
April	26	Confederate Memorial Day
May	31	Memorial Day
July	4	Independence Day
September	6	Labor Day
November	11	Veterans' Day
-	25	Thanksgiving Day
December	25	Christmas Day

If a holiday falls on a Sunday, the following Monday will be a legal holiday.

Pascagoula MS
Working hours:
Monday - Friday: 08:00-12:00 and 13:00-17:00.
Saturday, Sunday and Holidays: 00:00-00:00 at 50% overtime.

New Hampshire

January	1	New Year's Day
-	18	Martin Luther King Jr. Day
February	15	Washington's Birthday
May	31	Memorial Day
July	4	Independence Day
September	6	Labor Day
October	11	Columbus Day
November	11	Veterans' Day
-	25[1]	Thanksgiving Day
December	25	Christmas Day

If a holiday falls on a Sunday the following day will be observed as a holiday.

General elections are legal holidays.

[1] Subject to appointment

Portsmouth NH
Working hours:

Monday - Sunday: 00:00-00:00.

New Jersey

January	1	New Year's Day
-	18	Martin Luther King's Birthday
February	12	Lincoln's Birthday
-	15	Washington's Birthday
April	2	Good Friday
May	31	Memorial Day
June	18	Juneteenth
July	4	Independence Day
September	6	Labor Day
October	11	Columbus Day
November	11	Armistice Day
-	25	Thanksgiving Day
December	25	Christmas Day

All Saturdays are legal holidays.
If a holiday coincides with a Sunday, an additional holiday shall be observed on the following Monday.
If a holiday coincides with a Saturday, the government sector shall observe a holiday on the preceding Friday
General election days are legal holidays.

Camden NJ

Working hours:

Monday - Sunday: 08:00-12:00, 13:00-17:00. 17:00-08:00 at 50% overtime.
Breaks: 06:00-07:00, 12:00-13:00, 18:00-19:00, 00:00-01:00 workable at 100% overtime.
Work commencement 07.00, 08.00, 13.00, 17.00, 18.00 or 19.00; container and bulk ships also 01.00.

New York

January	1	New Year's Day
-	18	Martin Luther King Jr. Day
February	12	Lincoln's Birthday
-	15	Washington's Birthday
May	31	Memorial Day
June	13	Flag Day
-	19	Juneteenth
July	4	Independence Day
September	6	Labor Day
October	11	Columbus Day
November	11	Veterans' Day
-	25	Thanksgiving Day
December	25	Christmas Day

Holidays - other than Flag Day - falling on a Sunday will be observed the following Monday.
Saturday is half-holiday including the period from noon 12 to midnight.

Ogdensburg NY
Working hours:
Monday - Friday: 08:00-23:30.

North Carolina

January	1	New Year's Day
-	18	Martin Luther King Jr. Day
-	19	Robert E. Lee's Birthday
February	15	Washington's Birthday
March	25	Greek Independence Day
April	2	Good Friday
-	12	Anniversary of signing of Halifax Resolves
May	10	Confederate Memorial Day
-	20	Anniversary of Mecklenburg Declaration of Independence
-	31	Memorial Day
July	4	Independence Day
September	6	Labor Day
-	11	First Responders Day
-	16	Yom Kippur
October	11	Columbus Day
November	11	Veterans Day
-	25	Thanksgiving Day
December	25	Christmas Day

If a holiday falls on a Sunday, the following Monday is a public holiday.

Morehead City NC
Working hours:
Monday - Friday: 08:00-17:00. 17:00-08:00 at overtime. Break 12:00-13:00.
Saturday and Sunday: 00:00-00:00 at overtime.

Wilmington NC
Working hours:
Monday - Friday: 08:00-17:00. 17:00-08:00 at overtime. Break 12:00-13:00.
Saturday and Sunday: 00:00-00:00 at overtime.

Ohio

January	1	New Year's Day
-	18	Martin Luther King Day
February	15	Washington-Lincoln Day
May	31	Memorial Day
July	4	Independence Day
September	6	Labor Day
October	11	Columbus Day
November	11	Veterans' Day
-	25	Thanksgiving Day
December	25	Christmas Day

If a holiday falls on a Sunday, the following Monday is a legal holiday.

Ashtabula OH
Working hours:
Monday - Friday: 08:00-12:00 and 12:30-16:30. 18:00-22:00 at overtime.

Cleveland OH
Working hours:
Monday - Friday: 08:00-12:00 and 13:00-17:00. 18:00-22:00 at overtime.
Only general public holidays are observed in Ohio.

Toledo OH
Working hours:
Monday - Friday: 08:00-12:00 and 13:00-17:00.

Oregon

January	1	New Year's Day
-	18	Martin Luther King Jr. Day
February	15	Presidents' Day
May	31	Memorial Day
July	4	Independence Day
September	6	Labor Day
November	11	Veterans' Day
-	25	Thanksgiving Day
December	25	Christmas Day

If a holiday falls on a Saturday, the preceding Friday is a legal holiday. If a holiday falls on a Sunday, the following Monday is a legal holiday.
All Sundays are legal holidays.

Pennsylvania

January	1	New Year's Day
-	18	Martin Luther King Jr. Day
February	15	Presidents' Day
April	2	Good Friday
May	31	Memorial Day
June	14	Flag Day
July	4	Independence Day
September	6	Labor Day
October	11	Columbus Day
November	11	Veterans' Day
-	25	Thanksgiving Day
December	25	Christmas Day

If any of the following holidays falls on a Saturday, the following Monday shall be observed as a holidays:
January 1
June 14
July 4
November 11
December 25
Saturdays are half holidays from noon 12 to midnight.

Rhode Island

January	1	New Year's Day
-	18	Martin Luther King Jr. Day
February	15	Washington's Birthday
May	4	Rhode Island Independence Day
-	31	Memorial Day
July	4	Independence Day
August	9	Victory Day
September	6	Labor Day
October	11	Columbus Day
November	11	Veterans' Day
-	25	Thanksgiving Day
December	25	Christmas Day

When any of the following holidays falls on a Saturday or Sunday, State Employee will substitute the holiday on the following Monday:

New Year's Day
Independence Day
Veterans' Day
Christmas Day

All Sundays are considered holidays.

Providence RI

Working hours:

Monday - Friday: 08:00-17:00. Break 12:00-13:00. 19:00-06:00 at overtime.

Saturday and Sunday: 00:00-00:00 at overtime.

South Carolina

January	1	New Year's Day
-	20	Martin Luther King Jr. Day
February	17	Presidents' Day
May	10	Confederate Memorial Day
-	25	National Memorial Day
July	4	Independence Day
September	7	Labor Day
November	11	Veterans' Day
-	26	Thanksgiving Day
-	27	Day after Thanksgiving
December	24	Christmas Holiday
-	25	Christmas Day
-	26	Christmas Holiday

Charleston SC

Working hours:

Monday - Friday: 08:00-12:00 and 13:00-17:00. 12:00-13:00 and 18:00-19:00 at 100% overtime.

Saturday and Sunday: 00:00-00:00 at overtime.

Holidays: 00:00-00:00 at overtime. No work on New Year's Day, Independence Day, Labor Day and Christmas Day. Work will stop at 15:00: 24 December (Christmas Eve) and 31 December (New Year's Eve).

Holidays falling on a Saturday will be observed the Friday before and holidays falling on a Sunday will be observed the following Monday

Texas

January	1	New Year's Day
-	18	Martin Luther King Jr. Day
-	19	Confederate Heroes Day
February	15	Presidents' Day
March	2	Texas Independence Day
April	21	San Jacinto Day
May	31	Memorial Day
June	19	Emancipation Day
July	4	Independence Day
August	27	Lyndon B. Johnson Day
September	6	Labor Day
November	11	Veterans Day
-	25	Thanksgiving Day
-	26	Day after Thanksgiving
December	24	Christmas Eve
-	25	Christmas Day
-	26	Boxing Day

The following are note national or state holidays:

Rosh Hashanah
Yom Kippur
Good Friday
Cesar Chavez Day

Houston TX

Working hours:

Automated cargoes: Monday - Friday: 08:00-12:00 and 13:00-17:00. 17:00-08:00 at 50% overtime. Breaks: 06:00-07:00, 12:00-13:00, 18:00-19:00 and 00:01-01:00 workable at 100% overtime.

Non-automated cargoes: Monday - Saturday 07:00-12:00 and 13:00-18:00.

Virginia

January	1	New Year's Day
-	18	Martin Luther King Jr. Day
February	15	George Washington Day
May	31	Memorial Day
June	19	Juneteenth
July	4	Independence Day
September	6	Labor Day
October	11	Columbus Day & Yorktown Victory Day
November	11	Veterans Day
-	25	Thanksgiving Day
-	26	Day after Thanksgiving
December	25	Christmas Day

If a holiday falls on a Saturday, the preceeding Friday will be a legal holiday. If a holiday falls on a Sunday, the following Monday will be a legal holiday.

Hampton Roads VA

Working hours:

Monday - Friday: 08:00-12:00 and 13:00-17:00. 19:00-00:00 and 01:00-06:00 at overtime.

Saturday and Sunday: 00:00-00:00 at overtime.

Christmas: Work stops at 00:00 on 23 December and resumes at 06:00 on 26 December.

New Year's Eve: Work stops at 18:00 on 31 December.

Coal piers in Hampton Roads (Newport News and Norfolk)

Monday - Sunday: 00:00-00:00.

If a holiday, except a restricted holiday, falls on Saturday or Sunday, it will be observed on the following Monday.

Richmond VA

Working hours:

Monday - Friday: 08:00-12:00 and 13:00-17:00. 17:00-08:00 at overtime.

Breaks: 12:00-13:00, 18:00-19:00, 00:00-01:00, 06:00-07:00.

Saturday, Sunday and Holidays: 00:00-00:00 at overtime.

Washington

January	1	New Year's Day
-	18	Martin Luther King Jr. Day
February	18	Presidents' Day
May	31	Memorial Day
July	4	Independence Day
September	6	Labor Day
November	11	Veterans' Day
-	25	Thanksgiving Day
-	26	Native American Heritage Day
December	25	Christmas Day

If a holiday falls on a Saturday, it shall be observed the preceding Friday. If a holiday falls on a Sunday, it shall be observed the following Monday

All Sundays are state legal holidays.

Bellingham WA
Working hours:
Monday - Friday: 08:00-17:00 and 18:00-03:00. Breaks 12:00-13:00 and 22:00-23:00.
Saturday and Sunday: 00:00-00:00 at overtime.
Holidays: 00:00-00:00 at overtime. No work on New Year's Day, Labour Day, Thanksgiving and Christmas Day. Work stops at 15:00 on Christmas Eve and on New Year's Eve.

Everett WA
Working hours:
Monday - Friday: 08:00-17:00 and 17:00-03:00. Breaks 12:00-13:00 and 22:00-23:00.
Saturday and Sunday: 00:00-00:00 at overtime.
Holidays: 00:00-00:00 at overtime. No work on New Year's Day, Labour Day, Thanksgiving and Christmas Day. Work stops at 15:00 on Christmas Eve and on New Year's Eve.

Grays Harbor WA
Working hours:
Monday - Friday: 08:00-17:00 and 18:00-03:00. Breaks 12:00-13:00 and 22:00-23:00.
Saturday and Sunday: 00:00-00:00 at overtime.
Holidays: 00:00-00:00 at overtime. No work on New Year's Day, Labour Day, Thanksgiving and Christmas Day. Work stops at 15:00 on Christmas Eve and on New Year's Eve.

Olympia WA
Working hours:

Monday - Friday: 08:00-17:00 and 18:00-03:00. Breaks 12:00-13:00 and 22:00-23:00.
Saturday and Sunday: 00:00-00:00 at overtime.

Holidays: 00:00-00:00 at overtime. No work on New Year's Day, Labour Day,
Thanksgiving and Christmas Day. Work stops at 15:00 on Christmas Eve and on New
Year's Eve.

Seattle WA
Working hours:

Monday - Friday: 08:00-17:00 and 18:00-03:00. Breaks 12:00-13:00 and 22:00-23:00.

Holidays: 00:00-00:00 at overtime. No work on New Year's Day, Labour Day,
Thanksgiving and Christmas Day. Work stops at 15:00 on Christmas Eve and on New
Year's Eve.

Tacoma WA
Working hours:

Monday - Friday: 08:00-17:00 and 18:00-03:00. Breaks 12:00-13:00 and 22:00-23:00.
Saturday and Sunday: 00:00-00:00 at overtime.

Holidays: 00:00-00:00 at overtime. No work on New Year's Day, Labour Day,
Thanksgiving and Christmas Day. Work stops at 15:00 on Christmas Eve and on New
Year's Eve.

Wisconsin

January	1	New Year's Day
-	18	Martin Luther King Jr. Day
February	15	Presidents' Day
May	31	Memorial Day
June	19	Juneteenth Day
July	4	Independence Day
September	6	Labor Day
October	11	Columbus Day
November	11	Veterans' Day
-	25	Thanksgiving Day
December	25	Christmas Day

If a legal holiday falls on a Sunday, the following Monday shall be the legal holiday.
General elections are legal holidays.

Milwaukee WI
Working hours:
Monday - Friday: 08:00-17:00. 17:00-00:00 and 00:00-08:00 at overtime.
Saturday: 00:00-00:00 at overtime.

Vanuatu, Republic of

General holidays

January	1	New Year's Day
February	21	Dr. W.H. Lini Day Memorial Day
March	5	Custom Chiefs' Day
April	2	Good Friday
-	5	Easter Monday
May	1	Labour Day
-	13	Ascension
July	24	Childrens Day
-	30	Independence Day
August	15	Assumption Day
October	5	Constitution Day
November	29	Unity Day
December	25	Christmas Day
-	26	Family Day

Holidays falling on a Sunday will be observed the following Monday.

Port Vila

June	18	Shefa Day

Working hours:
Monday - Friday: 07:00-11:00 and 13:00-17:00. Breaks 11:00-13:00 and 17:00-18:00.
18:00-22:00 at overtime.
Saturday: 07:00-11:00. 11:00-15:00 at overtime.
Sunday and holidays: No work.

Venezuela

General holidays

January	1	New Year's Day
February	15	Carnival Monday
-	16	Carnival Tuesday
April	1	Maundy Thursday
-	2	Good Friday
-	19	Independence Declaration
May	1	Labour Day
June	24	Battle of Carabobo/St. John
July	5	Independence Day
-	24	Simon Bolivar's Birthday
October	12	Indigenous Resistance Day
December	24	Christmas Eve
-	25	Christmas Day
-	31	End of year holiday

Local holidays

Carupano

February	3	Anniversary of Antonio José de Sucre

La Guaira

February	28	La Guaira Day
March	10	José Maria Vargas Day

Lake Maracaibo

October	24	Rafael Urdaneta's Birthday
November	18	Maracaibo Virgin's Day

Orinoco River

April	11	Battle of St. Felix

Puerto Cabello

November	8	Puerto Cabello Battle
-	13	Provincial holidays

Puerto La Cruz

November	14	Anzoategui Day

Puerto Sucre

February	3	Mariscal Sucre's Day

Vietnam

General holidays

January	1	New Year's Day
-	11-15	Tet Holiday
April	22	Hung Kings Temple Festival
-	30	Victory Day
May	1	Labour Day
September	2	National Day Holiday

Campha
Working hours:
Monday - Sunday shifts: 00:00-06:00, 06:00-12:00, 12:00-18:00 and 18:00-00:00.

Danang
Working hours:
Monday - Sunday shifts: 00:00-06:00, 06:00-12:00, 12:00-18:00 and 18:00-00:00.

Haiphong
Working hours:
Monday - Sunday shifts: 00:00-06:00, 06:00-12:00, 12:00-18:00 and 18:00-00:00.

Ho Chi Minh City
Working hours:
Monday - Sunday and holidays: 00:00-00:00.

Hon Gai
Working hours:
Monday - Sunday shifts: 00:00-06:00, 06:00-12:00, 12:00-18:00 and 18:00-00:00.

Qui Nhon
Working hours:
Monday - Sunday shifts: 00:00-06:00, 06:00-12:00, 12:00-18:00 and 18:00-00:00.

Vung Tau

Working hours:

Monday - Sunday shifts: 00:00-06:00, 06:00-12:00, 12:00-18:00 and 18:00-00:00.

Virgin Islands

General holidays

January	1	New Year's Day
-	6	Epiphany
-	18	Birthday of Martin Luther King, Jr.
February	15	Washington's Birthday
March	31	Transfer Day
April	1	Maundy Thursday
-	2	Good Friday
-	5	Easter Monday
May	31	Memorial Day
July	3	Emancipation Day
-	4	Independence Day
September	6	Labor Day
October	11	Columbus Day / Puerto Rico Friendship Day
November	1	Hamilton Jackson Day
-	11	Veteran's Day
-	25	Thanksgiving Day
December	25	Christmas Day
-	26	Boxing Day

Yemen, Republic of

General holidays

May	1	Labour Day
-	11-15[1]	Eid-Al Fitr
-	22	Yemen Unification Day
July	19-23[1]	Eid-Al Adha
August	10[1]	Islamic New Year
September	26	Revolution Day
October	14	Liberation Day
November	30	Independence Day

[1] Exact date(s) subject to sighting of the moon.
If a holiday falls on a Friday, it will be substituted the immediate following working day.
All Fridays are holidays.

Aden
Working hours:
Monday - Sunday shifts: 06:00-18:00 and 18:00-06:00.
Breaks 12:00-13:00 and 00:00-01:00.

Hodeidah
Working hours:
Saturday - Thursday: 07:00-12:00, 14:00-00:00, 00:00-02:00.
Break 12:00-14:00.
Friday and holidays: 07:00-11:00, 11:00-00:00, 00:00-02:00.

Mokha
Working hours:
Monday - Sunday: 06:00-15:00, 15:00-19:00 extension hours at overtime.
Holidays: 05:30-11:00 at overtime.

Mukalla
Working hours:
Monday - Sunday: 06:00-15:00. 15:00-19:00 extension hours at overtime.
Holidays: 05:30-11:00 at overtime.

Saleef
Working hours:
Monday - Sunday: 07:00-11:00 and 16:00-00:00.

Index